VMware vRealize Configuration Manager Cookbook

Over 80 recipes to teach you the power of vRealize Configuration Manager 5.8 to provide automated and continuous configuration management

Abhijeet Shriram Janwalkar

BIRMINGHAM - MUMBAI

VMware vRealize Configuration Manager Cookbook

First published: July 2016

Production reference: 2040716

Published by Packt Publishing Ltd.

Livery Place

35 Livery Street

Birmingham B3 2PB, UK.

ISBN 978-1-78646-335-7

www.packtpub.com

Credits

Author
Abhijeet Shriram Janwalkar

Reviewer
Daniel Langenhan

Commissioning Editor
Pratik Shah

Acquisition Editor
Divya Poojari

Content Development Editor
Riddhi Tuljapurkar

Technical Editor
Gaurav Suri

Copy Editor
Madhusudan Uchil

Project Coordinator
Sanchita Mandal

Proofreader
Safis Editing

Indexer
Monica Ajmera Mehta

Graphics
Kirk D'Penha

Production Coordinator
Shantanu N. Zagade

Cover Work
Shantanu N. Zagade

About the Author

Abhijeet Shriram Janwalkar completed BTech in electrical engineering. He has 10 years' experience in IT, starting from desktop support, to server management, to technology lead in the cloud support team, and is now the lead consultant responsible for designing and deploying various VMware and Microsoft technologies. Meanwhile, he has performed technical trainings and was a Microsoft Certified Trainer. He is currently working for AtoS India Pvt Ltd as the Lead Consultant, mostly responsible for monitoring and checking compliance in the cloud deployment team. On the certification front, he has completed VCP-DCP, VCP-Cloud, VCP6-CMA, VCAP-DCA, and VCAP-DCD, and is waiting for the general availability of the VCAP6-DCD exam. He has been working on VCM for almost 3 years now and is responsible for the design, deployment, and maintenance of it in multiple deployments for customers. He is an MCT alumni and has a few other certifications in Microsoft technologies such as MCSE: Private Cloud and MCSA Server 2012, to name a couple. He used to train people on SCCM, SCOM, and Windows OS. He was invited by Microsoft to perform performance-based testing on Windows Server 2008 and then beta test SCCM 2012, which he passed successfully. You can find him at `http://abhijeet-janwal kar.blogspot.com` or `https://in.linkedin.com/in/abhijeet-janwalkar-364095 2`.

Acknowledgments

First of all, I would like to thank God for giving me wisdom and making sure that I share it with you in the form of this book.

Then, thanks to my parents and my brother and sister, who believed in me no matter what I did. Next, is my friend and mentor Pramod Pawar, who guided me to become a lead consultant and now an author.

Special thanks to the PacktPub team, Riddhi, Divya, Gaurav, and the background editorial team, for believing in my idea and giving me this opportunity.

My reviewer Daniel Langenhan for finding my errors and making sure that we deliver you a better book.

Thanks to all my friends and well-wishers who supported and encouraged me to finish this book.

Now comes the most important one to be thanked, my wife Pooja, for bearing with me and my long nights in front of the laptop to finish this book. For supporting me in all the things I do. Thanks to Aashka, my lovely daughter, for whom I wrote the whole book. I wrote this book because whenever I used to read any book, I used to start with this page, and I always wished my daughter's name to be here someday. Thanks for coming into my life and making sure that I write this; you are my true inspiration.

About the Reviewer

Daniel Langenhan is a virtualization expert with formidable skills in architecture, design, and implementation for large multi-tier systems. His experience and knowledge of process management, enterprise-level storage, and Linux and Windows operation systems, have made him and his business a highly sought-after international consultancy in the Asia-Pacific and European regions for multinational clientele in the areas of finance, communication, education, and government. Daniel has been working with VMware products since 2002 and is directly associated with VMware since 2008. He has a proven track record of successful integrations of virtualization into different business areas, while minimizing cost and maximizing the reliability and effectiveness of the solution for his clients.

Daniel's expertise and practical approach to VMware has resulted in the publication of the following books:

- *Instant VMware vCloud Starter, Packt Publishing*
- *VMware View Security Essentials, Packt Publishing*
- *VMware vCloud Director Cookbook, Packt Publishing*
- *VMware vRealize Orchestrator Cookbook, Packt Publishing*
- *VMware vRealize Orchestrator Essentials, Packt Publishing*

He has also lent his expertise to many other publishing projects as a technical editor.

www.PacktPub.com

Support files, eBooks, discount offers, and more

For support files and downloads related to your book, please visit www.PacktPub.com.

Did you know that Packt offers eBook versions of every book published, with PDF and ePub files available? You can upgrade to the eBook version at www.PacktPub.com and as a print book customer, you are entitled to a discount on the eBook copy. Get in touch with us at service@packtpub.com for more details.

At www.PacktPub.com, you can also read a collection of free technical articles, sign up for a range of free newsletters and receive exclusive discounts and offers on Packt books and eBooks.

https://www2.packtpub.com/books/subscription/packtlib

Do you need instant solutions to your IT questions? PacktLib is Packt's online digital book library. Here, you can search, access, and read Packt's entire library of books.

Why subscribe?

- Fully searchable across every book published by Packt
- Copy and paste, print, and bookmark content
- On demand and accessible via a web browser

Free access for Packt account holders

If you have an account with Packt at www.PacktPub.com, you can use this to access PacktLib today and view 9 entirely free books. Simply use your login credentials for immediate access.

Table of Contents

Preface

VMware is the pioneer and leader in SDDC with its various tools; VCM is responsible for policy-driven compliance management and the patching of infrastructure.

VCM helps in maintaining the compliance of infrastructure by automatically collecting data and analyzing it against industry standards such as VMware and Microsoft Hardening Guidelines, CIS Benchmarks, PCI DSS, and FISMA, to name a few. It helps you patch your machines with the latest patches released by OS vendors and automate software provisioning. You can see your compliance score on the vROps console after integrating both of them.

This book provides recipes for installing VCM and then the initial configuration, moving ahead with integration to another VMware tool. After this, it continues with configuring compliance and patching for Linux and Windows machines. We have a chapter that will help you configure VCM in order to deploy software from VCM.

You can use this book as a guide to completely explore all the features of VCM, and in the troubleshooting section, you can take a look at the issues you might face while working on VCM every day.

What this book covers

Chapter 1, *Installing VCM*, discusses the components of vRealize Configuration Manager (VCM), various options to install VCM; including the prerequisites; and ends with fine-tuning the database server used by VCM.

Chapter 2, *Configuring VCM to Manage Your Infrastructure*, discusses more about VCM configuration, and we start adding virtual infrastructure elements, installing agents, and configuring discovery.

Chapter 3, *Linux Patching*, shows you how to install the Software Content Repository (SCR), used to download and distribute patches, then follows all the steps required to configure, and distribute patches to managed Linux/Unix servers.

`Chapter` 4, *Windows Patching*, shows you how to configure VCM to synchronize patches with Microsoft servers, check the status of managed Windows machines, and finally install patches on demand or on schedule.

`Chapter` 5, *Software Provisioning for Windows*, discusses how VCM can be used to distribute software on managed Windows machines; whether servers or desktops, the process will be the same.

`Chapter` 6, *Compliance Management*, teaches you how to import and export compliance configurations, create compliance rules for Windows and Unix/Linux, and perform virtualization.

`Chapter` 7, *Maintenance of VCM*, discusses how to upgrade VCM, make changes in Service accounts, upgrade agents after the VCM upgrade, decommission managed machines, and offers some naming conventions to use.

`Chapter` 8, *Integration with vROps and Scheduling*, gives us more details of integrating VCM with vROps, and then using the scheduling feature of VCM to schedule reports, compliance, data collection, and so on.

`Chapter` 9, *Troubleshooting VCM*, is the final chapter and discuss various issues to troubleshoot in VCM, such as agent communication and agent upgrades. We list the basic tools used to troubleshoot, such as the job manager history and EcmDebugEventViewer.exe.

What you need for this book

If you are planning to go along with your practices as per the recipes in the book, which is highly recommended, you will need a good lab to work in. As VCM works with multiple VMware components, and you will want to test integration as well, then you will need a machine with at least 32 GB of RAM, supported by a minimum of a quad-core processor, 1 TB HDD, and 256 GB SSD. You can install your favorite OS and on top of it either VMware Workstation or Virtual box. You need to create a small lab that will include a Windows Domain controller, and a few Windows servers hosting SQL, vCenter, VCM, and so on. You can install other components such as vCloud Director, vROps, and vCNS. Sometimes, 32 GB of RAM may not be sufficient, so power on only those VMs that you will need. Basic functionalities can be tested with a portable lab on your laptop with 16 GB RAM, which excludes vCD, vROps, and VCNS.

Here are the specs for my lab:

Lab 01: This is a desktop I have at home with 32 GB DDR3 RAM, AMD FX6300 6 core processor, 256 GB SSD, and 1 TB HDD

Lab 02: This is my portable lab on my laptop with 16 GB DDR3 RAM, Intel i5 quad-core processor, and 256 GB HDD

Who this book is for

If you are a system administrator who is eager to provide better administration with VCM and are familiar with managing network users and resources, along with performing system maintenance, then this book is for you.

Sections

In this book, you will find several headings that appear frequently (Getting ready, How to do it, How it works, There's more, and See also).

To give clear instructions on how to complete a recipe, we use these sections as follows:

Getting ready

This section tells you what to expect in the recipe and describes how to set up any software or any preliminary settings required for the recipe.

How to do it...

This section contains the steps required to follow the recipe.

How it works...

This section usually consists of a detailed explanation of what happened in the previous section.

There's more...

This section consists of additional information about the recipe in order to make the reader more knowledgeable about the recipe.

See also

This section provides helpful links to other useful information for the recipe.

Conventions

In this book, you will find a number of text styles that distinguish between different kinds of information. Here are some examples of these styles and an explanation of their meaning.

Code words in text, database table names, folder names, filenames, file extensions, pathnames, dummy URLs, user input, and Twitter handles are shown as follows: "The agent is available at X: \Program Files (x86)\VMware\VCM\Installer\Packages\CMAgent.5.8.2.linux on the VCM Collector server."

A block of code is set as follows:

```
***   Installation Started 03/03/2016 3:57   ***
Title: EcmComSocketListenerService
Source: C:\windows\TEMP\GLB90C6.tmp | 03-03-2016 | 03:57:04 | 71680
Rem Wise Error Number: 141
Rem Function Name: EcmCreateService
Rem Error Message: Caught an exception from wise : Call to
EcmCreateService for service CSI Socket Listener failed with error code
of 1072 : error code 141
141
```

Any command-line input or output is written as follows:

```
cd "PatchRepo/Repos"/unix
rm SystemId*.xml
```

New terms and important words are shown in bold. Words that you see on the screen, for example, in menus or dialog boxes, appear in the text like this: "Click on **Add** to start the wizard."

Warnings or important notes appear in a box like this.

 Tips and tricks appear like this.

Reader feedback

Feedback from our readers is always welcome. Let us know what you think about this book—what you liked or disliked. Reader feedback is important for us as it helps us develop titles that you will really get the most out of. To send us general feedback, simply e-mail feedback@packtpub.com, and mention the book's title in the subject of your message. If there is a topic that you have expertise in and you are interested in either writing or contributing to a book, see our author guide at www.packtpub.com/authors.

Customer support

Now that you are the proud owner of a Packt book, we have a number of things to help you to get the most from your purchase.

Errata

Although we have taken every care to ensure the accuracy of our content, mistakes do happen. If you find a mistake in one of our books—maybe a mistake in the text or the code—we would be grateful if you could report this to us. By doing so, you can save other readers from frustration and help us improve subsequent versions of this book. If you find any errata, please report them by visiting http://www.packtpub.com/submit-errata, selecting your book, clicking on the **Errata Submission Form** link, and entering the details of your errata. Once your errata are verified, your submission will be accepted and the errata will be uploaded to our website or added to any list of existing errata under the **Errata** section of that title.

To view the previously submitted errata, go to https://www.packtpub.com/books/content/support and enter the name of the book in the search field. The required information will appear under the Errata section.

Piracy

Piracy of copyrighted material on the Internet is an ongoing problem across all media. At Packt, we take the protection of our copyright and licenses very seriously. If you come across any illegal copies of our works in any form on the Internet, please provide us with the location address or website name immediately so that we can pursue a remedy.

Please contact us at copyright@packtpub.com with a link to the suspected pirated material.

We appreciate your help in protecting our authors and our ability to bring you valuable content.

Questions

If you have a problem with any aspect of this book, you can contact us at questions@packtpub.com, and we will do our best to address the problem.

1
Installing VCM

In this chapter, we will cover the following recipes:

- Preparing our VCM deployment – installing SQL
- Preparing our VCM deployment – installing and configuring IIS
- Preparing our VCM deployment – configuring SSRS
- Preparing our VCM deployment – installing other prerequisites
- Installing VCM – single-tier deployment
- Installing VCM – two-tier deployment
- Installing VCM – three-tier deployment
- VCM post-installation tasks – database fine-tuning

Introduction

What is **vRealize Configuration Manager (VCM)** and what it can do for you?

vRealize Configuration Manager is a complete configuration management solution provided by VMware. This is a part of the vRealize Operations suite along with **vRealize Operations Manager**, **vRealize Hyperic**, and **vRealize Infrastructure Navigator**, to name a few. Being a part of the suite, VCM is responsible for compliance and patch management, these being its core functionalities.

VCM is a tool that collects data automatically from managed machines, which may be running Windows or Unix, and virtualization tools such as **vCenter**, **vShield**, and **vCloud Director**, and based on that data, VCM can perform compliance checks and help you manage your virtual machines from the console.

VCM can perform the patching of managed machines, which may either be physical or virtual, and Windows and many flavors of Unix/Linux are supported, such as **Red Hat Enterprise Linux** (**RHEL**), **SUSE**, **CentOS**, and **Mac OS**. To patch these operating systems, we need a RHEL server acting as a patch repository. For non-windows servers, this RHEL patch repository downloads the patches, and all the managed machines can come and download them over HTTP, HTTPS, FTP, or NFS. VCM can patch all the supported versions of Windows.

You can download various compliance packs created by VMware and others. Just download and import them, and they will be ready for use with your managed machines. The packages include but are not limited to security best practices developed by the **Defense Information Systems Agency** (**DISA**), the **National Institute of Standards and Technology** (**NIST**), the **Center for Internet Security** (**CIS**); regulatory mandates such as **Sarbanes-Oxley** (**SOX**), the **Payment Card Industry** (**PCI**) standard, the **Health Insurance Portability and Accountability Act** (**HIPAA**), and the **Federal Information Security Management Act** (**FISMA**); and hardening guidelines from VMware and Microsoft.

You not only can check the compliance of your infrastructure but also enforce it to enhance your compliance score. Enforcing compliance means VCM can make necessary changes to the server to make it compliant.

This does not limit you from creating your own rules and compliance templates; you can either create a completely new rule or combine rules from various rulesets provided by VMware.

VCM can be used to install an operating system on bare metal, or you can deploy a virtual machine. You can use VCM to deploy applications on managed machines, which is limited to Windows. With features such as **VCM Remote Client**, you can manage communication and management mechanisms for mobile Windows machines as they connect to and disconnect from the network.

With the **vRealize Operations** (**vROps**) **Manager** Management Pack, you can push the compliance score of managed virtual machines to the vROps console. vROps is a monitoring solution from VMware used to monitor virtual infrastructure; pushing the compliance score to the console gives us the view of the infrastructure under one console. Also, if required, an alert can be configured if the score goes beyond a certain limit.

Along with all this, we can use VCM to manage **Active Directory**. VCM for Active Directory collects Active Directory objects across domains and forests and displays them through a single console. The information is consolidated and organized under the Active Directory slider, allowing you to view your Active Directory structure, troubleshoot issues, detect changes, and ensure compliance.

Understanding VCM components

VCM is an application composed of multiple components, as described in the following figure:

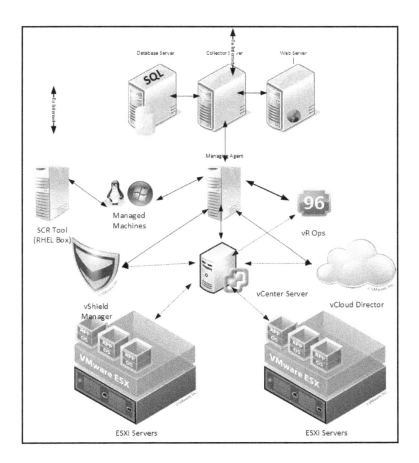

The database server

The database server contains the VCM, VCM_Coll, VCM_Raw, and VCM_UNIX databases. Using a shared SQL Server instance is supported by VCM. However, VCM makes heavy use of SQL Server for query and transaction processing. You must ensure that you have or can add enough capacity to a shared SQL Server instance so that VCM and any other databases on the shared server do not experience poor performance.

VCM operates with the Standard, Enterprise, or Datacenter editions of SQL Server. You must install the 64-bit SQL Server 2008 R2, 2012, or 2014 versions on the database server used by VCM.

The SQL Server license must include **SQL Server Reporting Services** (**SSRS**), which is used by VCM for the reporting feature.

The VCM Collector server

The **VCM Collector** is a standalone application that can run even when no other VCM components are active. This is particularly useful in the case of scheduled collections, because it means the VCM Portal does not have to be up and running. The Collector has all the necessary information and capabilities to perform the requested functions. You can stop the Collector and still look at data as the UI does not interact directly with the collector service; instead, it communicates with various executables that are installed on the same machine as the Collector.

Windows patches will be hosted on the VCM Collector as per the default configuration. Linux patches will be handled by the **Standby Continuous Replication** (**SCR**) server. We will have a look at Linux patching in Chapter 3, *Linux Patching*.

Supported operating systems for installing the VCM Collector are Windows Server 2008 R2, 2012, or 2012 R2. The VCM Collector must be installed on a AD domain member.

We will discuss the installation of the VCM Collector server in multiple recipes in this chapter.

The web server

The web server contains web applications such as IIS and SSRS, other services, and VCM software components. Before you install VCM, you must configure the web server. The Windows machine that hosts the web components must be running **Internet Information Services (IIS)** 7.5. Supported operating systems to install the web server to are Windows Server 2008 R2, 2012, or 2012 R2.

We will discuss the installation and configuration of the web server in the *Preparing our VCM deployment – installing and configuring IIS* recipe.

The managing agent

We need to install an agent to manage the machines through VCM. In the case of vCenter Server, vCloud Director, and vCloud Networking and Security Manager, VCM uses an intermediary **managing agent** for data collection. This intermediary collects data through the use of the vSphere VIMAPI, vCloud REST API, and vCloud Networking and Security Manager REST API, and it then passes it to VCM Server.

We need to install VCM agent 5.5 or higher on the system designated as being the managing agent. However, after the agent deployment, there is an additional step. Mutual two-way trust must be established with the system designated as the managing agent before the collection of any vCenter, vCloud Networking and Security, or vCloud Director data can be done.

The vCenter collection process via the managing agent is serial and very CPU intensive. For this reason, a separate managing agent is recommended for virtual infrastructures. If the number of vCenter or vCloud Server instances increases, the number of managing agents can be horizontally scaled.

We will see this in action in the Chapter 2, *Configuring VCM to Manage Your Infrastructure*, in the *Configuring a managing agent machine for virtual environment management* recipe.

The SCR Tool

To ensure that all patch dependencies are met when VCM deploys the patches, the SCR Tool downloads all of the necessary patches (except for patches that have been superseded by newer patches). VCM patching handles all the dependencies when the patches are deployed. If the patch was available when the SCR Tool was installed and configured, it would have been downloaded. If the patch was not available when the SCR Tool was last synchronized, it would not have been downloaded and hence not available for distribution to managed machines. If the patch is still available from the OS vendor, it will be available for download using the SCR Tool patch-replication process. The SCR server does not share or sync the details of the patches downloaded by it; VCM gets the details of the released patches from `http://www.vmware.com/`. So, we need to make sure is fully synced with vendors such as RHEL or SUSE and has all the patches downloaded in the repository.

The SCR Tool is not used to run patch assessments or deployments. It also does not assess the machine configuration or the downloaded patch content that is used for patch deployment. That job is done by the VCM server.

The SCR Tool downloads the patch signature files and OS vendor patch content from the **content distribution network** (**CDN**) and downloads subscription-only content from the OS vendor's content web sites. We will look at this in more detail in `Chapter 3`, *Linux Patching*.

Distributed VCM deployment

Depending upon the size of the infrastructure you manage, VCM can be deployed in multiple ways.

If you plan to install VCM on two or three tiers, check out this link for how to size your hardware environment: `http://kb.vmware.com/kb/2033894`.

Single-tier installation

A single-tier installation can be used by organizations smaller than 2,000 managed servers and POC/pilot engagements.

All the components, such as the VCM Database server, web server, and the VCM Collector, are installed on the same server, like this:

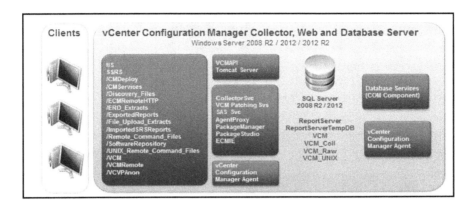

Two-tier installation

A two-tier installation can be used by organizations where the number of managed servers is between 2,000 and 5,000.

In this deployment, we have the application server (Collector) and IIS on one machine, SQL Server instance on the other machine, and SSRS on either system, as shown here:

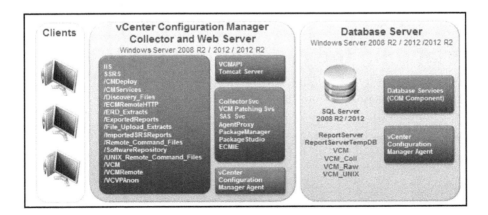

Three-tier installation

A three-tier installation can be used by organizations with more than 5,000 servers. It is constructed in this manner:

- The application server (Collector), IIS, and SQL Server instance are on separate machines
- SSRS can be either on the IIS or the SQL Server system

This figure depicts a three-tier installation:

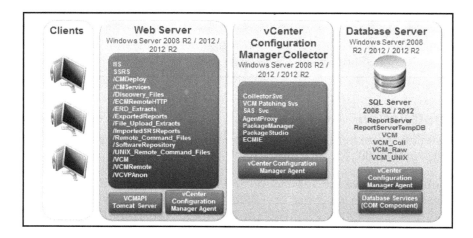

Understanding the requirements of VCM

Every software application we install has its own requirements for successful installation and functioning. VCM is no different. In this section, we will discuss the hardware and software requirements for getting VCM deployed.

Software requirements

We need the following software to install VCM:

Software component	Versions supported
Operating system for VCM Web, Collector, and Database server	Windows Server 2008 R2, Windows Server 2012, or Windows Server 2012 R2
SQL version	SQL Server 2008 R2, 2012, or 2014 Standard, Enterprise, or Datacenter Edition (64-bit)
SSRS version	SQL Server 2008 R2, 2012, or 2014 Reporting Services
OS for SCR*	RHEL 7.x

(*SCR: software content repository. It is used to download and store patches for non-Windows operating systems)

Minimum hardware requirements

Hosting the VCM has some hardware requirements as well, which are provided in the following tables:

Minimum hardware requirements to support 1-1,000 managed machines:

	Single Tier	2-Tier Database	2-Tier Web/Collector	3-Tier Database	3-Tier Web	3-Tier Collector
RAM	8 GB	8 GB	4 GB	8 GB	4 GB	4 GB
Processor	Dual Xeon or single dual-core 2 GHz	Dual Xeon or single dual-core 2 GHz	Dual Xeon or single dual-core 2 GHz	Dual Xeon or single dual-core 2 GHz	Single 2-GHz processor	Single 2-GHz processor

Minimum hardware requirements to support 1,001-2,000 managed machines:

	Single Tier	2-Tier Database	2-Tier Web/Collector	3-Tier Database	3-Tier Web	3-Tier Collector
RAM	12 GB	12 GB	4 GB	12 GB	4 GB	4 GB
Processor	Quad Xeon or two dual-core 2 GHz	Quad Xeon or two dual-core 2 GHz	Quad Xeon or two dual-core 2 GHz	Quad Xeon or two dual-core 2 GHz	Single 2-GHz processor	Dual Xeon or single dual-core 2 GHz

Minimum hardware requirements to support 2,001-5,000 managed machines:

	Single Tier	**2-Tier Database**	**2-Tier Web/Collector**	**3-Tier Database**	**3-Tier Web**	**3-Tier Collector**
RAM	16 GB	16 GB	8 GB	16 GB	4 GB	8 GB
Processor	Eight-way Xeon or four dual-core 2 GHz	Eight-way Xeon or four dual-core 2 GHz	Dual Xeon or single dual-core 2 GHz	Eight-way Xeon or four dual-core 2 GHz	Single 2-GHz processor	Dual Xeon or single dual-core 2 GHz

Service accounts

Let's look at the list of accounts and the privileges required for VCM to work properly.

You can reuse an account for more than one function, but dedicated accounts might be useful for troubleshooting and tracking.

The Collector, VCM Remote, Tomcat, and vSphere Client VCM plug-ins can be used from the same account. If you reuse one account, apply the permissions shown for the Collector service account.

Role	Permissions	Description
VCM Administrator	(During installation only) Local admin access on the VCM Collector and Web server. (During installation only) System admin access to the VCM SQL Server instance on the database server. This must be an interactive account and separate from the other accounts in this table.	The VCM Administrator account is the login account used when installing VCM and possibly post installation for the administration and maintenance of VCM.

VCM Collector Service	Local admin access on the VCM Collector and Web servers. This is not a domain administrator or interactive user account.	The Collector service account is the account under which the VCM Collector, VCM Database, and VCM Patch Management services run. During installation, VCM configures the Collector service account with DBO and bulk insert rights in SQL Server for the VCM databases.
VCM Remote Service	Local admin access on the VCM Web server. This is not a domain administrator or interactive user account.	The VCM Remote service account is used by the VCM Remote client for anonymous access to the VCM Remote virtual directory on the Web server.
VCM Tomcat Service	Local admin access on the VCM Database server. Public access on VCM databases. This is not an interactive user account.	The Tomcat service account serves as the VCM application programming interface for SQL login to the E12VCM Database server.
vSphere Client VCM Plug-in Service	Local admin on the VCM Web server. This is not an interactive user account.	The **vSphere Client VCM Plug-In** (**VCVP**) account provides vSphere access over HTTP to VCM managed machines. The **VCM Advanced Installation** option prompts for credentials for the VCVP account. Typical Installation does not.
VCM Default Network Authority	Local admin access on Windows machines that VCM collects from using the DCOM agent. Depending on the enterprise size and for convenience, a separate, domain administrator account with rights on the Windows machines. This is not an interactive user account.	The network authority account is for data collection from DCOM Windows machines.

IMPORTANT: Never use the service accounts for logging in to the VCM Console or for any other purpose. Logging in to VCM using a service account can lead to unexpected or inconsistent behavior. Services that use the same account as a logged-in user might modify the logged-in user's current role or machine group or log the user out of the system.

If for some reason you don't get a local admin account to be used as the NAA, you need at least the privileges mentioned in the following table. For VCM to make changes on licensed machines, such as rebooting and managing audit settings, the account used to interact with the VCM agent needs the following permissions and rights on each licensed machine:

Action	Required user right
Emergency repair disk	Back up files and directories
NTFS permissions	Manage auditing and security logs
Reboot	Shut down the system, force shutdown from a remote system
Services change	Shut down the system
Share permissions	Manage auditing and security logs

To check or set the appropriate rights on each machine, you can use either of these:

- **Local security policy**: **Security Settings** | **Local Policies** | **User Rights Assignment**
- **Group Policy plugin**: **Local Computer Policy** | **Computer Configuration** | **Windows Settings** | **Security Settings** | **Local Policies** | **User Rights Assignment**

VCM databases

There are four databases created by VCM; there is a list of them along with their purpose in the following table. The databases are created when we deploy VCM using the installer.

Make sure autogrowth is enabled on the databases.

Database name	Minimum size	Purpose
VCM	3 GB	This contains configuration data for the VCM application itself, collected data from Window systems and virtual infrastructure, change details from all systems, and results of patch and compliance assessments. The base name VCM is a default and may be changed.
VCM_Coll	1 GB	This provides operational state information for the Collector service and is mainly used to track details of running jobs and the last contact state of managed client systems.
VCM_Unix	1 GB	This contains the collected managed machine data gathered from any Linux, Unix, or Mac agents in the environment.
VCM_RAW	1 GB	To improve performance, this database temporarily holds collection data before it is transformed into the VCM and VCM_UNIX databases. The raw database should not be backed up or be included in maintenance plans.

OSes supported by VCM

The list of OSes supported by VCM is as per the following table, but this is not a comprehensive list.

You can take a look at the *Hardware and Operating System Requirements for VCM Managed Machines* chapter of the *VMware vRealize Configuration Manager Installation Guide* (http://www.vmware.com/pdf/vrealize-configuration-manager-58-installation-guide.pdf) for the complete list.

Supported operating system	Supported hardware platform
Microsoft Windows Server 2003 SP2	x86 and x64
Microsoft Windows Server 2008 R2 Enterprise Gold	x64
Microsoft Windows 7 Enterprise Gold	x86 and x64

Microsoft Windows 8.1 Enterprise	x86 and x64
Microsoft Windows Server 2012 R2 Datacenter	x64
Red Hat Enterprise Linux 5.0-5.11, 6.0-6.5, and 7.0 (x64) Server, Desktop with Workstation, and Advanced Platform	x86 and x64
SUSE Linux Enterprise Server (SLES) 10.0-10.2 (up to agent version 5.5.0 only) SUSE Linux Enterprise Server (SLES) 10.3-10.4, 11.0-11.3, and 12	x86 and x64
Windows 10	x86 and x64

vRealize Configuration Manager port and protocol summary

The following table shows the port and protocol requirements for proper functioning in the environment:

Source	Target	Port and protocol	Description
Managing agent	vCloud Management vCenter	HTTPS: 443	The web service connection to the vCenter API. Valid credentials and certificate thumbprint are required.
Managing agent	vCloud vCenter	HTTPS: 443	The web service connection to the vCenter API. Valid credentials and certificate thumbprint are required.
VCM Collector	VCM Database Server	SQL: 1433	Windows authenticated connection.
VCM Collector	VCM Database Server	DCOM: 135	DCOM is required between the Collector and the DB Server in a two-tier configuration so that the DB server can call back to the Collector at the end of various jobs.

VCM Collector	VCM Database Server	SMB: TCP ports 139 and 445	VCM creates a share to the DB server during installation.
VCM Collector	VCM Database Server	HTTP: 80	An SSRS connection from VCM Server to the DB SSRS instance.
VCM Collector	VCM Database Server	ICMP	Login details are not sent to the agent. Mutual authentication is used and the agent runs under LocalSystem. Data is pulled back to the Collector over a new TLS session.
VCM Collector	Agent	HTTP: 26542	Login details are not sent to the agent. Mutual authentication is used and the agent runs under LocalSystem. Data is pulled back to the Collector over a new TLS session.
VCM Collector	Agent	ICMP	Login details are not sent to the agent. Mutual authentication is used and the agent runs under LocalSystem. Data is pulled back to the Collector over a new TLS session.
VCM Collector	Agent	SMB: TCP ports 139 and 445	This is a mapped driver for Windows patch downloads.
Agent software	RedHat Patch Server	HTTPS: 443/80	This depends on how you have configured Apache, which will be used to download patches from the patch repository.

Licensing

vRealize Operations is available with two license models:

- **Per processor with unlimited VMs**: For virtual environments with high consolidation ratios, vRealize Operations is available per processor as a part of VMware vRealize Suite, VMware vCloud Suite, and VMware vSphere with Operations Management.
- **Per virtual machine or physical server**: For virtual environments with low consolidation ratios, vRealize Operations is also available à la carte in 25 VM or OS instance license packs.

The new release, VCM 5.8.2, supports Hybrid Cloud Suite license keys, as VCM will not be part of vCloud Suite anymore. This keeps changing; you can contact VMware for current pricing details or check out more details here: `https://www.vmware.com/products/vre alize-operations/pricing`.

Preparing our VCM deployment – installing SQL

VCM requires four databases on a dedicated SQL system. In this recipe, we will learn how to correctly install the SQL Server component.

Getting ready

Depending upon the deployment type we choose, we will need either a dedicated SQL Server (two- and three-tier deployment) or we can use the Windows server used for the VCM Collector server (single-tier deployment).

We will need an operating system-Windows Server 2012 (or better)-and SQL 2012.

For proof of concept or testing purposes, you can use shared SQL; or else, use dedicated SQL.

How to do it...

The steps to install SQL are the same for all the three types of VCM deployments–only the server will change depending upon the type of tier.

 As this is not a dedicated guide to installing and configuring SQL, we will not include all the screenshots; if you need further help, consult your DBA team for detailed instructions.

Follow these steps:

1. Start the SQL installer.
2. Under the installation menu, select **New SQL Server standalone installation or add features to an existing installation**.
3. Make sure all the setup support rules have been passed.
4. Ignore product update errors if you do not have an Internet connection.
5. Enter the product key.
6. Accept the EULA.
7. Under **Setup Role**, select **SQL Server Feature Installation**.
8. Select the following features:

   - **Instance Features**
     - **Database Engine Service**
       - **Full-Text and Semantic Extractions for Search**
     - **Reporting Service – Native**
   - **Shared Features**
     - **Documentation Components**
     - **Management Tools – Basic**
       - **Management Tools – Complete**

9. Choose the installation folder according to your server configuration.
10. Make sure all the installation rules have been passed.
11. Go with the default instance and again change the installation folder location if required.
12. It is always better to use a service account to run SQL services, and you need to have a domain account if you will be installing a two- or three-tier VCM instance.

In a multi-tier VCM deployment, the database is on a different server, and we need a domain service account so that SQL can communicate over the network.

Provide the correct service accounts to the SQL installation wizard.

13. The collation setting supported by VCM is `SQL_Latin1_General_CP1_CI_AS`; make sure this is selected.
14. Add the SQL admin group from Active Directory. Depending on company policy, enable **Mixed** mode and provide the `SA` account with a password.
15. For reporting services, we will be only installing SSRS and not configuring it.
16. Follow the wizard and install SQL.

How it works...

SQL will host all the four databases required for VCM. We don't need to create or configure any database right now; they will be created when we install VCM. We will need special permissions for SQL Server, as previously stated in the *Service accounts* subsection.

Also, all activities such as compliance check and patch status for a machine are performed using the data available in the database, so this puts extra workload on the database, which highlights the need for a dedicated SQL Server. All the schedules are stored as SQL jobs in SQL, putting another layer of work pressure on the SQL Server.

VCM uses SSRS to host the reporting feature; we installed SSRS as well while deploying SQL, and in the following recipes we will configure it.

Preparing our VCM deployment – installing and configuring IIS

Another important part after the SQL database is IIS. A VCM application is a web-based portal connected to a database, so all the actions are performed via the web interface, which needs IIS. In this recipe, we will install and configure IIS.

Getting ready

Again, depending upon the type of VCM deployment, you either need dedicated servers (two- or three-tier) or a single VCM server (single-tier) installation. We will need Windows Server 2012 R2 to start with the recipe.

As seen in the first diagram in this chapter (in the *Understanding VCM components* subsection) and the *Distributed VCM deployment* subsection, the placement of IIS changes according to the type of deployment.

How to do it...

The web components of VCM Collector contain web applications such as IIS and SSRS, other services, and VCM software components. Before you install VCM, you must configure the web components of VCM Collector.

 We will cover the installation process on Windows 2012 R2. Installation on Windows 2008 might differ.

Installing IIS

Follow these steps to install IIS:

1. Log in to the IIS server and launch **Server Manager**. Go to **Manage** | **Add roles and features**.

2. Add the **Web Server (IIS)** role.

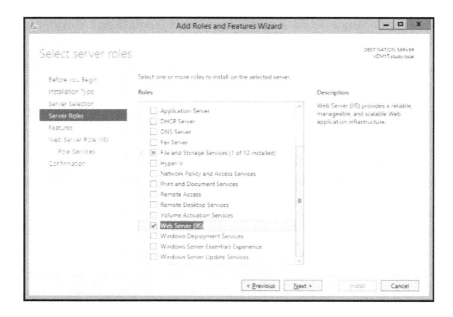

3. Add the **.NET Framework 3.5** feature.
4. Add the following components:

Sr. no.	Option	Action
1	Common HTTP features	Static Content Default Document Directory Browsing HTTP Errors HTTP Redirection
2	Application development	ASP.NET .NET Extensibility 3.5 .NET Extensibility 4.5 ASP ASP .NET 3.5 ASP .NET 4.5 ISAPI Extensions ISAPI Filters

3	Health and diagnostics	HTTP Logging Logging Tools Request Monitor Tracing
4	Security	Basic Authentication Windows Authentication Digest Authentication URL Authorization Request Filtering IP and Domain Restrictions
5	Performance	Static Content Compression Dynamic Content Compression
6	Management tools	IIS Management Console IIS Management Scripts and Tools Management Service

5. Provide a path to the Windows 2012 ISO if required.
6. Click on **Install** and let the installation begin; follow the wizard and make sure the installation is successful.

Configuring IIS

Once IIS has been installed, we need to configure it:

1. Click on **Start** and go to **All Programs** | **Administrative Tools** | **Internet Information Services (IIS) Manager**.
2. Expand **<server name>**, expand **Sites**, and click on **Default Web Site**.
3. In the **Actions** pane, under **Manage Web Site** and **Browse Web Site**, click on **Advanced Settings**.
4. Expand connection's **Limits** and set **Connection Time-out (seconds)** to 3600.

5. Click on **OK**

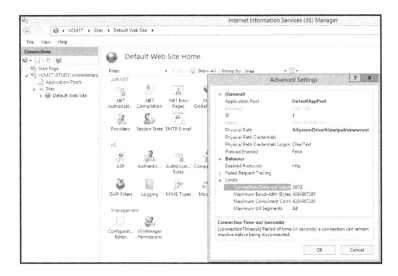

Configuring the IIS 7.5 default website

IIS 7.5 provides a default website, which defines the default authentication settings for applications and virtual directories. Verify that the IIS 7.5 default website has the correct settings.

Follow these steps to configure IIS:

1. Click on Start and go to **All Programs** | **Administrative Tools** | **Internet Information Services (IIS) Manager**.
2. Expand **<server name>**, expand **Sites**, and click on **Default Web Site**.
3. In the **Default Web Site** home pane, locate the IIS options.
4. Double click on **Authentication** and set the authentication settings as follows:

Sr. no.	Option	Action
1	**Anonymous Authentication**	Set to **Disabled**.
2	**ASP.NET Impersonation**	Set to **Disabled**.
3	**Basic Authentication**	Set to **Enabled**.
4	**Forms Authentication**	Set to **Disabled**

Your screen should look like this:

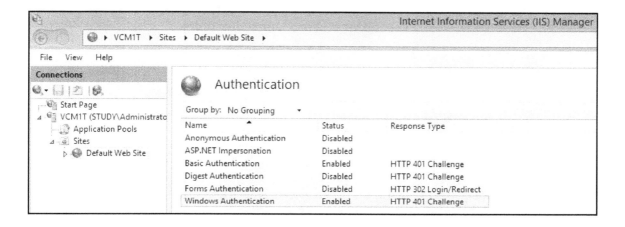

How it works...

VCM uses IIS to host the web applications that present the data. The web applications relay the commands we give from the VCM console to the database, the operations are performed, and the end result is again presented on the console GUI. VCM creates multiple applications inside IIS that are required for VCM. `CMAppPool` and `CMServices` are IIS application pools used for VCM virtual directories and web services.

Preparing our VCM deployment – configuring SSRS

SSRS is used by VCM for providing the reporting functionality.

Getting ready

In this recipe, we will configure SSRS to be used by VCM; as this is not a dedicated SQL guide, it is recommended you consult your DBA team while configuring SSRS.

To avoid getting charged for multiple licenses of SQL, it is recommended you install SSRS on the same server as the database server, which is what we did when we installed SQL Server.

We will need SSRS installed on the database server before we start.

How to do it…

Connect to the database server with the service account credentials, launch **Reporting Service Configuration Manager**, and follow the wizard:

1. Connect to the SQL Server instance where the reporting service is installed. Provide the correct server name and instance.
2. On the **Service Account** page, in this case, use the same service account which will be used by the VCM service. Click on **Apply**.

3. On the **Web Service URL** page, select port 80 and click on **Apply**.

4. Under **Database**, click on **Change Database** and follow another wizard to **Create a new report database**. It involves these steps:

    1. Select **Create a new report server database**.

    2. Under **Connect to the Database Server**, provide these values:

        • **Server Name**: The SQL database server name
        • **Authentication Type**: **Current User – Integrated Security**

    3. Use the default database name and language.

    4. Under **Credentials**, use **Service Credentials**.

    5. Accept the summary, click on **Next** and then on **Finish** on the next page to complete the database creation.

5. For the **Report Manager URL** tab, select **Virtual Directory:** Reports and click on **Apply**.

6. We don't need the rest of the parameters for VCM; you can check with your DBA team if they need to configure them and, if so, what the best options for you are.

7. Write down the URL (we will need this when we install VCM).

How it works...

The report manager and web service URLs will be provided when we install VCM and will then be used by VCM to present reports via its console.

When we install VCM, the installer will create default reports on the SSRS instance that will be accessed by users when they start using VCM.

Preparing our VCM deployment – installing other prerequisites

There are a few other prerequisites that we need to install before we can actually start installing VCM. We will install them in this recipe.

Getting ready

We need Internet access to download the following installers if they are not already available. We need to install them on all the servers in the VCM hierarchy.

We need to install them in the samesequence, or else they won't get installed.

The following links are used in this book; they might change if you change the SQL version, such as those of **SQL Native Client** and **SQL Command Line Utilities**:

Sr. no.	Description	Download location
1	SQL Native Client	`http://go.microsoft.com/fwlink/?LinkID=239648&clcid=0x409`
2	SQL Command Line Utilities	`http://go.microsoft.com/fwlink/?LinkID=239650&clcid=0x409`
3	SQLXML 4.0 SP1	`http://www.microsoft.com/en-us/download/details.aspx?id=30403`

How to do it...

This is a very simple installation and you just need to click on **Next** and **Finish**.

Just follow the sequence and install all the three utilities. You must install them on all the servers, that is, if you are deploying a three-tier VCM installation, these three must be installed on all the three servers.

How it works...

These utilities are used by VCM to communicate with the SQL database. If they are not present on the server, then the foundation checker will fail and you will have to install them and start the installer again.

Installing VCM – single-tier deployment

In this recipe, we will deploy vRealize Configuration Manager 5.8.2 on a Windows Server 2012 R2. As the title suggests, this is a single-tier installation; hence, all the VCM components will be installed on a single server. So, the VCM Database server, web server, and the VCM Collector components will reside on a single Windows Server 2008 R2, 2012, or 2012 R2 machine (in our case, Windows Server 2012 R2), which is referred to as the VCM Collector, as illustrated here:

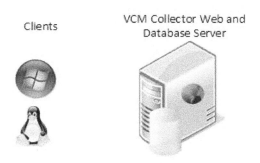

64-bit Windows Server 2008 R2 / 2012 / 2012 R2
SQL Server 2008 R2 / 2012 / 2014

Getting ready

In this case, we will need a single Windows Server 2012 R2 installation where we have already installed SQL, configured IIS, and installed all the prerequisites by following the previous recipes.

The VCM installer is available on http://www.vmware.com/. You need to have an account on my.vmware.com to download the installer.

You need to have all the required service accounts ready in Active Directory, and they should have the permissions described in the requirements document of VCM. The server should be a part of the Active Directory domain, and you must log in with an AD account that is a local administrator on the server.

How to do it...

You need to log in with the account that you want to have VCM admin rights to, as the account that is used to install VCM gets full admin rights on the VCM application, so you can choose either your account or any specifically created VCM administrator account.

Download the installer from the Internet and copy it to the VCM server. Then, follow these steps:

1. Mount the ISO and start the installation wizard by double clicking on `setup.exe`. Select **Typical Installation**.

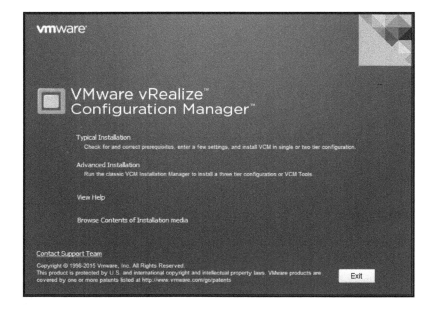

Typical Installation: This is mostly used for single- or two-tier installations and asks for less information.

Advanced Installation: This is mostly used for three-tier installations, as in this type, we need to spread the installation of the Collector and web server on different servers.

2. Read and accept the license agreement and select "**I am an authorised agent and/or representative of the customer/end user**" and "**I have read the terms and conditions stated above**".

3. It will perform the prerequisite checks and run a few tests for that; once the tests are complete, select **View full results of prerequisite check**.

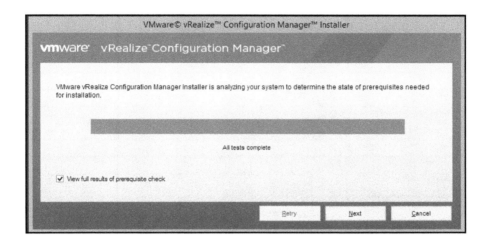

4. The results will be launched in Internet Explorer and check whether there are any errors and/or warnings; you can install if there are any warnings but can't proceed if there are errors.

5. Once you see any error, you can drill down by clicking on the error link in the report; it will then tell you why you faced the error.

In our case, we had not installed the `ServerSideIncludes` IIS role service, as shown in the following error report:

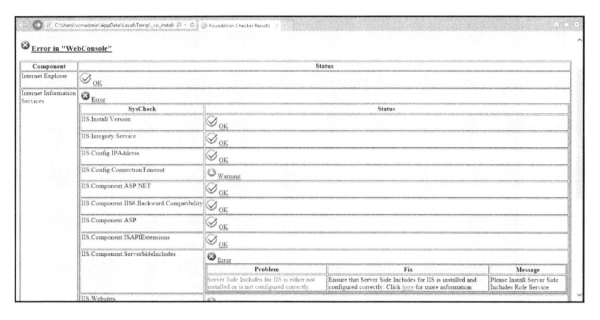

After installing the missing component, we can resume the installer.

1. In the next step, we need to provide the following details:

   - **VCM Database Server (a local or a remote SQL Server instance)**: The same server where we are installing as this is a single-tier installation.
   - **SQL Server Reporting Services WebService URL**: You must have noted this down while configuring SSRS; if not, go and launch the SSRS configuration wizard to check the URL. The default is `http://<Server-Name>/ReportServer`.

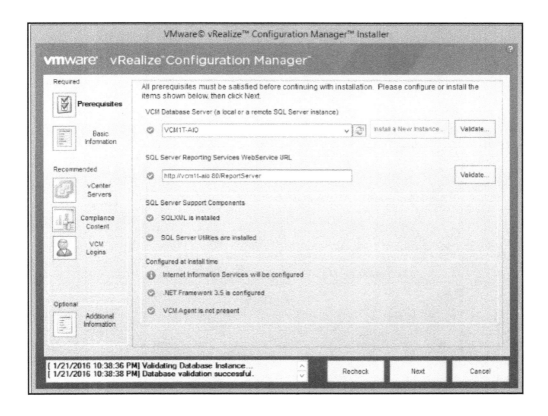

2. Click on **Validate...** under SSRS Web service, and provide the following information:

- **Database Server**: The hostname of the SSRS server
- **Domain**: The Active Directory domain
- **User Name**: The account to be used to can connect to the SSRS instance
- **Password**: Password for the user
- **Port**: The port configured while configuring SSRS
- **Virtual Directory**: Configured while configuring SSRS

Click on **Validate** and make sure the validation is successful.

After you fill in the details, the screen should look like this:

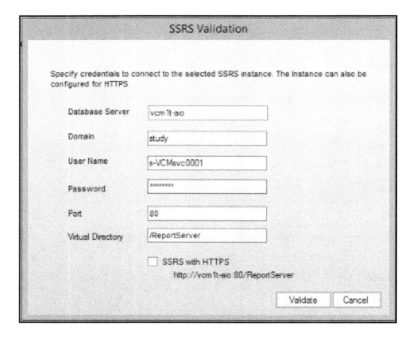

3. Enter the license key, provide the service account username and password, and click on **Validate**.
4. Provide the installation path.
5. Select **Use HTTPS. By default a self-signed certificate will be generated. Select an alternate certificate here.**

It will autogenerate a certificate; if you want, you can add your own certificate here:

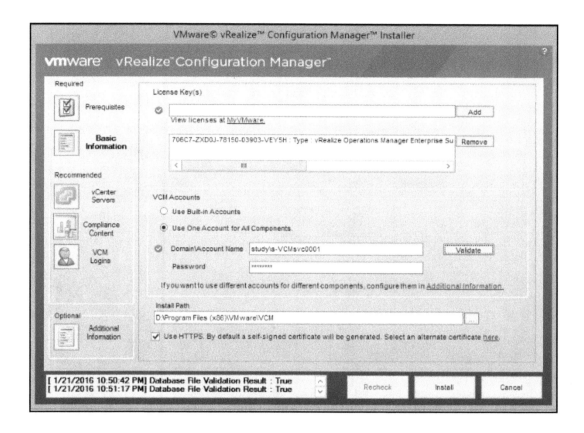

The installation can take upto an hour, depending upon the configuration of the server.

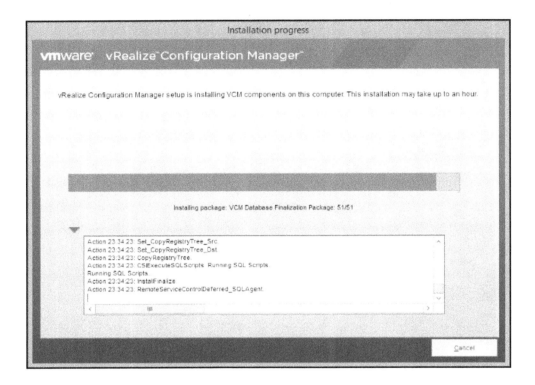

6. Once it is complete, launch the console using `https://<IP or Hostname of Collector>/VCM`.

7. As mentioned at the start of the recipe, only the account that has access to the VCM console is the one that is used for installation; we can add another users later.

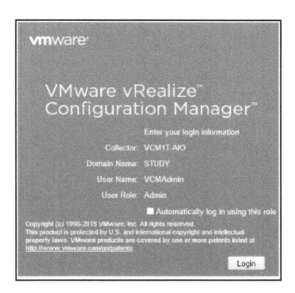

8. Click on **Login**, and you will be presented with the VCM console for the first time:

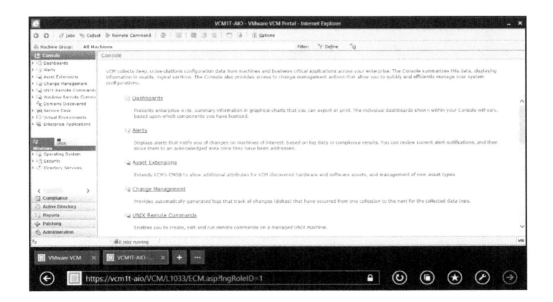

How it works...

We are installing VCM on a single server where we have already installed SQL, SSRS, and IIS. This console can then be used to manage the entire infrastructure. We will use this console to perform patching, checking compliance, publishing software exporting reports, and a lot more in the upcoming chapters.

Installing VCM – two-tier deployment

As you now know, VCM depends on SQL, and if we have a medium-sized infrastructure, it becomes too much load–the SQL, SSRS, web, and Collector server components–to carry on a single server. We can split the load in two by moving SQL databases to a dedicated server and the web and Collector components on another server.

This is how the two-tier deployment will look:

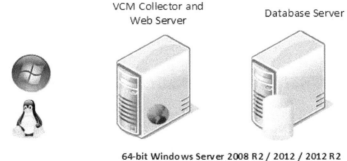

Getting ready

We will need two servers; on one, SQL Server 2012 should be installed with SSRS, and SSRS should be configured as per previous recipes.

Install all the prerequisites on both the SQL and Collector servers. Have all the mentioned service accounts ready and firewall ports open wherever required.

Install and configure IIS as per the *Preparing our VCM deployment – installing and configuring IIS* recipe.

How to do it...

As this is a two-tier VCM deployment recipe, you must have guessed that we need to perform the installation on two servers–not exactly correct; we just need to install SQL, configure SSRS, and install the prerequisites on the SQL Server; all the action happens on the VCM Collector server.

Log in to the collector server with a domain account that has local admin privileges; this is the account on which you want to have admin access on the VCM application.

Copy the downloaded ISO to the server and mount it.

Start the installation by double-clicking on `setup.exe` on the installer disk, and follow the wizard to install VCM, like this:

1. In this recipe, we will choose **Advanced Installation**.
2. Click on **Next** for the introduction page.
3. Click on **Next** for the patent information page.
4. Read and accept the license agreement and select "**I am an authorised agent and/or representative of the customer/end user**" and "**I have read the terms and conditions stated above**".
5. Under **Select Installation Type**, select the following:

   - **VMware vRealize Configuration Manager**
     - **VCM Web Console**
     - **VCM Collector Components**

- **Tools**

  - **ImportExport Utility**
  - **Foundation Checker**
  - **VMware VCM Package Manager for Windows**
  - **VMware VCM Package Studio**

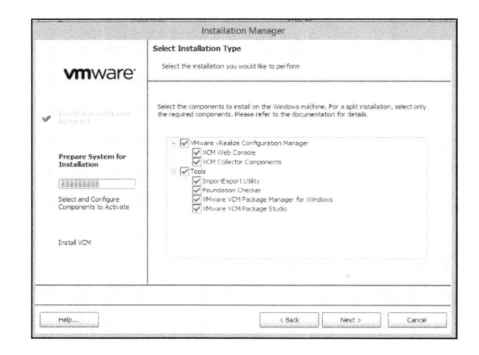

6. The installer will perform a prerequisite check and present the results; after the checks are successful, click on **Next**; if there are errors, click on **View Results**, remedy any errors and warnings, and perform a recheck.

7. Do not proceed further unless there are no errors; you can proceed if there are warnings, but it is not recommended. This is what a successful check looks like:

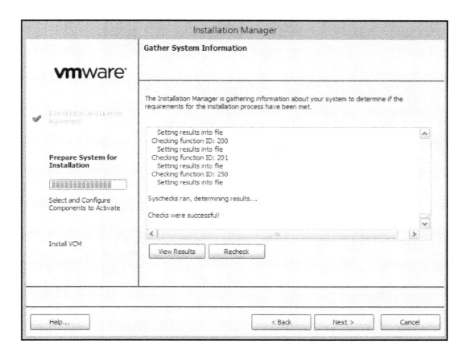

8. On the next page, enter the serial key.
9. On the **Configure Components** page, provide the hostname of the SQL Server and enter VCM as the database name; click on **Validate**.

If the validation is successful, it will provide you with the path for the data and log files, along with the **Size** and **Auto Grow** options. You can go with the defaults.

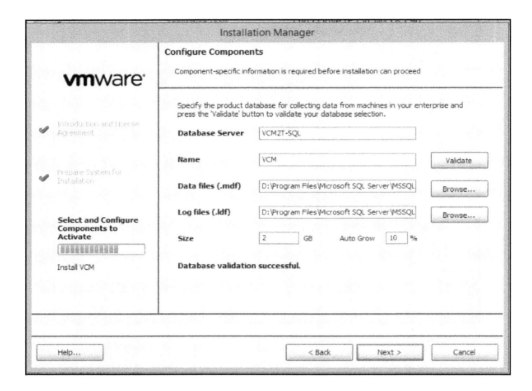

10. On the next page, provide the Tomcat service account and its password.

11. On the next page, provide the URL in **WebService URL**; credentials to validate the details include the **Domain**, **User Name**, and **Password**. Click on **Validate**. Accept the warning about insecure SRS, as we had configured it with port 80.

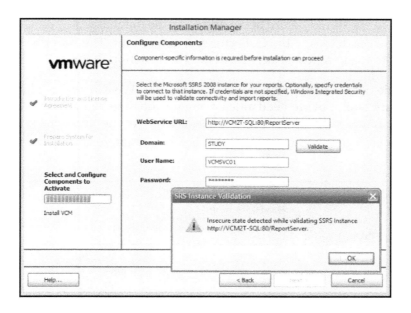

12. Provide the path to install the web console to.
13. Provide a URL to the application; the default /VCM is a good option.

    We can provide an SMTP address; the default is the collector server. If you don't know it now, it can be configured in the VCM console.

14. Provide a path to install the collector component to, and accept the SSL3 warning.

15. Provide a path to store the staging data to; this is the path where data is temporarily stored before being added to the database.

16. Provide the details of the Collector service account. This account will be given rights to log in as a service; accept the confirmation dialog.

17. Provide details of network authority accounts. We can add as many accounts as we want later, but we need at least one for the time being. More details about this can be found in the *Service accounts* subsection of this chapter's introduction.

18. The next page is about certificates. Click on **Generate** and then on **Next**.

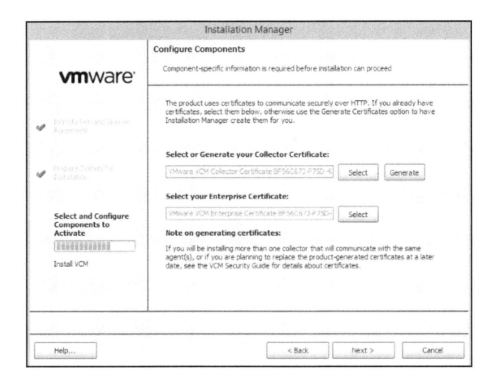

19. On the next page, which lets you select domains to run the discovery, select specific NetBIOS and AD domains.

 If you have multiple AD or NetBIOS domains, it will take more than 24 hours to detect all the domains, and the installation could eventually fail. To avoid such a scenario, select a few domains to start with and add the rest of them once VCM is ready.

20. Provide details about the virtual directory and credentials to access it.
21. Provide the credentials for the Virtualization Client plugin.
22. On the next page, provide the path to install package manager components to.
23. On the next page, provide the path to the local package cache.
24. On the next page, provide the path to the software repository and local cache.
25. Provide the name of the virtual directory.
26. Provide the path to the Package Studio components.

27. Finally, we will have reached the summary page; check the options and click on **Install**.

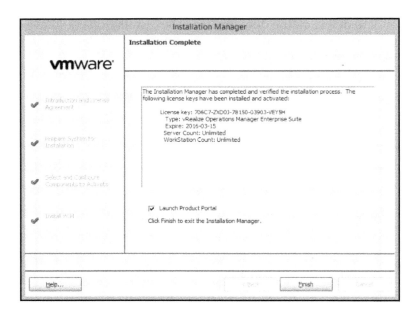

28. Log in to the portal and make sure the installation was successful.

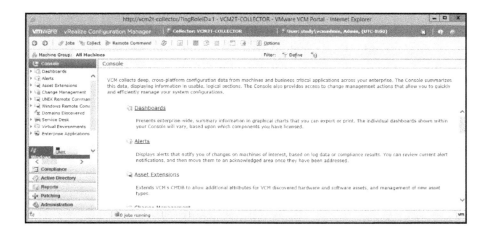

How it works...

We installed VCM on two servers; we had already installed SQL and SSRS on the SQL Server, while IIS for the web and collector components are on the Collector server. The console can then be used to manage the infrastructure. We will use this console to perform patching, compliance checking, publishing software exporting reports, and a lot more in upcoming chapters.

Installing VCM – three-tier deployment

So far, we have covered installing VCM on single and two-tier systems. There will be times when these are not sufficient, and you have a larger infrastructure to manage. To provide services to such large infrastructures, we can share the load across three tiers, namely, the database, web, and collector servers. In this recipe, we will install VCM on three different servers.

This is how the three-tier deployment will be configured:

Clients   Web Server   Collector Server   Database Server

64-bit Windows Server 2008 R2 / 2012 / 2012 R2
SQL Server 2008 R2 / 2012 / 2014

Getting ready

We will need three different servers to install the database, web, and collector components of the VCM server to.

We need all the prerequisites installed on all three servers. We should have all the mentioned service accounts ready, and firewall ports should be open wherever required.

IIS needs to be configured on the web server only.

SQL Server must be installed and SSRS configured as per previous recipes.

How to do it...

Even though this is a three-tier installation, we don't need to do much on the SQL Server; in addition to installing SQL Server 2012, we need to install the SQL Native Client, SQL Command Line Utilities, and SQLXML 4.0 SP1.

We will look at the web and collector servers in detail.

Let's cover the web server first.

Installing web components

We need to log in to the web server with a domain account that has local administrative privileges. Mount the VCM ISO and double-click on `setup.exe` on the installer disk. Follow the steps in the wizard to install the web component of VCM, as follows:

1. Select **Advanced Installation**, as this is a three-tier installation.
2. Click on **Next** for the introduction page.
3. Click on **Next** for the patent information page.
4. Read and accept the license agreement and select "**I am an authorized agent and/or representative of the customer/end user**" and "**I have read the terms and conditions stated above**".

5. Under **Select Installation Type**, select the following:

- **VMware vRealize Configuration Manager**
  - **VCM Web Console**
- **Tools**
  - **VMware VCM Package Manager for Windows**
  - **VMware VCM Package Studio**

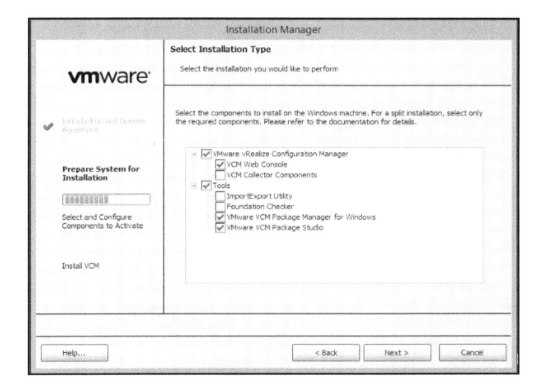

6. Accept that you have intentionally chosen to split the installation by clicking on **OK** in the dialog box that pops up.

7. The installer will perform a prerequisite check and present the results. If the check is successful, click on **Next**; if there are failures, click on **View Results**, remedy any errors and warnings, and perform a recheck. Do not proceed further until there are zero errors.

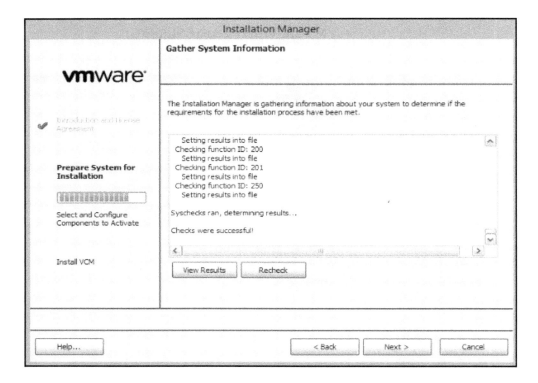

8. On the next page, enter the serial key.
9. On the **Configure Components** page, provide the hostname of the SQL Server and enter VCM as the database name; click on **Validate**.

   If the validation is successful, you will be provided with a path for the data and logfiles, along with the **Size** and **Auto Grow** options. You can go with the defaults.

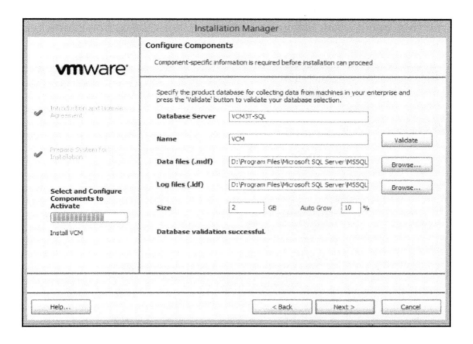

10. On the next page, provide the Tomcat service account details and its password.
11. On the next page, provide the URL in **WebService URL**. Credentials to validate the details include the **Domain**, **User Name**, and **Password**. Click on **Validate**. Accept the SRS insecure warning as we had configured it with port 80.
12. Provide the path to install the web console to.
13. Provide the URL to the application; it's okay to use the default value.

    We can provide an SMTP address. The default is the collector server. If you don't know it now, it can be configured in the VCM console.

14. Provide the credentials for the Virtualization Client plugin.
15. On the next page, provide the path to install the package manager components to.
16. On the next page, provide the path to the local package cache.
17. On the next page, provide the path to the software repository and local cache.
18. Provide the name of the virtual directory.

19. Provide the path for the Package Studio components.
20. After this, you'll reach the summary page. Check the options and click on **Install**.

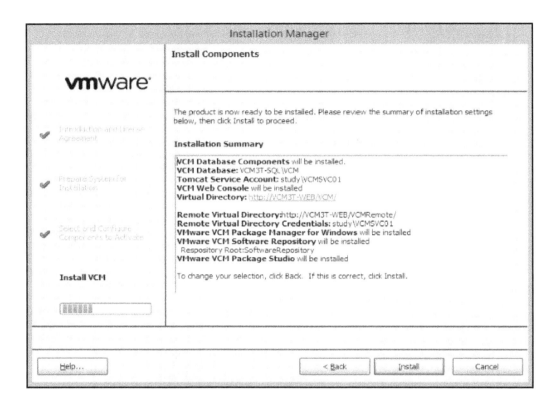

21. Click on **Finish** to exit the wizard.

This completes the web component installation; now, we have to perform similar steps on the Collector server.

Installing Collector server components

Once you are finished with the web server, log in to the Collector server with a domain account that has local administrative privileges. Copy the ISO of the VCM installer from the downloaded location and mount it.

Double-click on the `setup.exe` file from the installer media mounted, and follow these steps to complete the wizard.

1. Start with **Advanced Installation**.
2. Click on **Next** for the introduction page.
3. Click on **Next** for the patent information page.
4. Read and accept the license agreement and select "**I am an authorized agent and/or representative of the customer/end user**" and "**I have read the terms and conditions stated above**".
5. Under **Select Installation Type**, select the following:

   - **VMware vRealize Configuration Manager**
     - **VCM Collector Components**
   - **Tools**
       - **ImportExport Utility**
       - **Foundation Checker**
       - **VMware VCM Package Manager for Windows**

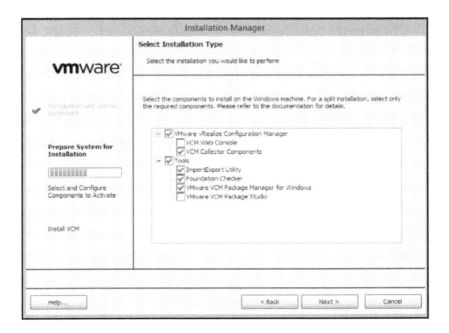

6. Accept that you have intentionally chosen to split the installation–click on **OK**.

7. The installer will perform a prerequisite check and present the results. If the check is successful, click on **Next**; if there are failures, click on **View Results**, remedy any errors and warnings, and perform a recheck. Do not proceed further until there are zero errors.

8. On the next page, enter the serial key.

9. Provide the path to install the collector component to and accept the SSL3 warning.

10. Specify the same database server and database name used when you installed the web components.

11. Provide details of a Collector service account; this account will be given rights to log in as a service; accept the corresponding dialog box.

12. Provide details of network authority accounts. We can add as many accounts as we want later, but we need at least one for the time being. More details about this can be found in the *Service accounts* subsection of this chapter's introduction.

13. The next page is for certificates; click on **Generate** and click on **Next**.

14. On the next page, in order to select domains to run the discovery, select **Specific NetBIOS and AD domains**.

 If you have multiple AD or NetBIOS domains, it will take more than 24 hours to detect all the domains, and the installation could eventually fail. To avoid such a scenario, select a few domains to start with and add the rest of them once VCM is ready.

15. On the next page, provide the path to install package manager components to.

16. On the next page, provide the path to the local package cache.

17. You will now reach the summary page; check the options and click on **Install**.

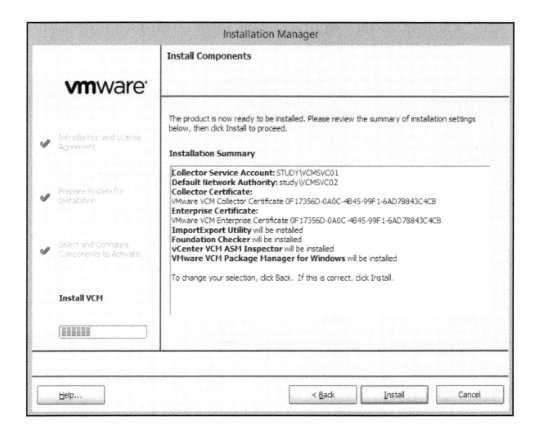

18. On the final page of the wizard, click on **Finish** to close it and launch the VCM console.

19. Once connected to the console, you will be able to notice the difference in single and two-tier deployments versus a three-tier deployment.

Earlier, our collector and web server were the same, but now, the Collector is different from the web server. Of course, this is expected as we just finished installing them separately.

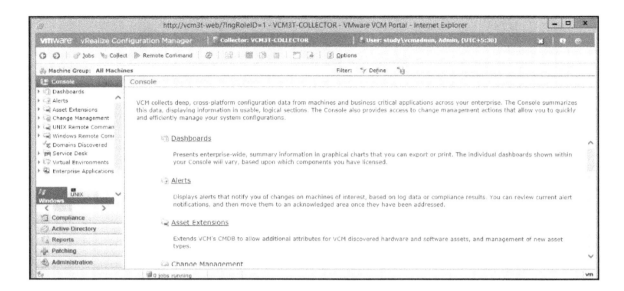

How it works...

For larger environments, such as where we need to manage more than 2,000 machines, it is recommended to have a three-tier deployment. Here, the Collector acts as middleware between the frontend IIS web component and the backend SQL database component. This distributes load between all the three components.

In a three-tier installation, when you want to connect to the VCM console, you need to use a web server and not a collector server. So, the link will be something like this:

```
https://<Web Server IP/Hostname>/VCM
```

VCM post-installation tasks – database fine tuning

VCM relies heavily on its SQL databases for operation. You must update the default settings in order to optimize SQL Server performance. We will create a maintenance plan for VCM databases.

Getting ready

Log in to SQL Server with an account that has SQL admin privileges.

How to do it...

We will perform the fine-tuning at three different levels, as detailed in the following subsections.

SQL Server – database settings

To ensure that VCM runs at peak performance and requires little operator intervention during its lifecycle, set up a routine maintenance plan. Take a look at the *VCM Administration Guide*.

Open SQL Server Management Studio and connect to the VCM SQL Server instance. Then, follow these steps:

1. Right-click on the SQL instance that you installed and select **Properties**.
2. In the **Select a page** area, select **Database Settings**.
3. Configure the following settings:

   - **Default index fill factor**: Set the fill factor to 80% in order to keep 20% free space available in each index page

Note: This sets a percentage value for the amount of free space in each index page when the page is rebuilt. Set the fill factor to 80% to keep 20% free space available in each index page. This setting is part of the SQL maintenance plan wizard. If you configure the default fill factor using this setting, keep space free in an index when you run a maintenance plan.

- **Recovery interval (minutes)**: Set the value to 5

Note: This configures the approximate amount of time that SQL Server takes to run the recovery process. The default setting is , which causes SQL Server to adjust this value and base the values on the historical operation of the server. In large environments, the recovery interval can affect the overall performance of VCM. Because VCM constantly updates how it interacts with SQL Server to process activities whose intervals differ, such as an inspection request and a compliance run, the server expends a lot of time constantly adjusting this value. By setting the recovery interval to 5 minutes, SQL Server no longer needs to tune this value.

4. Click on **OK** to save the settings.

SQL Server – maintenance plan

To ensure that VCM runs at peak performance and requires little operator intervention during its lifecycle, you must set up a routine maintenance plan. VCM relies heavily on its SQL databases for operation.

The maintenance plan uses the automated maintenance functions on the SQL Server instances that host the VCM database.

On the VCM SQL Server instance, follow these steps:

1. Click on **Start**.
2. Select **All Programs** | **Microsoft SQL Server {version}** | **SQL Server Management Studio**.
3. Expand the **Management** folder, right-click on **Maintenance Plans**, and select **Maintenance Plan Wizard**.
4. On the **Maintenance Plan Wizard** page, click on **Next**.
5. On the **Select Plan Properties** page, enter a maintenance plan name, select **Single schedule for the entire plan or no schedul**e, and click on **Change**.
6. On the **Job Schedule Properties – Maintenance Plan** page, set the scheduling properties to run the maintenance plan when the SQL Server is idle or has low usage.

7. Click on **OK** to return to the **Select Plan Properties** page, and click on **Next**.

8. On the **Select Maintenance Tasks** page, select the following maintenance tasks and click on **Next**:

   - **Check Database Integrity**
   - **Rebuild Index**
   - **Update Statistics**
   - **Clean Up History**

9. On the **Select Maintenance Task Order** page, order the maintenance tasks and click on **Next**.

10. On the **Define Database Check Integrity Task** page, define how the maintenance plan will check database integrity:
    1. Click on the **Databases** drop-down menu.
    2. Select the following databases and click on **OK**:

       - VCM
       - VCM_Coll
       - VCM_Raw
       - VCM_UNIX

Note: You must select the VCM_Raw database, because it contains transient data that the other databases consume.

    3. Select **Include indexes** and click on **Next**.

11. On the **Define Rebuild Index Task** page, define how the maintenance plan will rebuild the index:
    1. Click on the **Databases** drop-down menu.
    2. Select the following databases and click on **OK**:

       - VCM
       - VCM_Coll
       - VCM_UNIX

Note: Do not rebuild the index for the VCM_Raw database.

    3. In the **Advanced Options** area, select **Sort results in tempdb** and click on **Next**.

12. On the **Define Update Statistics Task** page, define how the maintenance plan will update database statistics:

    1. Click on the **Databases** drop-down menu.

    2. Select the following databases and click on **OK**:

- VCM
- VCM_Coll
- VCM_UNIX

Note: Do not update statistics for the VCM_Raw database.

13. On the **Define History Cleanup Task** page, define how the maintenance plan will clean up historical data from the SQL Server machine, and click on **Next**:

    1. Select **Backup and restore history**.

    2. Select **SQL Server Agent job history**.

    3. Select **Maintenance plan history**.

    4. Set the cleanup task to remove historical data older than 4 months.

14. On the **Select Report Options** page, save a report of the maintenance plan actions:

    1. Select **Write a report to a text file**.

    2. Select a folder for the report and click **Next**.

15. On the **Complete the Wizard** page, verify your selections in the **Maintenance Plan Wizard** summary, expand the selections to view the settings, and click on **Finish**.

16. When the **Maintenance Plan Wizard** progress has finished, verify that each action was successful.

How it works...

In this recipe, we tried to make sure that our SQL Server for VCM is performing optimally and we don't need much operator intervention for VCM maintenance.

We scheduled a maintenance plan to keep our database clutter free and help it perform better.

2
Configuring VCM to Manage Your Infrastructure

In this chapter, we will cover the following recipes:

- Adding a vCenter Server instance
- Adding a vCloud Director and vShield instance
- Collecting data from managed machines
- Adding a discovery rule
- Adding a network authority account to manage machines in multiple domains
- Configuring a managing agent machine for virtual environment management
- Installing an agent on Windows servers
- Installing an agent on Linux servers
- Creating machine groups

Introduction

Once VCM has been installed, we need to configure it to make it work for our environment; the default configurations need to be changed for environment-specific changes. To manage our infrastructure, we need to install agents on the Windows and Linux servers. This can be achieved in many ways, such as installing via scripts or, if we are using automation to deploy the machines, we could use that itself or push it to the servers identified by VCM.

We need to add vCenter, vCloud, and vShield server instances to VCM so that we can start utilizing the details available in those systems, such as machines and vApps deployed, which can be used to create various reports. Also, the captured details include the virtual machines deployed in the infrastructure, which can be used by VCM to deploy agents and bring them under management.

We need to create various machine groups; a machine group is basically a collection of machines that can be grouped into a single entity for various purposes, such as patching, reporting, and checking compliance.

In this chapter, we will start configuring VCM so that it is ready for day-to-day operations.

Let's begin.

Adding a vCenter Server instance

Before we start managing our virtual infrastructure, we need to add the components to VCM. We will start adding them in the following recipes, starting with vCenter.

Getting ready

We will need a user with administrative access to the vCenter instance that we want to add to VCM as well as its **fully qualified domain name** (**FQDN**) or IP address.

How to do it...

To add the vCenter instance to VCM, log in to the VCM server UI and follow these steps:

1. Log in to VCM with an administrative account.
2. Go to **Administration** | **Machines Manager** | **Licensed Machines** | **Licensed Virtual Environments**.

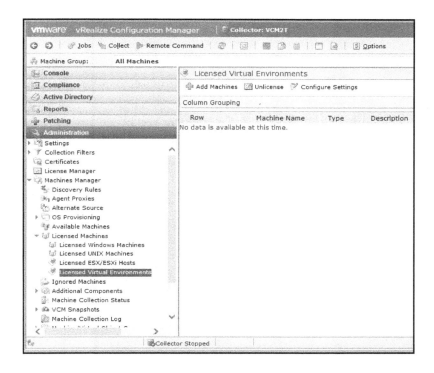

3. Click on **Add Machines**.
4. Select **Basic** on the first page of the wizard.
5. Enter the hostname (not FQDN here) for the machine name, select **Domain** from the dropdown which the machine belongs to, select **DNS** for **Type**, and **vCenter Windows** for **Machine Type**.
6. Click on **Add**, and then click on **Next**.
7. Click on **Finish** to close the wizard.

> With these steps, we added the vCenter instance to VCM, but we still need to configure it so that we can collect the details.

8. Now, select the vCenter instance we just added and click on **Configure Settings**.
9. In this wizard, select the vCenter instance.

10. Provide the following information:

   - **Managing Agent**: Your Collector server
   - **Port**: 443
   - **User ID**: A user with administrative access to vCenter
   - **Password**: The password for the user; enter it twice to confirm
   - **Ignore untrusted SSL Certificate**: Yes

11. Click on **Next** once all the details have been filled in.

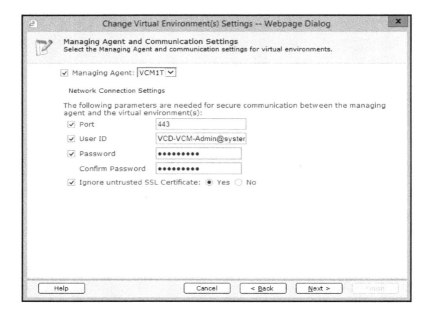

 Note: The user must have a vCenter Server administrative role or a read-only role. However, you cannot run actions with a read-only role.

12. Click on **Finish** to close the wizard.
13. There should be a green circle in front of the vCenter instance's name on the VCM console.

How it works...

We are adding vCenter to VCM so that we can collect information about all the ESXi hosts in the instance, all the virtual machines, and so on, and based on this information, we can create compliance checks for our virtual infrastructure, discover the virtual machines as managed machines in VCM so that we can install agents, and collect information about them as well.

VCM collects the following information from vCenter:

- vCenter Summary
- vCenter Custom Information
- vCenter Guests
- vCenter Hosts
- vCenter Host Profiles
- vCenter Inventory
- vCenter Networking
- vCenter Settings
- vCenter Resource Pools
- vCenter Roles

Adding a vCloud Director and vShield instance

There are three virtual elements that can be managed by VCM: vCenter, vShield, and vCloud. In the previous recipe, we added vCenter. In this one, we will continue with **vShield** and **vCloud Director** (**vCD**).

VMware vShield is a suite of virtual security appliances built for VMware vCenter Server integration. A vShield security group is a logical trust zone that you create and assign resources to for vShield protection.

By adding vCloud to VCM, you can use the vCloud Director properties to create machine groups and so on.

Getting ready

We will need the IP address of the vShield Manager and vCloud Director instances and a user account with administrative privileges.

Before adding vShield, you must collect data for your vCenter instance, as described in the next recipe.

How to do it...

We will split this recipe into two sections, as follows.

- *Adding a vShield instance*
- *Adding a vCloud Director instance*

Adding a vShield instance

This is a bit different than adding vCenter. After adding a vCenter instance and collecting data from it, VCM identifies the vShield VM and it makes it available on the VCM console for configuration, so we don't need to perform any additional steps as we did for vCenter; we just need to configure it, which we will do as follows:

1. Go to **Administration** | **Machines Manager** | **Licensed Machines** | **Licensed Virtual Environments**.
2. Select the vShield device identified by VCM, and click on **Configure Settings**.

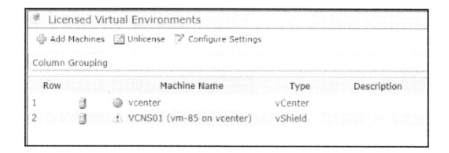

3. Make sure the vShield instance is selected in the wizard launched.

4. Provide information as follows:

- **Managing Agent**: Your Collector server
- **Port**: 443
- **User ID**: A user with administrative access to vShield
- **Password**: The password for the user; enter it twice to confirm it
- **Ignore untrusted SSL Certificate**: **Yes**
- Provide the name of the vCenter Server instance this vShield instance is responsible for

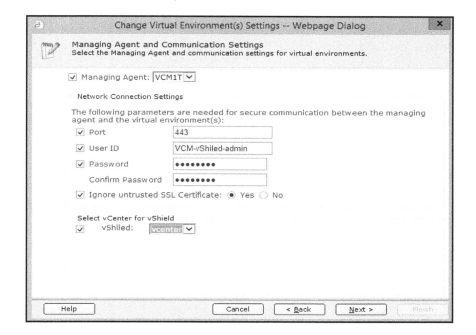

 Note: The user must have a vShield Manager administrative role or an unrestricted read-only role.

5. Click on **Finish** to close the wizard.

> Once again, you should see a green circle in front of the vShield instance you just configured.
>
> If there isn't one, make sure you have provided the correct username and password.

Adding a vCloud Director instance

Log in to VCM server and follow these steps:

1. Go to **Administration** | **Machines Manager** | **Licensed Machines** | **Licensed Virtual Environments**.
2. Click on **Add Machines**.
3. Select **Basic** from the first page of the wizard.
4. Enter your hostname in **Machine Name**, select **Domain** from the dropdown that the machine belongs to, select **DNS** as **Type** and **vCloud Director** as **Machine Type**.
5. Click on **Add**, and then click on **Next**.
6. Click on **Finish** to end the wizard.

 With these steps, we added the vCloud instance to VCM, but we still need to configure it so that we can collect the details.

7. Now, select the vCloud Director instance we just added and click on **Configure Settings**.
8. In this wizard, select the vCloud Director machine.
9. Provide information as follows:

   - **Managing Agent**: Your Collector server
   - **Port**: 443
   - **User ID**: A user with administrative access to vCloud Director

- Local user in the format user@System
- **Password**: The password for the user; enter it again to confirm it
- **Ignore untrusted SSL Certificate: Yes**

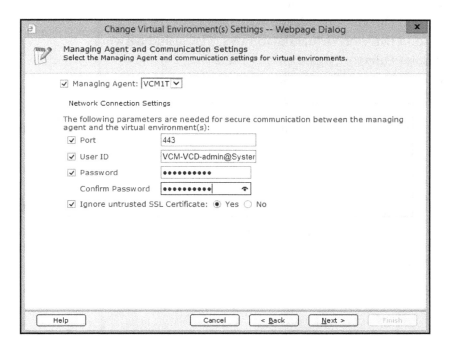

10. Click on **Finish** to close the wizard.
11. There should be a green circle in front of the vCloud Director instance's name on the VCM console.

How it works...

We make information available in the vShield instance, that is, security groups and its members exposed to VCM. The details are stored in the VCM database as well and can be used when required.

After adding and performing a collection, we have the following information from the vCloud Director database in the VCM console:

- vCloud Director Organizations
- vCloud Director virtual machines and vApps
- vCloud Director organization catalogs
- vCloud Director Virtual datacenters (vDCs) and networks
- vCloud Director Organizations Users
- vCloud Director Organizations Groups
- vCloud Director Organizations Settings

This information can be used to create machine groups based on vCloud organizations in order to manage them accordingly.

Collecting data from managed machines

Once we are done adding and configuring virtual environments, we can start collecting data, which can be further used to check compliance, create necessary machine groups, export reports, and so on.

We need to collect data from virtual environments as well as from all the machines that we plan to manage, that is, Windows or Linux servers.

Getting ready

All the servers we want to manage should be added to the VCM console, either by following earlier recipes for virtual infrastructures or by installing agents by following the recipes in this chapter.

How to do it...

We will split this recipe into two sections:

- *Collecting data from virtual infrastructures*
- *Collecting data from managed machines*

Collecting data from virtual infrastructures

To collect all data off a vCenter, vShield Manager, or vCD instance, follow these steps:

1. Log in to VCM and follow the steps to collect virtual infrastructure data.
2. You can be anywhere in the VCM console; make sure the machine group is **All Machines** (to understand more about machine groups, have a look at the *Creating machine groups* recipe), and click on **Collect** in the top-left corner.
3. This will launch a wizard; select **Machine Data** under **Collection Type**.
4. Select the machines you want to collect data from, in this case, any or all of vCenter, vShield, and vCloud servers. Select them and make sure they are on the right-hand side, and then click on **Next**.
5. Select **Select Data Types** to collect from these machines.

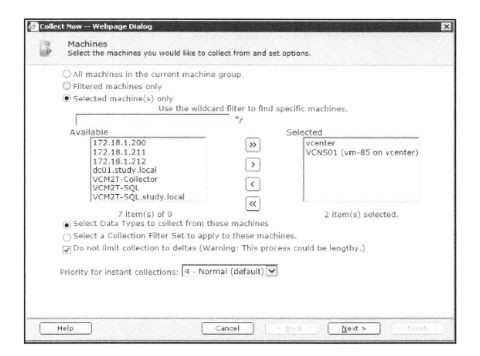

6. Under **Data Types**, tick each checkbox underneath **Virtualization**:

7. Make sure there are no conflicts, and click on **Finish**.
8. Click on **Jobs** in the left-hand corner of the VCM console.
9. Make sure the job to collect the data has completed successfully.

Collecting data from managed machines

In this subsection, we will collect data from managed machines, such as Windows and Linux servers. Follow these steps:

1. Log in to VCM and follow the steps to collect virtual infrastructure data.
2. You can be anywhere in the VCM console; make sure the machine group is **All Machines** (to understand more about machine groups, have a look at the *Creating machine groups* recipe) and click on **Collect** in the top-left corner.
3. This will launch a wizard; select **Machine Data** under **Collection Type**.

4. On the next page, select the machine/machines whose data you want to collect. The machines must be on the right-hand side.

5. You have two options for deciding how data will be collected: based on the data type or based on the collection filter set.

Note: If you select data type then you are presented with options to select from various entities of the OS such as accounts, account policies, disk space, device drives, and so on that are relevant to the OS of the machine we selected.

If you select filter sets, VCM has precreated sets of filters, which can be used to collect data from the managed machine. The filter sets can be created manually, while installing VCM, or when you import any compliance template.

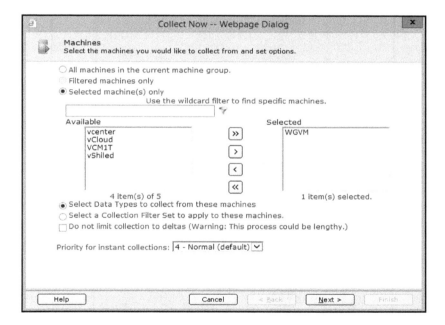

6. Depending upon what you select, the next page will differ.

7. For the **Data Types** window, select individual data types or select all of them.

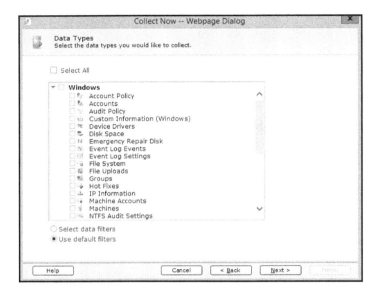

8. For the **Filter Sets** window, select the appropriate filter set to collect the data.

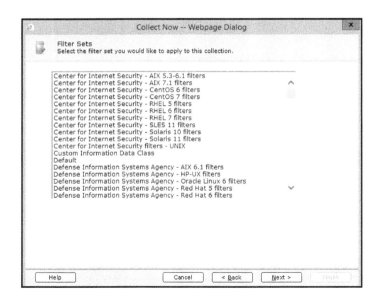

9. Make sure there are no conflicts, and close the wizard. It will start a collection job, and VCM will go to the specified machines and collect details either according to data types or selected filter sets.

How it works...

In the previous recipes, we added vCenter, vCD, and vShield Manager; now, we need the data to import into all those elements. By performing a collection, we are adding the details available on those systems to VCM so that we can have a single interface where we can see all the details.

The details fetched from those systems have been mentioned in the earlier recipes. When VCM performs a collection operation, it goes into each application's database, pulls all the relevant information, and then places it in its own database. For example, when we perform a vCenter collection, it collects details about all the VMs, ESXi hosts, their versions, snapshot details for VMs, VM configuration, and so on. All the data is presented in the VCM console under **Console** | **Virtual Environments**.

In case of vCD, VCM fetches information about the vApps, VMs, catalogs, local users, groups, and so on.

This information can then be exported via reports, used for compliance checks. This can also be used in creating dynamic filters for creating machine groups.

Details captured from managed machines such as Windows and Linux servers will be used in analyzing their current compliance and patch status.

There's more...

Have a look at the following article by VMware if you want details about filter sets:

```
https://www.vmware.com/support/vcm/doc/help/vcm581/Content/Core_CS/Admi
nSettingsCollFltr.htm
```

Adding a discovery rule

VCM must discover machines in your environment before you can collect data from them. You can create a **discovery rule** to discover all machines, or you can apply a filter to limit the machines that VCM discovers. Discovery rules are used to discover managed machines automatically.

Getting ready

You must have configured and collected data from vCenter and vCloud to add a database discovery rule.

You must license the virtual environments and Windows, Unix, and Linux machines to use for data collection. When you license these virtual or physical machines, they appear in the **Licensed Machines** list.

VCM can discover machines from Active Directory, browse lists, domain controllers, databases, or by IP address.

We will perform database discovery in this recipe; you can check remaining options in your lab.

How to do it...

We will configure VCM to discover vCenter VMs by following these steps:

1. Log in to VCM as an administrative user.
2. Go to **Administrator** | **Machines Manager** | **Discovery Rule**; click on the green plus button to add a new discovery rule.
3. This will launch a wizard; provide a name and description.
4. Select the **By DB Discovery:** checkbox.

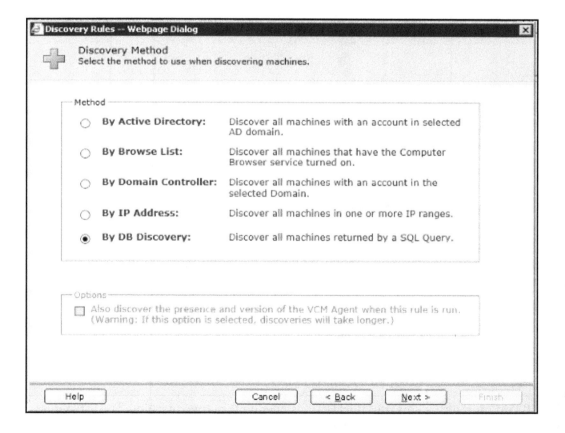

5. Select **vCenter Guest Systems** under **Discovery Query**.
6. The other two options are using vCloud Director or directly from the host.

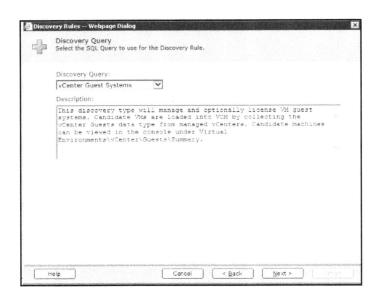

7. On the next page, select/fill in options according to this table:

Option	Description
Machine Name Format	The format for VCM to display guest machines. You can select the **NetBIOS**, **DNS**, or **VM/vCenter** name format.
Domain Name	The domain under which to add the new machine. This domain is the same as the **Domain Name** property when you add machines using manual discovery.
Domain Type	Select one out of **Active Directory**, **DNS**, or **NetBIOS** domain types.
Protocol	Select **DCOM** or **HTTP**.
HTTP Port (default used if blank)	This uses the HTTP listener on the target machine. The listener is configured to listen on the designated port. Port 26542 is the default setting. Accepted port values range from 1 to 65535. Other applications must not use this port.
Use a proxy server	No

Connection String	This is the address of the virtual machine to contact. This address can differ from the address that resolves by machine name from DNS or other name-resolution systems. Use this address when VCM must contact a vApp virtual machine through a Network Address Translation (**NAT**) address.
ESX Host Name Filter	This filters the query to ESX host machine names in the virtual environment based on the information you type.
VM Guest Name Filter	This filters the query to guest VM names on the ESX host machine in the virtual environment based on the information you type.
Guest DNS Name Filter	This filters the query to domain name servers based on the information you type.
Guest OS Name Filter	This filters the query to the guest operating systems in the virtual environment based on the information you type.
Power State	This filters the query to the state of the guest virtual machine in the virtual environment based on the information you type.

After you make appropriate selections as described in the table, your screen should look like this:

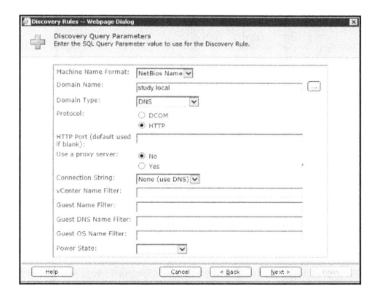

8. Select **Yes** to start the discovery once the rule creation is over, and if you want, you can select **License** and install **Agent** on **Discovered Machines**.

9. Click **Finish** to close the wizard.

How it works...

As this is a query run against the VCM database, we must perform a collection against at least one vCenter Server before we run this discovery rule.

VCM adds the machines either to the available machines in the machine manager if you choose not to license the machine; and if you choose to license it as part of the discovery rule, then they go to either licensed Windows or Unix machines.

There's more...

This is the table describing all the available methods taken from the VCM help document on http://www.vmware.com/:

Sr. No.	Method	Description
1	**By Active Directory**	This discovers all the machines that have an account on the selected AD domain. The discovery process identifies machines based on the current domain controller data.
2	**By Browse List**	This discovers all the machines that have the **Computer Browser** service turned on. When the rule discovers machines through the browse list, VCM returns the NetBIOS domain name for each machine.
3	**By Domain Controller**	This discovers all the machines that have an account on the selected domain. When the domain controller performs a periodic update, existing machines might not appear, while deleted machines might.
4	**By IP Address**	This discovers all the machines in your network that exist in specific IP address ranges. Discovered machines appear in the list of available machines.
5	**By DB Discovery**	This discovers machines based on the SQL query used for the discovery rule. This discovery type uses data that VCM has already collected from other sources as the basis for finding new systems to manage. You can discover vCD-managed virtual machines, virtual machine guests, and virtual machine hosts.

Refer here for more:

```
https://www.vmware.com/support/vcm/doc/help/vcm581/Content/Core_CS/Admi
nMachMngrDiscAECWiz.htm
```

Adding a network authority account to manage machines in multiple domains

For medium to large infrastructures, there are always multiple Active Directory domains available. We can use VCM to manage servers in multiple domains. This recipe explains what you need to do for that.

Getting ready

There should be a proper name resolution. If there is a firewall in between, then the ports stated in the first chapter must be open.

We need a **network authority account** per domain in order to manage the machines in that domain and VCM functions such as collecting data, patching, and so on.

How to do it...

We need to add the domains and network authority account and finally associate them with one another.

Go to **Administration** | **Settings** | **Network Authority**

We have three options:

- **Available Domains** (identified while performing the installation); we can add new ones if required
- **Available Accounts** (we assigned one NAA while performing VCM deployment)
- **Assigned Accounts**

Available Domains

Domains are identified in one of the steps when we perform the VCM server installation; now, we can add extra domains. Click on **Add** under **Available Domains**, and provide the domain **Name** and **Type**.

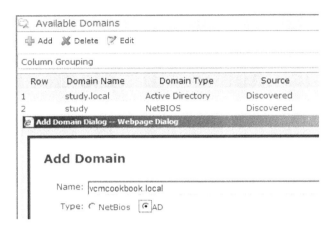

Available Accounts

Under **Available Accounts**, we can see which network authority accounts are available and then add any extra accounts or remove unwanted ones.

Assigned Accounts

This is the place where we associate available accounts with available domains.

Go to **Assigned Accounts** | **By Domain** | **Active Directory**, and then click on **Edit Assigned Accounts** and associate the available accounts with this domain.

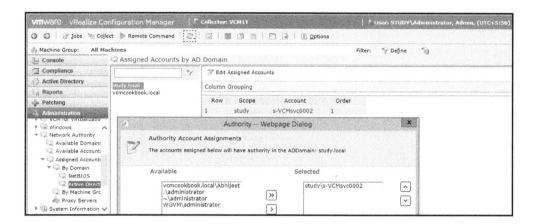

How it works...

Basically, by following this process, we assigned an account that has local admin privileges or the rights explained in the first chapter to all the machines in the respective domain that will be managed by VCM.

We can assign as many accounts as required. When a VCM function is started, assigned accounts will be tried in the specified order. When something starts a subsequent time, the last successfully used account will be used first. Accounts are listed in the order in which they are assigned, from top to bottom.

If a machine is in multiple lists (such as a domain and a machine group), the authority account that will be used to contact it will be in the following order:

- The last account that worked
- The accounts assigned to the domain
- The accounts assigned any machine group (including the default **All Machines** group) to which the machine belongs

We need to do this for Windows only, as in the case of Linux, we need to accept the certificate in the VCM console. Unless we accept the certificate, we will not be able to patch the Linux machine from VCM. To accept the certificate, on the VCM console, go to **Administration** | **Certificates**, select the machine, and click on **Change Trust Status**. Follow the wizard, and you will see a handshake symbol in front of the machine. This will allow you to patch the Linux machine from the VCM console. The steps to perform this action are a part of the next recipe.

Configuring a managing agent machine for virtual environment management

Managing agents are systems that manage the communication between the collector and the virtual environment we manage via VCM, that is, vCenter Server, vCD, and vShield Manager. In this recipe, we will assign a system the role of a management agent.

Getting ready

We need to have the version 5.5 or later agent installed on the machine and data collected from it, which will be designated as the managing agent. Refer to the next recipe.

The managing agent machines must have the version 5.5 or later agent installed.

We can designate any server that can communicate with VCM as well as vCD, vShield, and vCenter Server as a managing agent.

How to do it...

Log in to VCM and follow these steps to designate a managing agent and then change it to a managed virtual environment:

1. Navigate to **Administration | Certificates**.

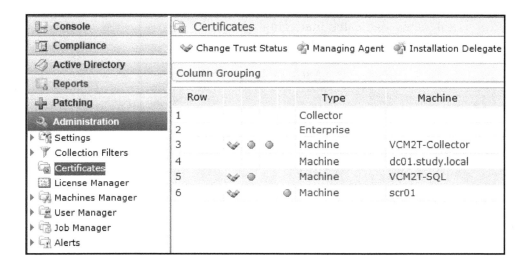

2. Select the machine that you want to designate as a managing agent.
3. Select **Change Trust Status**.
4. Check to trust or uncheck to untrust the selected machines box, click on **Next**, and click on **Finish** on the next page to complete the wizard.
5. Select the machine again and click on **Managing Agent** in the top menu.

6. Select **Enable**, click on **Next**, and then click on **Finish** on the next page to complete the wizard.

Note: The choice of managing agent solely depends on the size of the infrastructure you manage; you can use your collector as a managing agent, or you can use another Windows machine. If your individual vCenter instance manages between 1 to 30 hosts and a maximum of 1,000 guests, then you can use the collector as your managing agent. Otherwise, designate a dedicated managing agent.

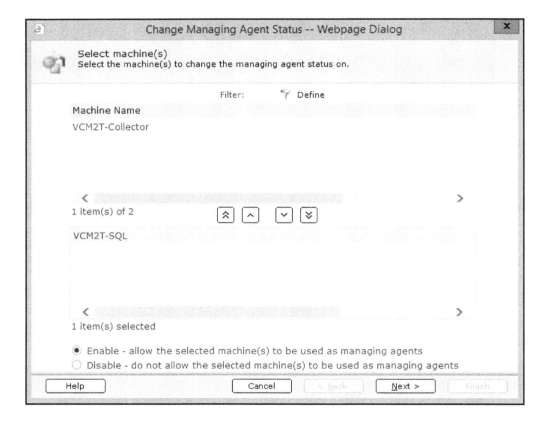

7. The selected server will become the managing agent now.
8. Once the managing agent has been designated, we can change it for the managed virtual environment.
9. Go to **Administration** | **Machines Manager** | **Licensed Machines** | **Licensed Virtual Environments**. Select the machine whose managing agent you want to change, and click on **Configure Settings**.
10. Select the machine added if required.
11. On the top, there is a dropdown to select either of the available managing agents. Change to a new one and click on **Next** (not visible in the screenshot), and click on **Finish** on next page to close the wizard.

12. Repeat steps 8 through 10 for the remaining virtual environments in the infrastructure.

How it works...

The managing agents are systems that manage the communication between the collector and the virtual environment using the VMware APIs of the various products. They must be configured to manage secure communication between virtual environment instances and the collector.

It is recommended that VCM collector act as the managing agent if any of the vCenter instances it is managing has 1 to 30 hosts and upto 1,000 guests. The default managing agent is the Collector server, but as the workload increases, we can start adding them. In this recipe, we looked at designating a managed machine to a managed agent.

We are designating another server to communicate with the virtual environment so that some of the work can be offloaded from VCM Collector. The server must have connectivity to the virtual environment servers and VCM Collector.

Installing an agent on Windows servers

Before we start managing any machine, we need to install an agent on it. This can be done in multiple ways, such as pushing it from the VCM console, installing it manually, or installing it with a script.

In this recipe, we will have a look at installing the agent manually and with a script on a Windows server.

Getting ready

Prepare a server to install the agent; the installer is available on the VCM Collector server, at `X:\Program Files (x86)\Vmware\VCM\AgentFiles` and the certificate is available at `X:\Program Files (x86)\Vmware\VCM\CollectorData`, where `X` is the drive where VCM is installed.

Copy the installer and certificate on a shared location from where it can be copied to the server where we want to install it.

We need administrative access on the server where we will be installing the agent.

The local firewall should be disabled (not recommended) or port `26542` must be open between the managed machine and VCM Collector.

For an agent push, we need the machines to be registered as licensed machines on the VCM console and the network authority account to be a part of the local administrators group, and port `26542` should be open on the machine where we are pushing the agent.

How to do it...

We will split this recipe into three sections, as follows

- *Manual agent installation*
- *Agent push from the console*
- *Licensing Windows machines*

Manual agent installation

Log in to the server with an administrative account, copy the installer with a certificate locally, and follow this process:

1. Start `VCMAgentInstall.exe`.
2. Click on **Next**, again on **Next**, and on the destination location screen, continue with the default `C:\Windows\CMAgent` value.
3. Select **Allow HTTP**, and go with the default port, `26542`.
4. On this page, browse to the location where the certificate is copied.
5. Click on **Next** three more times, and it will start installing the agent.
6. Once the agent has been installed, log in to VCM console.
7. Go to **Administration** | **Machines Manager** | **Licensed Machines** | **Licensed Windows Machines**, and click on **Add Machine**.
8. Select **Basic** and select automatically license machines.
9. Provide details about the machine where you installed the agent, as follows:

   - Provide the hostname for the **Machine Name** parameter
   - Select the domain from the dropdown which the machine belongs to
   - Select **DNS** as **Type**
   - Select **Windows Server** as **Machine Type**

10. Click on **Next** and then on **Finish** to close the wizard.

11. Once the machine has been added to VCM, we need to hit the **Refresh** button on the console and click on **Collect** to start data collection.
12. Monitor the data collection job, and finally, we are done with adding a machine to VCM.

Agent push from the console

The machine should be in the VCM console either by running a discovery rule or adding it manually. Now, we can perform a push of the agent from the console.

Log in to the VCM console and follow these steps to install the agent on the machine:

1. Go to **Administration** | **Machines Manager** | **Licensed Machines** | **Licensed Windows Machines**, and select the machine which you want to add the agent to.
2. Click on **Install** in the menu.

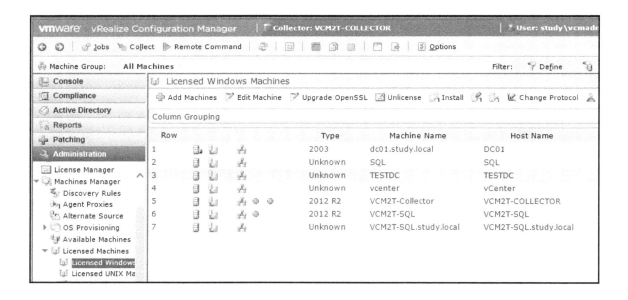

3. The wizard will open. Make sure the machine appears in the **Selected** box.
4. On the next page, set the following values:

   - **Install At:** Keep this default.
   - **Install From:** Keep this default.
   - **Options:** Select **HTTP** and set the port to `26542`. Keep the rest default.

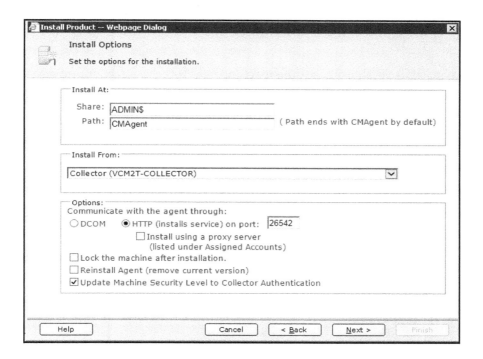

5. On the schedule screen, select **Run Now**.
6. Confirm the selection and click on **Finish**.
7. Click on **Jobs** to see whether the job is successful, and after that, go back to the console, scroll to the right, and check whether the machine has its agent state changed from **Unknown** to **Current Agent** and shows its agent version as **5.8.2**.
8. Once the machine has its agent installed, perform an initial collection.

Licensing Windows machines

We will perform the following steps to license a managed machine. The steps are the same for Windows and Linux/Unix machines.

1. Log in to the VCM console with an admin account.
2. Click on **Administration**.
3. Go to **Machines Manager** | **Available Machines**.
4. Select the Windows machines to license.
5. Click on **License**.

Follow the wizard to finish licensing the machine, and if the available number is below zero and in red, contact VMware to purchase more licenses.

How it works...

With this recipe, we are making sure that the machine we want to manage has an agent installed, is licensed in VCM, and that we have performed the data collection.

VCM has enough information about managed machines to start deploying software; put the machine in the correct machine group. We can perform further specific collections to find out the compliance status or patching status, and based on that, we can fix the machine or install missing patches.

There's more...

We can install the agent with a script.

Here is the code for the script:

```
cd C:\VCM_Agent
CMAgentInstall.exe /s INSTALLPATH=C:\Windows\CMAgent PORT=26542
CERT=C:\VCM_Agent\VMware_VCM_Enterprise_Certificate_E5D8927D-
A9A7-43E8-8E6F-5C88D1E40F12.pem
```

Here is what the options stand for:

Sr. No.	Option	Description
1	C:\VCM_Agent	The location where the BAT file, installer, and certificate are copied
2	CMAgentInstall.exe	The VCM agent installer
3	/s	Option for a silent installation
4	INSTALLPATH	The location to install the VCM agent on the server
5	PORT	The port for the VCM agent to communicate
6	CERT	The VCM Enterprise certificate path

Just run the batch file and then follow steps 6 to 11 to complete the agent installation.

You can also use the PowerCLI commands Copy.VMGuestFile and Invoke-VMSCript to automate the deployment.

Installing an agent on Linux servers

We need an agent to manage Linux/Unix machines; in this recipe, we will install it manually on a Linux machine.

Getting ready

In case of a Linux installer, make sure that it is copied from the same VCM server where the managed machine will get managed, as VCM certificates are embedded in the installer. If we use an installer from another VCM server and then try to manage it from a different server, it will fail.

Copy the correct installer from the VCM server to the Linux server.

Install the prerequisites and verify that the glibc.i686, net-tools, and redhat-lsb-core packages have been installed on the target machine.

Open port 26542 if a firewall is enabled.

We need the root password of the machine where the agent will be installed.

The agent is available at `X: \Program Files (x86)\VMware\VCM\Installer\Packages\CMAgent.5.8.2.linux` on the VCM Collector server. We don't need to copy the certificate the way we did in Windows as the certificate is built into the installer.

How to do it...

Follow the steps to install the agent on a Linux machine:

1. Copy the installer with `scp` or `winscp` on the server.
2. Log in to the Linux server as root.
3. Run `chmod u+x CMAgent.5.8.2.linux`.
4. Run `./CMAgent.5.8.2.linux`.
5. Copy the modified and `savedcsi.config` file to the extracted location.

   Note: `csi.config` is a configuration file used by the VCM agent to install the agent.

   More details about the configuration options can be found at `https://ww w.vmware.com/support/vcm/doc/help/vcm581/Content/NIX/CM_R ef_UNIX_csi_config_options.htm`.

   There are lots of options available to configure the `csi.config` file.

   We need to set `CSI_AGENT_RUN_OPTION = daemon` to start this as a daemon; for the rest, you can consult with your Linux admin and decide.

   An example: `# cp /<Shared_location> csi.config /<extractedlocation>/CSIInstall/csi.config`.

6. Once this is done, run the installer script using `./CSIInstall/InstallCMAgent -s`.

Once the agent has been installed, follow the previous recipe from step 6 onward; just change the location from **Licensed Windows Machines** to **Licensed UNIX Machines**, and when entering details, set **Machine Type** as **Red Hat Server** or any other, depending upon the OS and as per the following screenshot:

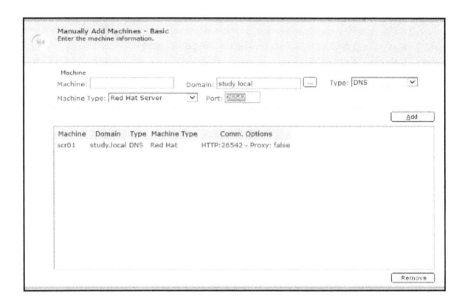

How it works...

We added the agent to the Linux/Unix machines as well so that we can collect the details of the managed machines; then, those details will be used to check compliance and patch status.

There's more...

We can create a preconfigured `csi-config` file and copy it to `/opt/CMAgent` along with the installer.

Copy the content of the following script into a `.sh` file.

Give it execute permission: `chmod CMAgentInstall.sh 755`.

Then, run the ./CMAgentInstall.sh command.

```
IPTABLES="/sbin/iptables"
grep -i suse /etc/issue >/dev/null || rc=$?
if [ $rc -ne 0 ]; then
  IPTABLES="/usr/sbin/iptables"
fi

${IPTABLES}-save > /opt/APPL/iptables.CMAgent.preinstall
${IPTABLES} -I INPUT -m state --state NEW -p tcp --dport 26542 -j ACCEPT

grep -i suse /etc/issue >/dev/null || rc=$?
if [ $rc -ne 0 ]; then
  /sbin/SuSEfirewall2 open EXT TCP 26542
else
  grep -i maipo /etc/redhat-release >/dev/null || rc=$?
  if [ $rc -ne 0 ]; then
    /sbin/firewall-cmd --zone=public --add-port=26542/tcp --permanent
  else
    /sbin/service iptables save
  fi
fi

cd /opt; /opt/APPL/CMAgent.5.8.2.Linux
cp /opt/CMAgent/csi.config.CMAgent /opt/CSIInstall/csi.config
/opt/CSIInstall/InstallCMAgent -s
```

The script identifies the OS of the machine and, based on that, opens port 26542 on the local firewall. Then, it copies the preconfigured csi.config file and, finally, installs the agent from the /opt/CSIInstall folder.

Creating machine groups

Machine/virtual object groups are used to organize managed machines and virtual objects into small logical groups. There are default groups available from VCM when it is deployed (more details are in the *There's More...* section).

Getting ready

As an administrator, you must have some idea of which machine you should put together. You can use this concept and create machine groups as per your requirement.

How to do it...

Once you have a basic understanding of what you want to achieve with the group, log in to the VCM console and follow the steps detailed shortly.

We will create a machine group that will include all the machines that are a part of the `Study.local` Active Directory group, and it will keep on adding machines as soon as a new machine is added to VCM from the same domain.

1. Go to **Administration** | **Machines Manager** | **Machine/Virtual Object Group** | **All Machines** and click on **Add Group**.

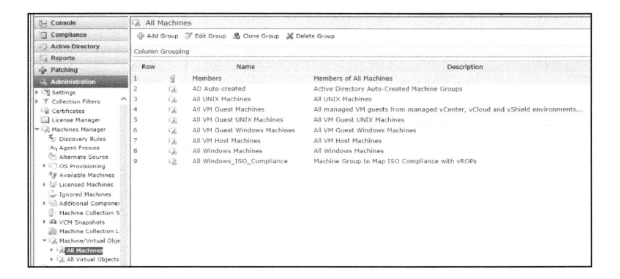

2. Provide a name and proper description, and click on **Next**.
3. Set **Membership Type** as **Dynamic** or **Static**.
4. In our case, we are going ahead with **Dynamic**, so click on **Finish** on the next page to complete the wizard.
5. Follow step 1 again, but this time, go to the machine group we just created. Click on the group and then click on **Filters**. This is where we will define the criteria to add machines to this group.

6. Under **Filters**, click on **Add Filter**.

7. Provide a meaningful name and description, and click on **Next**.

8. Now, all the details we collected from vCenter, vCloud, and all the managed machines are available here to filter.

9. Your imagination is the limit for creating filters, and you can use all the information you can gather from VCM. In our case, we have selected Machines as the data type; this is where your experience and expectations will meet together to make the exact machine group you want.

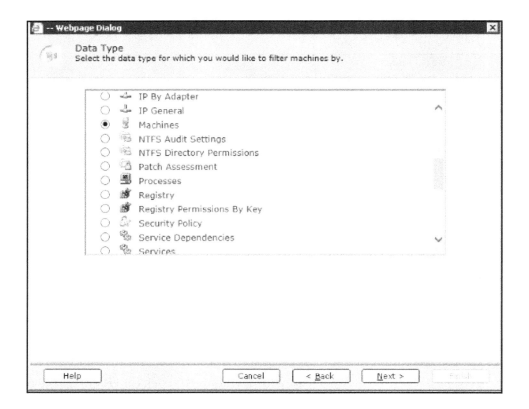

10. Select **Basic** under**Rule Type**.

11. Now, add your condition, such as **Domain Name** = 'STUDY'.

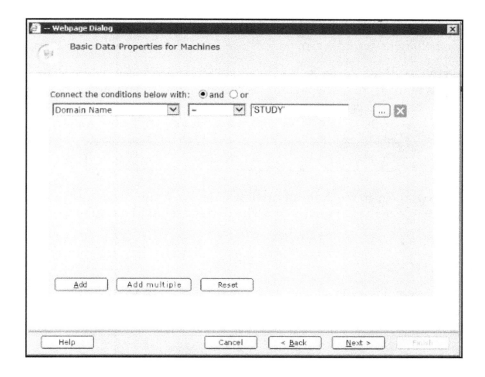

12. Click on **Next**, and then click on **Finish** to close the wizard.
13. Now, go to the machine group, and a refresh will give you all the machines that are a part of the STUDY domain.

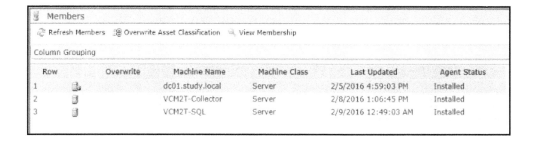

How it works...

When you work with managed machines, you can create static groups, where members are selected manually, or dynamic groups, where filters dynamically determine membership. Machines can belong to multiple groups.

You set the active machine group on the main toolbar, and you can define a machine filter with the options to the right of the textbox, as shown in this screenshot. A machine group filter further limits the selected machine group.

In all nodes except those in the **Administration** slider, an active machine group limits the displayed data to the managed machines defined in the selected machine group.

There's more...

This is the list of default groups created with an installation of VCM:

Name	Description
All machines	All the licensed machines in VCM
AD auto-created	Active Directory auto-created machine groups
All Unix machines	All Unix machines
All VM guest machines	All managed VM guests from managed vCenter, vCloud, and vShield environments
All VM guest Unix machines	All VM guest Unix machines
All VM guest Windows machines	All VM guest Windows machines
All VM host machines	All VM host machines
All Windows machines	All Windows machines

Dynamic groups

In dynamic groups, we define single or multiple filters, and based on the filters, the group is populated. If we are defining multiple filters, then a logical AND operation is performed on them.

Your imagination is the limit, considering the amount of data you have in VCM and all that of it is available to play with while creating filters for groups.

Static groups

In static groups, we define the members when we create the group, and then, we need to update them as and when required. There are no filters associated with them.

The best use case is creating a static group for all the vCenter Server instances, as we won't be adding members on a daily basis, and if we add anyone, we can add them manually.

3
Linux Patching

In this chapter, we will cover the following recipes:

- Installing SCR prerequisites
- Installing the SCR Tool
- Setting up the SCR configuration file
- Scheduling content downloads
- Configuring Apache
- Configuring patching repository options in VCM
- Configuring staging options in VCM
- Configuring the SCR Tool base path for the patching repository
- Creating a patch assessment template
- Deploying patches on Linux machines – on demand
- Deploying patches on Linux machines – scheduled

Introduction

Before patching Linux/Unix or Macintosh, we need to configure a repository into which we can download the patches in vendor-provided format. Once they've been downloaded, we need to make them available for the machines we plan to patch. This is where the VMware **Software Content Repository** (**SCR**) tool comes into picture. SCR is a Java-based tool that is installed on a separate RHEL 7 VM. SCR downloads the patch signature files and OS vendor patch content from the **content distribution network** (**CDN**) and downloads subscription-only content from the OS vendor content websites.

Since the release of SCR 6.1, which was shipped with VCM 5.7.3, VMware supports the installation only on RHEL 7.x (refer to the VCM 7.5.3 release notes).

Note that you must have a basic understanding of RHEL 7 or basic Linux commands to work through this chapter.

Note that if you need to patch your RHEL 7 target machines, then you must have the new SCR Tool 6.1 version based on RHEL 7 Server (64-bit). However, VCM continues to support SCR Tool on RHEL 6 Server (64-bit) for patching earlier Linux platforms.

SCR is not involved in patch management, configuration, or deployment. It just acts as a repository that will be accessed by various methods such as HTTP, HTTPS, FTP, and NFS by the clients that need those patches. As a VCM administrator, we need to define the way in which the managed machines will access the content, such as downloading via HTTP, HTTPS, or NFS. We need to make the necessary changes on the SCR server, such as installing a web server to make patches available over HTTP, add proper certificates so that they can be accessed over HTTPS, and so on.

How Linux patching works

The following figure from the VMware documentation depicts how VCM works with SCR:

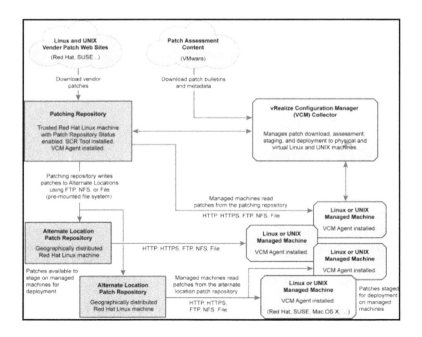

The following is the procedure of getting Linux patching working according to the previous figure:

1. We configure the SCR Tool on an RHEL machine (the biggest blue box); we can have several of them for load balancing.
2. Patches are downloaded either via a CDN or from the vendor into respective configured folders on the SCR server.
3. Meanwhile, VCM server (the biggest green box) checks the patch status of the managed Linux machines (the smaller green boxes). The VCM admin then decides which patches to install. VCM downloads patch bulletins from `http://w ww.vmware.com/` to get the latest information about the patches.
4. Once the VCM administrator decides which patches to install, all the Unix/Linux machines reach the SCR server to get those patches.
5. Managed machines install the patches and inform the VCM server about the latest status; based on this, if required, the VCM admin can take further action, for instance, troubleshooting and getting a patch installed if it failed to.

SCR VM requirements

Let's look at some values you should consider to plan for the SCR VM.

Estimated required SCR storage by platform

Supported platform	Minimum storage required for patch content files and payload
AIX	130 GB
CentOS	80 GB
HP-UX	15 GB
Mac OS X	210 GB
Oracle Enterprise Linux (OEL)	80 GB
RedHat	80 GB
Solaris	325 GB
SUSE	60 GB

SCR VM hardware requirements

Here are the base hardware requirements for deploying SCR:

Hardware	Specification
OS	RHEL 7.x x86_64
HDD	20 GB base OS + extra disk as per the previous table. This needs to be mounted at `/opt/vcmpatches` on the server. Follow the `http://www.techotopia.com/index.php/Adding_a_New_Dis` `k_Drive_to_an_RHEL_6_System` this is for RHEL 6 blog. This is for RHEL 6 but works well with RHEL 7.
Processor	2 vCPUs if going for virtual
RAM	4 GB
NIC	1 GBps with Internet access

List of patch sites for SCR

This is the list of websites we need access to for downloading patches for the respective OSes:

Platform	Download URL

All platforms	`http://configuresoft.cdn.lumension.com/configuresoft`
	`http://novell.cdn.lumension.com/`
	`https://a248.e.akamai.net/f/60/59258/2d/`
	`http://vmware.cdn.lumension.com/`

CentOS	`http://vault.centos.org`
	You can also use the mirrors returned from the Web service:
	`http://mirrorlist.centos.org`

RedHat	`http://xmlrpc.rhn.redhat.com/XMLRPC`
SUSE	`https://you.novell.com/update/` `https://nu.novell.com/repo/$RCE/`

Check `http://www.vmware.com/pdf/vrealize-configuration-man ager-software-content-repository-tool-61-guide.pdf` for details of more OSes supported by SCR.

Installing SCR prerequisites

As mentioned earlier, SCR is a Java-based tool, so it has some prerequisites, such as the latest JRE and JDK versions installed on the base OS. We will now check all the requirements that we need to get SCR going.

Getting ready

Before we start, we must have an RHEL 7 server deployed, the minimum install option of the RHEL installer installs the necessary features we need to start with. We will need to install Apache and a few other utilities, but those we can install later. The latest JRE and JDK RPMs can be downloaded from Oracle.com. We also need root credentials to install the patches.

How to do it...

Log in to the RHEL server with an SSH tool such as **PuTTY** and go to the folder where the installers have been copied. Then, follow these steps:

1. **Downloading**:

    Visit `http://www.oracle.com/index.html` and download the latest RPMs for JRE and JDK for RHEL 7 x64.

    Once the RPMs have been downloaded, you can use a tool such as **winscp** to copy the installer to the SCR server.

2. **Installing JDK using RPM**:

    Use the `cd` command to go to the folder where you have copied both the installers and run this command:

    ```
    rpm -ivh <jdk Installer filename>.rpm
    ```

3. **Installing JRE**:

    Continue from where you left off earlier and run this command to install JRE:

    ```
    rpm -ivh <jre Installer filename>.rpm
    ```

4. **Verify the Java Cryptography Extension (JCE)**:

By default, when you install the Java tool that comes with JCE, you don't need to separately install it again.

Run the following command to validate whether JCE has been installed:

```
find / -iname US_export_policy.jar
```

```
[root@scr ~]# find / -iname US_export_policy.jar
/usr/lib/jvm/java-1.8.0-openjdk-1.8.0.65-3.b17.el7.x86_64/jre/lib/security/US_export_policy.jar
/usr/java/jdk1.8.0_72/jre/lib/security/US_export_policy.jar
/usr/java/jre1.8.0_72/lib/security/US_export_policy.jar
[root@scr ~]#
```

How it works...

As SCR is a Java-based tool, we need the latest JRE installed to make the tool work.

The minimum Java version you can safely install without worrying about breaking the application is JRE 8u72, which is what we will use in this book. The JCE is required for AIX, HP-UX, RedHat, Solaris, and SUSE. It encrypts passwords when we use third-party credentials in the properties files used to download patch content.

VCM downloads the metadata about the patches from http://www.vmware.com/.

VCM is not at all aware what patches are available on the SCR server; it gets its data from http://www.vmware.com/, and SCR gets its updates from other locations.

There is no synchronization between what is available on SCR and what is required on VCM, so it is recommended that you synchronize your SCR server overnight to make sure all the patches are downloaded and then start pushing the patches from VCM.

Installing the SCR Tool

In this recipe, we will install the SCR Tool on the RHEL VM we prepared earlier.

Getting ready

You should have made sure that all the prerequisites form the previous recipes have been met.

Download the latest version of SCR from `http://www.vmware.com/`, at the time of writing, it was SCR 6.1.21. Copy the ZIP file to the `/tmp` directory of the SCR VM.

We also need login credentials for vendors such as RHEL and SUSE so that we can encrypt the password for later use in the configuration files.

How to do it...

Log in to the SCR VM with root credentials and follow these steps to install and perform base configuration of SCR.

Installing SCR

1. Create the `/opt/SCR` folder with this command:

   ```
   mkdir /opt/SCR
   ```

   From now on, we will refer to this location as `scr_root`

2. Unzip the SCR installation files:

   ```
   tar -zxvf /tmp/SCR-vmware-6.1.21.tar.gz -c /opt/SCR
   ```

Encrypting the password for the content repository

Continue from where we left off at step 2, and start the process of encrypting the password with the following commands:

1. Go to `/opt/SCR/bin` using this command:

   ```
   cd /opt/SCR/bin
   ```

2. Run the script that will encrypt the password:

   ```
   ./lumension_encryptor_tool.sh
   ```

3. Provide the password (and confirm it).

4. Copy the encrypted password string and keep it handy for the upcoming configuration steps in the following recipe.

```
[root@scr bin]# ./lumension_encryptor_tool.sh
MyPassword
Please enter the password:
RHN_Password_Here
Please re-enter the password:
RHN_Password_Here
RHN_Password_Here
Encrypted Password is : 000108000afc82fd40f6c7947f898b9fb76376e529b6ccb342c79c7c92906aa3
[root@scr bin]#
```

Not only the vendor connection password, but also the proxy password, if required, needs to be encrypted in this way.

 Note that if you provide a non-encrypted password, SCR assumes it is encrypted and will fail to connect and download patches.

How it works...

We are now getting ready by unzipping the installer and encrypting all the required passwords, such as the RedHat network access password, the password required to download content from SUSE, or the password required to get past our proxy.

We need to enter the password in the plaintext properties file used by SCR as configuration input when it starts downloading patches. If we enter our password unencrypted, then anyone with access to the file can read it. To avoid this situation, there is a script that encrypts the password, and we can provided this encrypted password in the configuration file.

These passwords can be set in a plaintext configuration file for further processing of SCR.

The SCR server must have execute permission for all of the repository application files in order to access and update the properties files. To provide those privileges, follow these steps:

1. On the SCR server, change to the `scr_root` directory.
2. To change the mode, run the `chmod -R a+x **/*` command.

Setting up the SCR configuration file

The meat of SCR is its configuration file; if we make a mistake here, we will never have those patches downloaded, and we can't have our SCR instance ready. Pay attention to what you choose; if a channel is not required, don't mention it the configuration file.

In this recipe, we will have a look at the various configuration options we have, what they mean, and how to configure them.

Getting ready

Follow the *Installing SCR* recipe to install SCR and prepare the encrypted passwords.

Consult your OS support teams about which Linux/Unix OSes will be patched by VCM so that you can download those patches beforehand.

How to do it...

In this recipe, we will prepare for RedHat Linux patching; however, the same principle applies for all Linux operating systems.

The example properties files are available in the `scr_root/conf/` directory.

If you have been following along properly so far, then the RHEL properties file will be at `/opt/SCR/redhat-rt.properties`.

As stated earlier, we want to configure a properties file that will be used by the SCR Tool to obtain configuration details and act accordingly.

To configure the file, open it with your favorite Linux editor.

The options that we will keep at their default values are not discussed here.

Here are the options to configure:

- `platform`

    The `platform` parameter specifies the type of patch content to download.

    ```
    platform=LINUX
    ```

- `arch`

    The `arch` parameter specifies valid architecture strings for the specified platform.

    ```
    arch=X86, X86_64
    ```

- `dist`

    The `dist` parameter specifies the distribution of Linux. Multiple values must be comma separated without spaces.

    ```
    dist=REDHAT
    ```

- `folder`

    The `folder` parameter specifies the **root folder** where the SCR Tool output is stored. By default, this `folder` is `/tmp/SCR/download`.

    Change it to `folder=/opt/vcmpatches` (we have mounted our second HDD under this folder; if you don't understand this, consult your Linux admin)

    The SCR Tool creates the subdirectory tree under the root output folder.

- `thirdparty`

    Set the value to `true` to support third-party downloads for CentOS, Oracle Linux, RedHat, Solaris, and SUSE.

    ```
    thirdparty=true or false
    ```

- user

  The user parameter specifies the user ID for third-party vendor downloads, such as SUSE or RHEL.

  ```
  user=string
  ```

- pwd

  The pwd parameter specifies an encrypted password for the user id specified by the user parameter. Check the *Installing SCR recipe* for more details.

  ```
  pwd=[encrypted password string]
  ```

- configlog

  This parameter specifies an output file, which contains a list of parameters and values. These values reflect the parameter configuration used during the previous or current execution of the SCR Tool and can be used to troubleshoot problems.

  ```
  configlog=config_log_file_path/filename.log
  ```

- checkPayload

  ```
  checkPayload=true or false
  ```

  Set this to true.

- dependencyCheck

  This turns off dependent RPM downloads for Linux platforms.

  ```
  dependencyCheck= Valid values (not case sensitive): NONE, DIRECT,
  and TRANSITIVE
  ```

  VMware recommends using TRANSITIVE, as this will download all the dependent patches.

- channels

  Channels are basically versions of the Linux/Unix operating system; for example, in the case of RHEL, we either have `client-x`, `server-x`, or `workstation-x`.

  An example for RedHat:

  ```
  channels=es-4, server-5
  ```

  If you want to download patches only for RHEL 7, then select `server-7`. SCR will then download patches for any other version.

  This is where you need to consult your Linux team about which OS versions they support to add only those as channels and avoid unnecessary patch download.

- downloadPayload

  If the value is `true`, all patches are downloaded. If the value is `false`, only the patches with UIDs that are included in the cache request folder are downloaded. If the value is `false` and there is no cache request XML, the content is processed but no patches are downloaded.

  ```
  downloadPayload=true or false
  ```

  It is recommended to keep this `true`.

- cacheRequestFolder

  ```
  cacheRequestFolder=path/CacheRequest.xml
  ```

  - /opt/SCR/cacherequest

  The cache request XML file is used to limit the downloaded patches to only those for which you obtain UIDs from the `ecm_sysdat_patch_pls` table in the VCM database.

  Even if you are not using this, don't hash out this option; or else, the patch download will fail.

- proxyServer

    This specifies the proxy server IP address in your infrastructure for internet access.

    ```
    proxyServer=IP_address
    ```

- proxyPort

    This specifies the proxy server port in your infrastructure for internet access.

    ```
    proxyPort=port_number
    ```

- proxyUser

    This specifies the user ID for proxy server authentication, if applicable.

- proxyPwd

    This specifies the encrypted password for the proxy server if you need a proxy user. This password is generated using the lumension_encryptor_tool.sh script, as explained in the earlier recipe.

    ```
    proxyPwd=string
    ```

- Certificate

    Point this to the file containing your RedHat entitlement certificate. This file is created in /etc/pki/entitlement by the subscription manager when you attach a subscription to your registered RedHat system. The filename of the certificate varies but is always in the form XXXXXXXXXXXXXXXXXXX.pem, where X is a decimal digit.

    If you attempt to download RedHat 7 RPMs without setting a certificate, the following error message appears:

    ```
    java.lang.IllegalArgumentException: certificate cannot be null or
    not a file
    ```

    Example values for this parameter:

    ```
    certificate=/etc/pki/entitlement/5280746408908734973.pem
    privateKey=/etc/pki/entitlement/5280746408908734973-key.pem
    ```

The following command is used to register RHEL 7 with RedHat Subscription Management:

```
subscription-manager register --username <User_Name> --password <Pass_Word>
-auto-attach
```

This is the reason we can't use any other version of Linux as the SCR server.

 Most of these details have been taken from `http://www.vmware.com/pd f/vrealize-configuration-manager-software-content-reposit ory-tool-61-guide.pdf`.

Save the properties file.

There is another problem with this file; we need to copy the working `redhat-rt.properties` file to the `REDHAT-rt.properties` file, as it has been observed in error logs that VCM tries to find the file with uppercase `REDHAT` and it fails, and in Linux, `REDHAT-rt.properties` and `redhat-rt.properties` are two different files.

Once configured, the file looks something like this:

```
platform=LINUX
arch=X86, X86_64
dist=REDHAT
folder=/opt/vcmpatches
keyfile=./vmware.plk
key=Y341H8i7arr8915580oepd
index=VMware58.xml
program="."
thirdparty=true
user=RHN_User
pwd=Encrypted_RHN_User_password
configlog=../logs/RedHat-Config.log
checkPayload=true

#Patch Dependency Check
#  Valid values (not case sensitive): NONE || DIRECT || TRANSITIVE
dependencyCheck=TRANSITIVE
channels=server-7
downloadPayload=false
cacheRequestFolder=../cacherequest

#Connection Timeout in seconds.
#  Valid range: 0..3600 (1 hour), where default=60 and Infinite=0. No separator characters.
connectionTimeout=60

# Logging settings
handlers=java.util.logging.FileHandler
java.util.logging.FileHandler.pattern = ../logs/scr-redhat-log-%g.log
java.util.logging.FileHandler.limit = 10000000
java.util.logging.FileHandler.count = 3
java.util.logging.FileHandler.level = INFO
-- INSERT --
```

Once the file has been saved, go to `/opt/SCR/bin` and run the following command:

```
./startup.sh redhat-rt
```

Then, check the logfiles and the download folder; if there are no error logs in the logfile, then SCR will start synchronizing the patches.

How it works...

When we start downloading patches with the SCR Tool, it uses the information provided in the configuration file and then acts on it; for example, it will use the proxy provided in the configuration file and the credentials configured to authenticate.

It will use the folder path to download the patches and the credentials shared to authenticate with the OS vendor.

It will download only patches for the OS versions mentioned in the channel configuration; it might not download any patch if we configure the file like that, and we might get failures while performing the deployment with VCM.

The SCR Tool first attempts to download the payload from the CDN. If the patch is not found in the CDN, the SCR Tool downloads it from the vendor's website, such as RedHat, SUSE, or Solaris, using the credentials provided in the user and password parameters.

If something like that happens now, you know where to look first. The logfile location mentioned here comes in handy, assuming you have configured everything correctly. If SCR is not downloading the patches, have a look at the logfile generated at the location mentioned in the configuration file.

If you are new to Linux, then use a tool called winscp; this allows you to browse the Linux filesystem and manipulate files.

Open the logfile in winscp and look for something that tells you the system is getting registered to RHN in order to make sure everything is going well:

```
/opt/SCR/logs/scr-redhat-log-0.log - 192.168.1.140 - Editor - WinSCP          [_][□][23]

    Encoding ▾  □ Color ▾  {}  ?

INFO: Downloading repodata for channel rhel-i386-server-5
Apr 10, 2016 5:57:01 PM com.lumension.scr.log.CommonsLogging info
INFO:  Processing Architecture X86_64
Apr 10, 2016 5:58:33 PM com.lumension.scr.log.CommonsLogging info
INFO: Downloading YUM repo for LST: redhat-nca-Server-5.0/x86_64/es50.lst
Apr 10, 2016 6:02:00 PM com.lumension.scr.log.CommonsLogging info
INFO: vendor RedHat release Server version 5 Architecture x86_64
Apr 10, 2016 6:02:08 PM com.lumension.scr.log.CommonsLogging info
INFO: vendor RedHat release Server version 5 Architecture x86_64
Apr 10, 2016 6:02:08 PM com.lumension.scr.log.CommonsLogging info
INFO: System doesnt exist and automatically registering.. /opt/vcmpatches/unix/System
Apr 10, 2016 6:02:08 PM com.lumension.scr.log.CommonsLogging info
INFO:  Details redhat-nca-Server-5.0-x86_64 - x86_64 - 5Server
Apr 10, 2016 6:02:11 PM com.lumension.scr.log.CommonsLogging info
INFO: Register Response <?xml version='1.0'?>
```

We will look at a recipe on troubleshooting SCR download issues in Chapter 9, *Troubleshooting VCM*.

Scheduling content downloads

OS vendors keep generating patches. We can't just log in to SCR and synchronize them manually; we can set a schedule and let SCR take care of downloading all the required patches.

Getting ready

The SCR VM must have access to the Internet and be configured as per the previous two recipes.

Configure the `redhat-rt.properties` file with the correct settings, such as user details for RHN and proxy details, and save it.

How to do it...

To set up the scheduling, we need to a create scripts that then can be run automatically.

Follow these steps to create the script and schedule it.

1. Once logged in to the SCR server, go to the location where SCR is installed (for us, it is /opt/SCR)

2. **Copy the following content into the file:**

   ```
   vi /opt/SCR/bin/start_all_nix_replication.sh
   ```

   press *i*

   Enter or copy the following content:

   ```
   #echo Running startup.sh hp-rt
   #./startup.sh hp-rt
   #echo Running startup.sh osx-rt
   #./startup.sh osx-rt
   echo Running startup.sh redhat-rt
   ./startup.sh redhat-rt
   #echo Running startup.sh solaris-rt
   #./startup.sh solaris-rt
   #echo Running startup.sh suse-rt
   #./startup.sh suse-rt
   ```

   Remove the # in front of the RedHat entry as we want to synchronize the patches for it, and if you have another version of Linux, do the same for that.

   After you finished press [*ESC*] and then *:wq* to write the content and exit vi

3. **Assign executable permissions to the created file:**

   ```
   chmod +x   /opt/SCR/bin/start_all_nix_replication.sh
   ```

   Once the script is ready, we need to schedule it.

4. **Schedule a cron job to download it daily**:

```
cd /etc/cron.daily
touch /etc/cron.daily/SCR
chmod +x /etc/cron.daily/SCR
```

Note that the following script runs daily and synchronizes your patch content:

```
vim /etc/cron.daily/SCR
```

5. **Add the following code to the file**:

```
#!/bin/sh
cd /opt/SCR/bin
echo "### Get all new Unix content"
./start_all_nix_replication.sh
```

The host machine must have execute permission for all of the repository application files in order to access and update the properties files. To grant this permission, you run a command on the host machine.

Change directory to the SCR root directory (/opt/SCR).

Note that execute the following command in the /opt/SCR directory:
cd /opt/SCR
chmod -R a+x **/*

Run the SCR file to create the directory structure:

1. Change directory to /etc/cron.daily.

   ```
   cd /etc/cron.daily
   ```

2. Run the SCR file to create the directory structure and download the content:

   ```
   ./SCR
   ```

3. Monitor the size for a while by running this:

   ```
   du -sh /opt/vcmpatches
   ```

How it works...

We create a daily schedule that will run at 12:00 am and will then use the configuration settings provided in the properties file and download the patches to the SCR server. The patches can then be used to deploy using VCM. Before starting to deploy patches with VCM, you must download them to the SCR server, as VCM will not know which patches are available and which are not.

Configuring Apache

By now, we will have all the patches downloaded to the SCR server; now, we need a mechanism to make them available to the managed machines when they need them for installation.

We can configure a web server to distribute the patches from the SCR repository.

As discussed in the introduction, we can distribute the patches over HTTP/HTTPS; we will configure the Apache web server such that the folder containing patches (/opt/vcmpatches) will be available over HTTP. We will make the necessary changes in the VCM server to instruct the Linux/Unix machines to download patches according to our web server configuration.

Getting ready

As you have already registered your SCR server with the RedHat network, which is a prerequisite for downloading RHEL 7 patches, you have a repository ready to install Apache.

Security-Enhanced Linux (SELinux) should be disabled or configured such that we can connect on port 80 or 443.

If you are not aware how this can be achieved, have a look at the following article:

```
https://access.redhat.com/documentation/en-US/Red_Hat_Enterprise_Linux/
7/html/SELinux_Users_and_Administrators_Guide/chap-Managing_Confined_Se
rvices-The_Apache_HTTP_Server.html#sect-Managing_Confined_Services-The_
Apache_HTTP_Server-The_Apache_HTTP_Server_and_SELinux
```

The firewall should be disabled or configured so that we can access patches over port 80/443.

Have a look at this article for details on how to work with the RHEL firewall:

```
https://access.redhat.com/documentation/en-US/Red_Hat_Enterprise_Linux/
7/html/Security_Guide/sec-Using_Firewalls.html
```

You could also use the following article for port 80 and make the necessary changes for port 443:

```
https://linuxconfig.org/how-to-open-http-port-80-on-redhat-7-linux-usin
g-firewall-cmd
```

How to do it...

This is a pretty long recipe, and we will break it into multiple sections, as follows:

- *Installing Apache*
- *Configuring httpd.conf for Apache*
- *Configuring the .htaccess file*
- *Configuring HTTPS in Apache*

Installing Apache

To make the patches available in our infrastructure, we can make the SCR server act as a web server and then configure it in VCM such that the managed machines access the patches over port 80 or 443 from the SCR server.

We will achieve this by following these steps:

1. Log in to SCR server with the root account.
2. Install Apache:

   ```
   # yum install httpd
   ```

3. Make sure that httpd starts with the OS boot:

   ```
   # systemctl enable httpd
   ```

4. Start the httpd service now:

   ```
   # systemctl start httpd.service
   ```

Now, we need to configure the `httpd.conf` file, located in `/etc/https/conf`, to make Apache work as per our requirements.

Configuring httpd.conf for Apache

The Apache configuration is stored in the `httpd.conf` file, located in `/etc/https/conf`. Continue with the following steps to make the necessary changes in the configuration file.

1. Before making changes to `httpd.conf`, we need to add a symbolic link between the folder we used to download the patches (`/opt/vcmpatches`) and the folder exposed under `httpd.conf` (`/var/www/html`).
2. Log in to the SCR server with the root account.
3. Go to `/var/www/html` using `cd /var/www/html`.
4. Run the `ln -s /opt/vcmpatchs vcmpatches` command.
5. Edit `httpd.conf`:

   # vi /etc/httpd/conf/httpd.conf

6. Enter *I* to go into edit mode, and add the following line under the `AccessFileName` section:

   AccessFileName /vcmpatches/.htaccess

Note that we will be creating this `.httaccess` file in the next section of this recipe.

Configuring the .htaccess file

To make this secure, we can add a `.htaccess` file so that only configured users can access the patches.

Create and edit the `.htaccess` file at `/opt/vcmpatches`:

 # vi /opt/vcmpatches/.htaccess

Add the following lines to the file:

```
AuthType Basic
AuthName "Restricted Area"
AuthUserFile /opt/vcmpatches/.htpasswd
require valid-user
```

Now, create an encrypted password for the `httpuser` user:

```
#  htpasswd -c /opt/vcmpatches/.htpasswd  httpuser
```

It will prompt you for a password; type the password you want to set.

This creates another file at the same location called .htpasswd, and it stores the encrypted password, which you can see using the following command:

```
# cat /opt/vcmpatches/.htpasswd
httpuser:$apr1$1UgtgyfY$ed2kr8fDOB7XVd6UoytgE0
```

Configuring HTTPS in Apache

The default installation of Apache will give us an HTTP connection to the patch repository. We need to create and configure a certificate in Apache so that our managed VMs can securely download the patches from the SCR server. To configure HTTPS, we follow these steps:

1. **Install Mod SSL**

   In order to set up the self-signed certificate, we first have to be sure that Apache and Mod SSL are installed. You can install both with one command:

   ```
   rpm -ivh mod_ssl-2.2.15-29.e16_4.x86_64.rpm
   ```

2. **Create a new directory**

   Next, we need to create a new directory, where we will store the server key and certificate:

   ```
   mkdir /etc/httpd/ssl
   ```

3. **Create a self-signed certificate**

When we request a new certificate, we can specify how long it should remain valid by changing the `1000` parameter to the number of days we prefer:

```
Openssl req -x509 -nodes -days 1000 -newkey rsa:2048 -keyout
/etc/httpd/ssl/apache.key -out /etc/httpd/ssl/apache.crt
```

With this command, we will both be creating the self-signed SSL certificate and the server key that protects it and placing both of them into the new directory. This command will prompt the terminal to display a list of fields that need to be filled in. The most important line is **Common Name**. Enter your official domain name here or, if you don't have one yet, use your site's IP address.

You will be asked to enter information that will be incorporated into your certificate request.

Provide the following details:

- **Country Name (two-letter code)**: IN
- **State or province name (full name)**: Maharashtra
- **Locality name (for example, a city)**: Pune
- **Organization name (such as a company)**: VCM_Cookbook
- **Organizational unit name (for example, a section)**: Information Technology
- **Common name (for example, a server FQDN or your name)**: VCMCookbook.com
- **Email address**: Abhijeet@vcmcookbook.com

 Note that the example values need to be changed as per your infrastructure.

4. **Set up the certificate**:

We now have all of the required components of the finished certificate. The next thing to do is to set up the virtual hosts to display the new certificate.

Open up the SSL config file:

```
vi /etc/httpd/conf.d/ssl.conf
```

Now, add the following block of code to the file:

```
## SSL Virtual Host Context
<VirtualHost *:443>
    ServerAdmin root@localhost
    DocumentRoot /var/www/html
    ServerName SCR Server FQDN
    ServerAlias SCR Server hostname
    SSLEngine on
    SSLCertificateFile /etc/httpd/ssl/apache.crt
    SSLCertificateKeyFile /etc/httpd/ssl/apache.key

</VirtualHost>
<VirtualHost _default_:443>
```

5. **Restart Apache**:

   You are done. Restarting the Apache server will reload it with all of your changes in place.

   #systemctl restart httpd.service

After this, you should access the VCM patches folder over the network via a browser, and it should look something like the following screenshot.

When you access the link, it will ask for authentication. Use the `httpuser` user and password created in the earlier step.

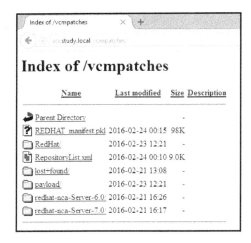

How it works...

Linux and Unix managed machines can use HTTP/HTTPS to retrieve patches directly from the RedHat Linux patching repository machine.

The VCM Collector orchestrates and coordinates the tasks required to download, stage, and deploy the patches and the custom predeployment, postdeployment, and reboot actions using the VCM agent installed on the patching repository machine and the VCM agent on the target managed machines.

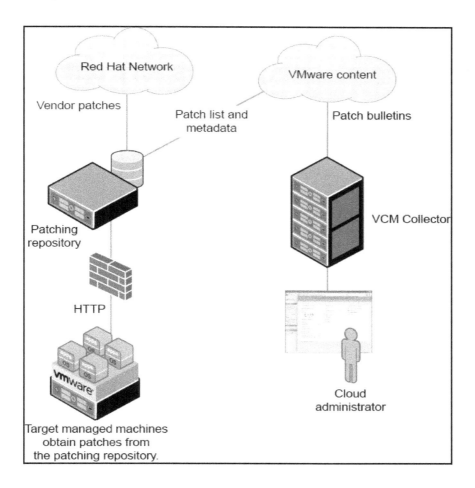

The patches are available on the SCR server, and with the help of the Apache server, we created a web server that will present the patches to the managed machines.

There's more...

Once this has been configured, we need to make the necessary configuration changes in the VCM console and add the staging option as HTTP and redirect the managed machines to the `/opt/vcmpatches` folder to download patches. We will do this in the following recipes, *Configuring patching repository options in VCM* and *Configuring staging options*.

Configuring patching repository options in VCM

Once everything is configured and ready on the SCR front, we should start configuring the repository in VCM. This is where we set the machine (SCR server) that will act as the repository.

Getting ready

We should have finished all the previous recipes before we start this, as this is dependent on all of them. Install the VCM agent as described in Chapter 2, *Configuring VCM to Manage Your Infrastructure*, in the *Installing an agent on Linux servers* recipe, and perform an initial data collection for the SCR machine.

How to do it...

To set up a patch repository in VCM, log in to the VCM console and follow these steps:

1. Go to **Administration | Certificate** and select the SCR server. Click on **Change Trust Status** at the top of the screen.

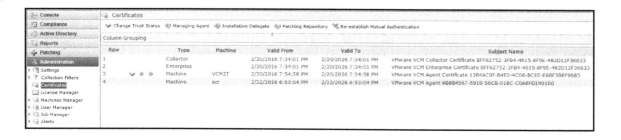

2. In the wizard, select the SCR machine and tick the **Check to trust and uncheck to untrust the selected machine** option.
3. You should see a handshake sign in front of the SCR server.
4. Now, keep the SCR machine selected and click on **Patching Repository** at the top of the screen.
5. Make sure the SCR server is selected and choose **Enable – Allow the selected machine to be used as Patch Repository**. Click on **Next**.
6. Click on **Finish** to close the wizard.
7. The end result should look something like this:

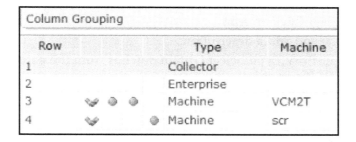

How it works...

We set the patching repository as the designated patch repository for all the Linux/Unix machines we will be managing. Now, VCMknows where to redirect the machines if they want to be patched; we need to perform further configuration changes such as setting the path from where the machines can download the patches, but that is for the next recipe.

Configuring staging options in VCM

Staging options are where we set VCM to exactly redirect the VM to `https://<SCR Server>/<Patch location>`. So far, we have downloaded the patches and added a server as the repository, and now, we will set the name of the folder and configure machine group mappings to the staging options.

Getting ready

We are building on previous recipes, so before we go ahead with this recipe, we should have finished all of them. If there are any special machine groups required, then they should be ready before we start with this recipe.

How to do it...

Log in to the VCM server console and follow these steps to configure patch staging:

1. Login as a VCM administrator in VCM console.
2. Navigate to **Administration** | **Settings** | **General Settings** | **Patching** | **UNIX** | **Patch Staging**. Click on **Add**.
3. Give a name and add a description.
4. Under **Repository Type**, select **Obtain patches from the patching repository : <Name of SCR server>**.

5. On the next page, provide details as follows:

   - **Repository Path:** /vcmpatches (this is the relative path to which we have downloaded the patches)
   - **Protocol:** Choose **HTTPS**
   - **Port:** Type 443 unless you have made some changes in httpd.conf and are using some other port
   - Select credentials required
   - **Username :** httpuser (or any user set in the .htaccess file)
   - **Password :** A plaintext password (don't use an encrypted password here)

6. Click on **Finish**.

Now that we have set a staging option, we need to assign it to the machine groups so that the machines will know where to download the patches from.

1. Navigate to **Administration** | **Settings** | **General Settings** | **Patching** | **UNIX** | **Machine Group Mapping**.
2. Select the **Machine Group** and click on **Edit**.
3. Set the patch path value to **Standard Deployment and Source** for staged patches to **SCR-HTTP**.
4. The protocol and path will populate automatically, that is, if you have not created the certificate, then it will assign port 80, and if you have secured your Apache setup by creating a self-signed certificate, then it will look like one of these:

   - HTTP://scr:80/vcmpatches
   - HTTPS://scr:443/vcmpatches

5. Click on **Next** and **Finish** to save the settings.
6. Do this for all the machine groups that have Linux/Unix machines and will be patched with VCM.

How it works...

If we don't set staging options, then machine patching will fail as the machines won't know from where to get the installers. As a best practice, use HTTPS.

Configuring the SCR Tool base path for the patching repository

The setting for the SCR Tool base path in VCM must point to the location where you installed the SCR Tool on the patching repository machine.

The base path directory contains directories for the SCR binary files, configuration files, and logs.

Getting ready

As usual, we are building a patching mechanism, so all previous recipes are important to continue with subsequent ones. The same is applicable for this recipe: complete all the previous recipes before starting this one.

How to do it...

In this recipe, we will make a few changes to the VCM configuration; just follow these steps:

1. Navigate to **Administration** | **Settings** | **General Settings** | **Patching** |**UNIX** | **Additional Settings**.
2. Select **Default Machine Group Mapping for Temporary files during patching** and change it to a folder you know will have enough space to download the patches before installation.

   How much space is enough will depend on how many patches are getting deployed.

   If you have standard partitions across the entire Linux/Unix server, select a path where you will have enough space.

In our case, it is /var/tmp, as shown here:

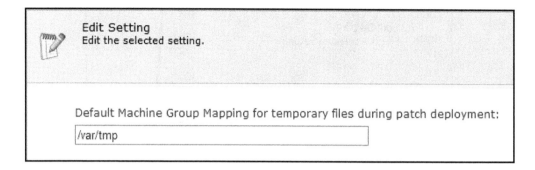

3. Click on **Next** (not visible in the screenshot) and **Finish** to close and save the setting.
4. Next in the list is **Default UNIX>Linux package Repository path**.
5. This is the path to which we are *downloading the patches*; in our case, it is /opt/vcmpatches.

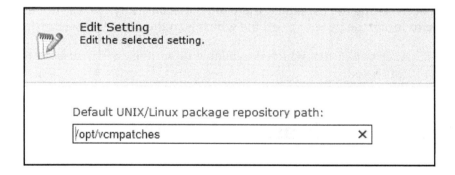

6. Click on **Next** (not visible in the screenshot) and **Finish** to close and save the setting.
7. The final setting in the list is **Default UNIX/Linux package repository SCR base path**.
8. This is the location to which we *untarred or installed the SCR files* downloaded from http://www.vmware.com.

9. In our case, it is `/opt/SCR`.

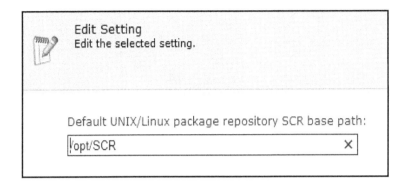

10. Click on **Next** (not visible in the screenshot) and **Finish** to close and save the setting.

How it works...

The details of each setting are explained there only; this basically makes sure of the location of the SCR file to locate the `properties` file which is in the `/opt/SCR/conf` folder.

To check the `manifest.pkl` file, which is available under the `/opt/vcmpatches` folder, this has all the RPMs listed.

Creating a patch assessment template

A patch assessment template is basically list of patches that will be installed on managed machines or will be used to check patch compliance against.

Getting ready

We need internet access on the Collector server to download patch metadata.

How to do it...

Log in to the VCM console and follow these steps to create the required assessment template:

1. Navigate to **Patching** | **All UNIX/Linux Platforms** | **Assessment Templates** and click on **Add**.
2. Templates can be created under individual Unix/Linux platforms as well.
3. Give the template a descriptive name and add a description.
4. Select **Static** as the type of template. Here is the difference between a static and dynamic template:

    - **Static template:** With this, we can choose which patches are to be included in the template.
    - **Dynamic template:** With this, VCM selects patches depending upon the query we set.

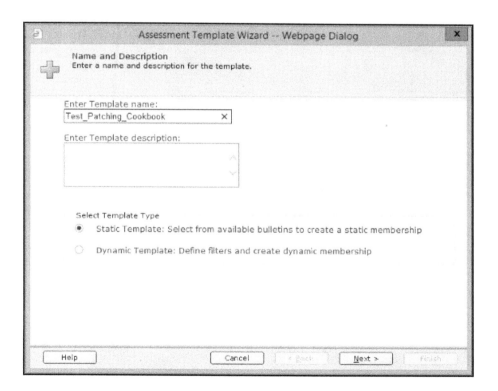

5. If we selected a dynamic template, we have options to formulate queries, such as **OS Name**, **OS Version**, and **Severity**, and we can create multiple queries and select the **and/or** operator.

 Note that you can have only one **and/or** operator for all queries.

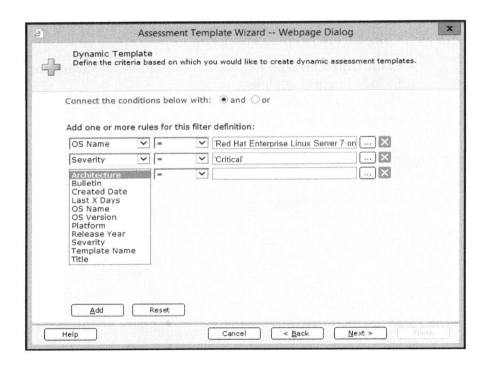

6. If we select **Static**, we are free to choose all the patches we want.
7. There is a temporary filter we can apply to limit the number of patches to select from.

 Note that multiple product bulletins can be wrapped up in this way. VCM will only attempt to patch an affected product, that is, if a VM is running RedHat 6, then VCM will not attempt to apply RedHat 7 bulletins.

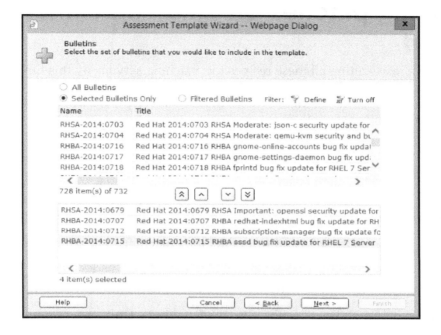

8. Click on **Next** once all the required patches have been selected.
9. Close the wizard by clicking on **Finish.**

How it works...

We cannot deploy patches without creating assessment templates; these will be used for assessing the status of the machines, checking missing patches, and then deploying them.

We cannot make sure whether the patch we are selecting in the template will be there on the SCR server, so to avoid failures, we should always download all the patches to the SCR server.

See also

- This patch assessment template will be used in *Deploying patches on Linux machines – on demand* and *Deploying patches on Linux machines – scheduled* recipes.

Deploying patches on Linux machines – on demand

This is what we're executing all these recipes for: patching servers. By this time, we will be ready to install the patches on the managed machines. We can either schedule the patch to be installed or we can install them on demand. In this recipe, we will install the missing patches directly from the console.

Getting ready

Make sure the VM you want to patch is trusted in VCM; if it isn't, follow the same steps we followed to trust the SCR server in the *Configuring patching repository options in VCM* recipe.

We must have DNS resolution to and from the Linux machine to be patched and the SCR and VCM servers.

The managed machine must reach the VCM and SCR server on their IPs.

We should have performed a collection with the **Patching – Unix Assessment Result** as the **Filter Set** option, as explained in the *Collecting data from managed machines* recipe in Chapter 2, *Configuring VCM to Manage Your Infrastructure*.

How to do it...

Log in to the VCM console with admin privileges and start installing patches by following these steps:

1. Go to **Patching | RedHat | AssessmentTemplates** and select the assessment template you have created.
2. Click on **View Report** in the top corner.
3. Once you see the report, drag **Recommended Action** to the **Filter** bar; now, the default view changes and you can see that it is arranged depending upon the **Recommended Action**.
4. Click on the small arrow in front of **Install Path**, select the patch and hit **Deploy** from the topmost menu.

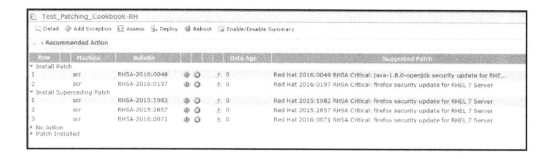

5. Select the items and click on **include prerequisite patches**.
6. Validate the patches.
7. Click on **advanced** and check whether this interests you or your Linux admin.
8. Confirm the patch deployment and select the staging option.

 Note that if the machine you want to patch belongs to a machine group that you did not assign a staging option to, you will see only one option enabled for you, that is, **None: Stage patches manually**.

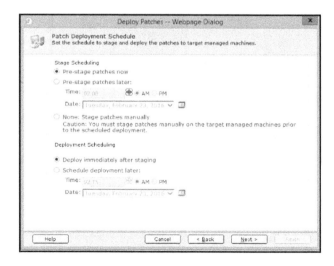

9. On the next page, choose whether you want to reboot the server.
10. Click on **Finish** to close the wizard.

11. VCM will start installing the patch and you can check the status of the jobs it runs: all the three jobs–**Download**, **Stage**, and **Deployment**–should end with a **Succeeded** result.

    If you chose to reboot the server, then after a reboot, check the status like we did in steps 3 and 4 of the recipe; it should say **Success** and list the name of the path we just installed.

    This is how it will look in the job history under **Administration** | **Job** | **Manager** | **Other jobs** | **Past 24 Hours**:

12. You can check the status of the patch in the VCM console and it will show you that the patch has been installed. To check the status, go to **Patching** | **RedHat** | **Assessment Template** | "Template name ":

How it works...

When we push the patch from the VCM console, it first assesses the machine to check whether the patch has been installed since the last assessment. If it is still required, then the patch that was staged at the location configured in the staging option gets installed, and then the VCM agent checks whether the patch was installed properly.

If we schedule a reboot after that, then another job is configured in VCM and it starts, depending upon the configuration we select when deploying the patch. If the patch installation takes more time than the scheduled fixed reboot time, then the reboot job fails.

Deploying patches on Linux machines – scheduled

When we performed on-demand patching, we made sure the infrastructure we set up for patching Linux or Unix machines was working fine. Now, we need to take this to the next level by performing all the stuff automatically. In this recipe, we will configure all the required jobs so that VCM will perform patching of Linux/Unix machines on schedule.

Getting ready

Preparation will be the same as earlier. Make sure the VM you want to patch is trusted in VCM; if it isn't, take the same steps we followed to trust the SCR server in the *Configuring patching repository options in VCM* recipe.

We should have DNS resolution to and from the Linux machine to be patched and the SCR and VCM server.

The machine group where the VMs belong should have proper staging configured.

How to do it...

We now know patching Linux is a three-step process:

- Collecting the latest data with **Patching – Unix Assessment Result** as the **Filter Set** option
- Performing the actual patching
- Again collecting the data (this is kind of optional as VCM also collects the data–it's just a precaution)

So, let's begin by scheduling the required tasks in VCM so that our machines will get patched automatically:

Sr. No.	Name	Schedule	Reason
1	Initial collection	First Sunday 08:00 am	12 hours before the actual patch
2	Deploying the patch	First Sunday 08:00 pm	Scheduled patch maintenance window
3	Final assessment	First Sunday 11:00 pm	3 hours after patching to give time for automated collection (happens after 30 minutes of patching and reboot)

Step 1 – the initial collection

1. Log in to the VCM console and go to **Administration** | **JobManager** | **Scheduled**.
2. Click on **Add**, select **Collection** once the wizard starts, and click on **Next**.
3. Provide a proper name and description.
4. Select **Patching – Unix Assessment Result** as the **Filter Set** option.
5. Select the machine group you want to patch in this schedule.
6. Select a schedule, preferably one upto 24 hours before the actual patching.
7. Click on **Next** and finally, after validating there are no conflicts, click on **Finish**.
8. This completes our first phase. The next is the actual patching schedule.

Step 2 – deploying the patch

To schedule patching, follow these steps:

1. Go to **Patching** | **AllUnix/Linux Platforms** | **Automatic Deployment**
2. Give the deployment a name and add a description.
3. Select the **Machine Group** we want to patch and whose data was collected in the earlier initial collection step.
4. Select the **Assessment Template** to deploy the patches with.

5. On the next page, select the following:

- **Scheduled Automatic Deployment Run**
- Depending upon the organization's policy, select whether you want to reboot or not.
- **Threshold Data Age**: 2 days should be fine as we are performing the data collection for the past 24 hours. If the data is older than the number of configured days, the server will not be patched.

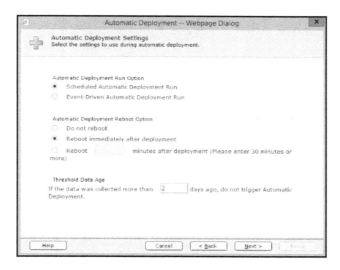

6. Select the schedule and click on **Finish** on the last page to save the scheduled patching.

Step 3 – final assessment

- Once patching is done, VCM performs a collection with **Patching – Unix Assessment Result** as the **Filter Set** option. Still, we can schedule one more task to collect the details.
- Follow the same steps we did for configuring prepatch data collection, but this time, change the name and the collection schedule so that this collection will start a few hours after the patching has finished.

How it works...

Basically, we are scheduling the things we were doing manually to save us some time and to not be awake at midnight to patch the server. VCM starts the scheduled jobs on time, collects the data, checks which patches are missing, installs them, and finally collects post-patch data so that when we run patch reports, we will have the latest status of the managed machine.

To check the reports, have a look at the *Patching Reports* recipe in Chapter 4, *Windows Patching*. The only difference we can expect there is that the name is different; we need to replace Windows with Unix.

4
Windows Patching

In this chapter, we will cover the following recipes:

- Configuring VCM to use Microsoft updates
- An introduction to automated patching
- Creating a patch assessment template
- Windows patching – on demand
- Windows patching – scheduled
- Patching machines in multi-domain environments and workgroups
- Patching VM templates
- Patching reports

Introduction

So far, we have covered how to deploy VCM on one or multiple tiers, how to configure it, and how to deploy agents on the machines we want to manage. In this chapter, we will have a look at patching Windows servers and desktops.

Even though all products go through rigorous quality tests, there are always some bugs left that can be exploited if they aren't fixed. Patch management comes into the picture to do this job. With the help of VCM, we can perform an automated, scheduled analysis of the infrastructure for missing patches and then deploy them as necessary. There are many tools in the market, such as Microsoft System Center Configuration Manager or BMC BSA, that can do this job, but the benefit of using VCM is that it's an integral part of the vRealize Operation suite, so you don't need to pay extra for VCM. It can not only patch Windows and Linux but can also be used to patch Unix and Mac OS. We can schedule the patching job, and VCM will perform the patching and update the status on the central console.

With the help of vRealize Automation and vRealize Orchestrator, we can automate the deployment of Windows patching. We can create a registry entry in the VM that will be captured by VCM while performing the collection, and based on that registry entry, the VM will be placed in the correct machine group, which is created for the sole purpose of patching the VMs on the same schedule.

In order to perform scheduled patching, we need to configure at least four jobs. The first one is the initial collection, which will collect status details against the **Patching – Windows Security Bulletins** filter set. Once those details are in the VCM database, another job will start the initial assessment and check which patches are missing on the server. Once VCM has the details of which patches from the patch assessment template are missing on the server, it will start the actual patching job. After each patching job is finished, VCM starts its own data collection job to obtain the updated status of the server. Finally, we need to schedule a final assessment, which will update the patch status of the after patch deployment.

Configuring VCM to use Microsoft updates

In this recipe, we will configure VCM to synchronize patch metadata with Microsoft so that we can select one or more patches and check the compliance of our infrastructure. If VCM detects non-compliance, we can deploy the patches.

Getting ready

We will need a fully deployed VCM server to work on this recipe. In order to use VCM for patching, we need Internet access to download patches from Microsoft onto the VCM Collector server. We should have proxy details available, such as IP address, port name, and user credentials. If you are on a secure network, make sure you have Internet access, at least to https://www.microsoft.com/ and http://www.vmware.com/.

Firewall requirements are discussed in the *vRealize Configuration Manager port and protocol summary* section of Chapter 1, *Installing VCM*.

 Note that before you patch Windows Server 2008 and Windows 7 machines, you need to verify that the Windows Update service is running, which means that it is set to something other than **Disabled**.

How to do it...

To prepare for Microsoft patching, we will break the recipe into several steps. The proxy steps only need to be performed if you are using a proxy to access the Internet.

Configuring a proxy

In a real-life scenario, the VCM server would need a proxy to access patching sites on the Internet; we need to update those settings in vRealize Configuration Manager. We can do that by following these steps:

1. Log in to VCM with admin privileges.
2. Go to **Administration** | **Settings** | **General Settings** | **Patching** | **Internet**.
3. Select **HTTP Proxy Server** and **Logon** individually. Hit the **Edit** button at the top and provide the proxy details.

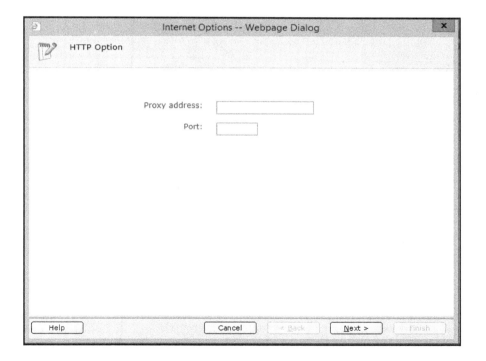

4. Enter the credentials acquired in the **Getting Ready** stage.

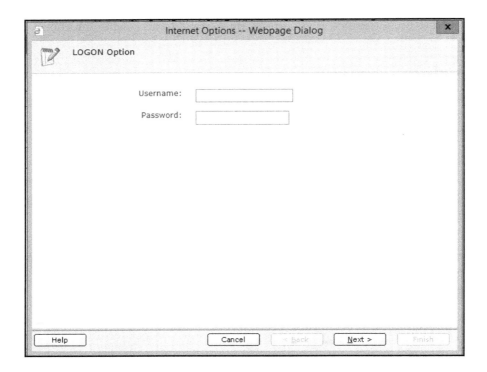

5. Hit **Next** and then **Finish**.

Once we have filled in the proxy options, VCM can connect to the Internet and download Microsoft patches.

If you have direct access to the Internet, you don't need to fill in these details. You can skip this section. Once the proxy has been configured, we can set the frequency with which to check for updates and the languages we need to download the patches.

VCM will not download any patch on the collector unless it is required while deploying it on the managed machine and the administrator opts to download it. VCM only syncs metadata for Windows and Linux/Unix machines from http://www.vmware.com/, and then, those details are presented to the VCM administrator as available patches for distribution.

Downloading settings

The download settings are where we define the synchronization schedule and additional languages if required. Patches are available in various languages for the operating systems we have installed; here, we can choose the language required by our infrastructure. Microsoft patches are released every second Tuesday, also known as *Patch Tuesday*, but there are patches that can be released out of band, so we can set the schedule to daily to make sure we don't miss those out-of-band patch details.

To configure download settings, follow these steps:

1. Go to **Administration** | **Settings** | **General Settings** | **Patching** | **Windows** | **Bulletin and Updates**.
2. Change the schedule to suit your needs, or go with the defaults.

Superseded Patches

Some of these updates might *supersede* previously installed updates, that is, Microsoft might re-release a patch or release a patch that supersedes/replaces a previous patch. The new version of the patch is the only one that needs to be installed.

An example would be Patch MS15-024 superseding Patch MS15-016, which in turn supersedes Patch MS14-085. This would mean that only Patch MS15-024 needs to be downloaded.

Microsoft's supersedence information can be found in the **Updates Replaced** column of the **Affected Software** table at the top of the security bulletins:

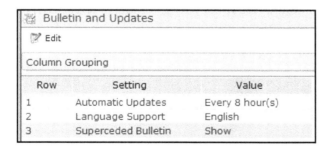

The network authority account

As explained in the *Service accounts* subsection of `Chapter 1`, *Installing VCM,* we need the network authority account. Now, we will associate those accounts with either machine groups or domains.

Start by following these steps:

1. Go to **Administration | Settings | Network Authority**.
2. We now have the following options:

   Available Domains Identified

   We added domains when we installed VCM. Have a look at step 19 of the *Installing VCM – two-tier deployment* recipe from `Chapter 1`, *Installing VCM* for more details.

   Available Accounts

   We assigned one network authority account during VCM deployment; have a look at step 17 of the *Installing VCM – two-tier deployment* recipe from `Chapter 1`, *Installing VCM* for more details.

   Assigned Accounts

   For this recipe, we will chose **Assigned Accounts**.

   To make it possible to patch machines in multiple domains, we need to assign available accounts to available domains or machine groups. To do this, go to **Assigned Accounts | By Domain | Active Directory**.

   The following screenshot shows the assigned network authority account for the `study.local` Active Directory domain:

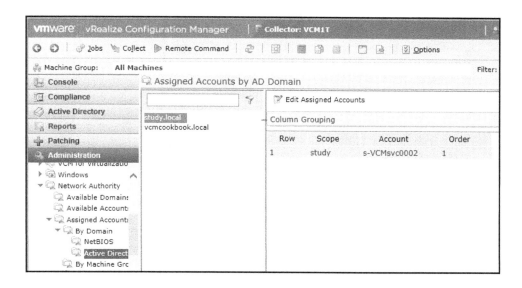

Synchronizing patches with Microsoft

Once we have an Internet connection (either natively or using a proxy), we can synchronize patch metadata with Microsoft by following these steps:

1. Go to **Patching** I **Windows** I **Bulletins** I **By Bulletin** and click on **Check for Update**.

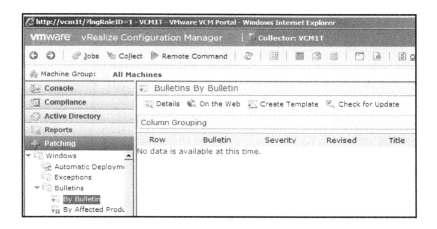

2. To monitor the status of the sync, go to **Patching** | **Job Management** | **Windows** | **Job Manager** | **Running**.

3. Once the job is done, you can look at the bulletins under **Patching** | **Windows** | **Bulletins** | **By Bulletin**, which can be used to create a patch assessment template.

You will be able to see the patch details on the right-hand side now:

In earlier releases of VCM, there was an issue with synchronization. Patches were not visible even after synchronization was complete. Here is the *Knowledge Base* article for the resolution: `http://kb.vmware.com/selfservice/microsites/search.do?language=en_US&cmd=displayKC&externalId=2053975`. Fortunately, we don't need to do this in the latest version of VCM.

How it works...

We are performing necessary initial configuration so that VCM can reach the Internet and synchronize patch metadata that can be used to check which patches are missing and which are not required on the machines in the infrastructure.

The proxy configuration in VCM is for the synchronization and downloading of patches once we start deploying them; they are downloaded to the collector server from the Internet.

The download directory

The default download directory is `X:\Program Files (x86)VMware\VCM\WebConsole\L1033\Files\SUM Downloads`.

This directory is shared as `\\collector_name\cmfiles$\SUM Downloads`.

Note that if no Internet access is available, you must obtain the patches manually and store them in `\\collector_name\cmfiles$\SUM Downloads` on the VCM Collector.

See also

- More details about the network authority account can be found in the *Adding a network authority account to manage machines in multiple domains* recipe from `Chapter 2`, *Configuring VCM to Manage Your Infrastructure*

An introduction to automated patching

Once we are finished with the preparation, we will have a look at how we can use VCM to automatically populate specific machine groups so that they can be patched automatically on a schedule. As discussed in the introduction of the chapter, if you are using vRealize Automation and vRealize Orchestrator to deploy new VMs, you can use them to create a registry entry that will be captured by VCM during the initial data collection. Based on that registry entry, individual VMs will be placed in their respective machine groups, which will be used for automated patching.

If you are not using an automated deploy tool to create registry entries, you have to devise a way to manually populate the machine groups every time a new machine/server is deployed.

Getting ready

Get help from a vRA and vRO expert, who will present an option on the portal for users when they request a machine; otherwise, create scripts that will add required registry entries to the managed machines.

For this recipe, we will do it manually in order to simulate the process.

How to do it...

An explanation of utilizing vRA and vRO for automated patching is out of the scope of this book; get in touch with your vRA and vRO experts for that.

An example script that can be used to add a registry entry is as follows. Each line represents a single script and will add required registry entry:

```
REG ADD HKLM\Software\VCM-CookBook /v VCMPatchWindow /t REG_SZ /d "MW01"
REG ADD HKLM\Software\VCM-CookBook /v VCMPatchWindow /t REG_SZ /d "MW02"
REG ADD HKLM\Software\VCM-CookBook /v VCMPatchWindow /t REG_SZ /d "MW03"
REG ADD HKLM\Software\VCM-CookBook /v VCMPatchWindow /t REG_SZ /d "MW04"
```

You can use any tool to do this, or run them manually on each machine. We had a look at how this can be used to create a machine group in the *Creating machine groups* recipe in `Chapter 2`, *Configuring VCM to Manage Your Infrastructure*.

How it works...

It gives us a variable that will be used to create filters in machine groups, and then, those filters will make sure the machines in the respective machine groups can be patched on a schedule. To create a machine group based on this captured registry entry, have a look at the *Creating machine groups* recipe in `Chapter 2`, *Configuring VCM to Manage Your Infrastructure*.

See also

- As mentioned in the recipe, have a look at *Creating machine groups* recipe in `Chapter 2`, *Configuring VCM to Manage Your Infrastructure*
- For setting up scheduled patching, go through the *Windows patching – scheduled* recipe later in this chapter

Creating a patch assessment template

A patch assessment template is basically a list of patches grouped together, for example, all patches for Windows Server 2008, all security patches for a specific month, or only security updates for all Windows operating systems. We can create either a static template or a dynamic template. In a static template, we choose patches manually, while in a dynamic template, we define criteria based on the patch release date, severity of the patch, product, and so on.

Getting ready

Before starting this recipe, we need a fully functional VCM setup and to follow the steps mentioned in *Configuring VCM to use Microsoft updates.*

How to do it...

You are tasked with implementing your organization's patch policy for Windows servers, and your security team will test and provide you with a list of approved patches on a monthly basis. You need to create a patch template and make sure all your servers are patched according to approved patches.

To start with, you need to create a patch template and update it on a monthly basis. As you will get a list of approved patches, it's better you create a static template and keep adding patches every month.

To create the patch assessment template, follow this process:

1. After logging in to VCM, go to **Patching** | **Windows** | **Assessment Template** and click on **Add**. This will launch the wizard.
2. Give a name, proper description, and, depending on your requirements, select **Dynamic Template** or **Static Template**.
3. In our case, we need to select **Static Template**.

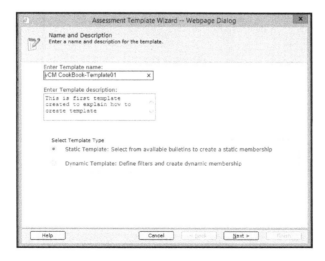

- For **Static Template**, select the required patches and save the template.

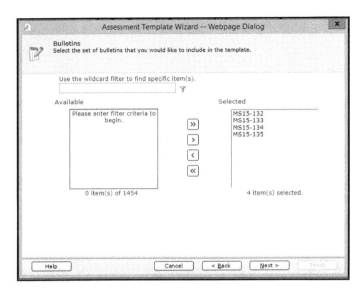

- For **Dynamic Template**, define criteria; VCM will then populate the patches on that basis.

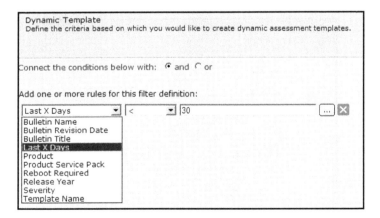

Note that once a template type is selected and saved, it cannot be changed to another type.

How it works...

We cannot deploy patches without creating assessment templates; these will be used for assessing the status of the machines, checking missing patches, and then deploying them.

As explained, you can create a dynamic monthly template to assess and update Windows templates in vCenter, as those will be patched monthly and we don't need them to be assessed with a big, long assessment template.

We can create a big assessment template that can be used to scan and check the entire infrastructure with live machines and will include only those patches that are approved by the company's security team.

You should note that if some users with administrative access uninstall a patch, then this big assessment template comes in handy, as it will have the uninstalled patch listed, and then VCM will reinstall the patch.

Here is a comparison of the template types:

Dynamic template: This updates the patch list based on the conditions we provide while creating it. Refer to the previous screenshot: we have options to filter patches based on parameters such as **Bulletin Name** or **Last X Days**, so we can have a monthly assessment template ready for the current month; or by severity, so we can have security patches only.

Static template: This template does not update itself on its own; the administrator needs to log in to VCM to add/remove the patches from the list. If your security team releases a list of approved patches every month, you can create a master template and keep adding new patches, removing patches that are superseded, and keep an updated assessment template ready for deployment.

Every template has a unique ID associated with it in the VCM database; if we create a template, use it in deployment, delete it, and then recreate a template with the same name, then this newly created template will be treated as a different template by VCM and will not be used automatically in the deployment that had been using the old template.

Windows patching – on demand

Once the patch assessment template is ready, we need to first assess machines for missing patches and then use that to patch them. The assessment will also be used to check patch compliance in the form of reports, which we will cover at the end of this chapter.

Getting ready

We will need the VCM server connected to the Internet and configured as in the *Configuring VCM to use Microsoft updates* and *Creating a patch assessment template* recipes. We can either use the default machine groups created by VCM or create groups as necessary; the process was explained in the *Creating machine groups* recipe in Chapter 2, *Configuring VCM to Manage Your Infrastructure*.

How to do it...

We will use the default machine groups listed in the recipe just mentioned and will not create any new ones for now. So, we will start by logging in to VCM and following these steps:

1. Go to **Patching** | **Windows** | **Assessment Template**.
2. Select the assessment template, making sure the proper machine group is selected at the top (machine groups are used to filter selected machines instead of showing all the machines managed by VCM).
3. If you click on the data grid, you will be able to see the status of all the machines on which the VCM agent is installed and which are a part of the selected machine group. If **Data Age** is **N/A**, then we need to perform a data collection for those machines. The following screenshot shows the **Suggested Patch** value as **Must reassess – Machine Added After Assessment run** for the dc01 machine:

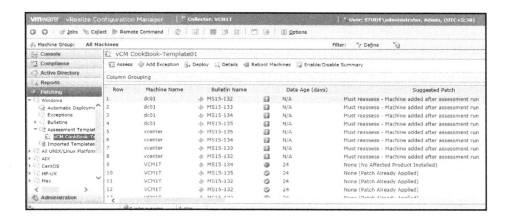

4. Simply select the machine(s) and click on **Collect** in the top-left corner. This will launch a wizard; make sure all the required machine(s) are part of the **Selected** box on the right-hand side.

5. Select **Select a collection Filter set to apply to those machines** and **do not Limit collection to Deltas**; any priority is fine, so go with the default.

6. Under **Filter Sets**, select **Patching – Windows Security Bulletins**.

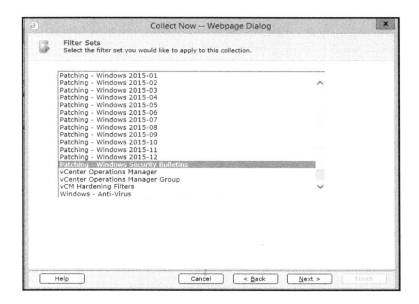

Make sure the job is completed successfully; it will take 10 minutes to add the details to the VCM database.

7. Once the collection is complete, click on **Assess**. This will check the patch status of each machine. The content of the assessment template will be checked against the managed machine's patch status. The results will then be presented with details of missing or installed patches.

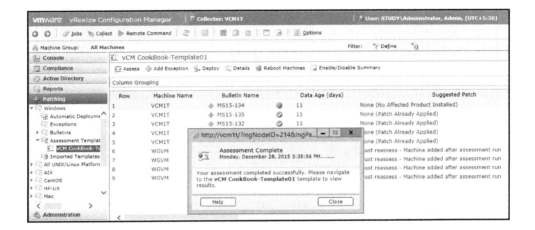

8. After the assessment, you will be given options such as **Installing the missing patches** or **No Affected Product Installed**. To install missing patches, select them and click on **Deploy**. This will again launch a wizard.

9. On the first page, select the patches you want to deploy.

10. In the next step, it will try to find the location of the patches. It will report whether the patch was found and include the bulletin number:

   - **Found on Collector**: The Windows patch file was found in the download directory.

   - **Found on the Internet**: The Windows patch file was found on the download site and must be downloaded.

   - **Not Found**: The Windows patch file was not found on the Collector or the Internet.

11. We need to download a patch before installing, so select **Download Now**:

- **Download at run time**: This pulls the patch down to the default download directory or the alternate local patch path when the patch is deployed. Because the deployment can be scheduled, you can run the deployment and download the files when heavy loads do not occur on your network.
- **Download now**: This pulls the patch files down to the default download directory or the alternate local patch path immediately. Depending on your network load and the number of files to download, you can download the patch files immediately.

12. As this is on-demand patching, select **Copy patches to target machines during deployment** and **Run Action now**.

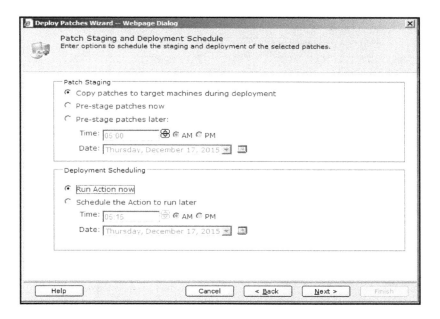

13. Select **Reboot Options** as required.

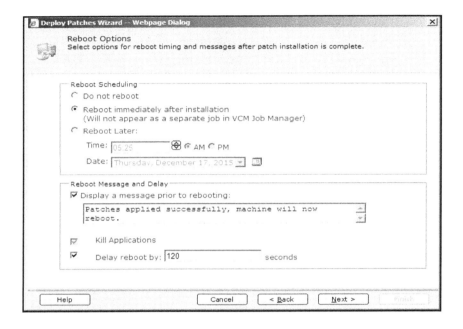

14. Download the patches, and the deployment will start.

The deployment can be monitored at **Patching** | **Job Management** | **Windows** | **Job Manager** | **Running**.

15. Once the patches are deployed on the target machine, it will display a message like this:

After we have started the deployment, we probably want to monitor how it's going. To do so, click on **Jobs** on the VCM console and follow the **Patching** job. Once the patch has been deployed, we need to check the status being updated in VCM console, that is, earlier under **Suggested Patch**, it showed **Install the Patch**, and now, it should show **None (Patch Already Applied)**. For that, go back to **Patching | Windows | Assessment Template** | <The patch template you used at the start> and start the collection. Once the collection is complete, perform an assessment (click on **Assess** in the top menu), and a refresh will give you the desired result, that is, the status of the managed machines–whether the patch was deployed or the machine failed or is still waiting for a reboot (if not, set to reboot when deploying patches).

The following screenshot shows the status after running the assessment on a managed machine after patch deployment, reboot, and data collection:

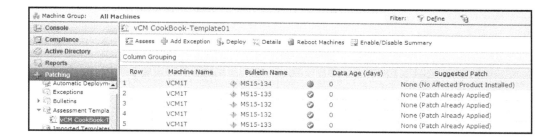

 Note that VCM runs **Job Summary: Patching Automated Collection – Patching – Windows Security Bulletins** to run a collection after patching, but it sometimes takes a while to run this collection. We can run the collection the same way we did at the start of the recipe and perform an assessment.

How it works...

After the initial assessment, VCM identifies which patches are missing on the server, based on which it gives you the Suggested Patch advice, such as installing missing patches. You can choose to install missing patches. Now, VCM tries to find out whether the patch is available on the Collector server–downloaded for installation on another server–or is available on Internet; this is where proxy configuration comes in handy. If the patch is not available on the Collector server, it offers to download the patch.

Once the patch download is complete, it stages the patch on the managed machine and starts installing it. Once the patch installation is over and if the patch requires a reboot, depending upon the options we have selected, it will reboot the server. After the server is rebooted, it performs a post-patch collection and then updates the status to VCM regarding the patch we installed. If we perform another assessment after the patching and data collection, we can check the current status of the patch: it must be installed.

Windows patching – scheduled

In the previous recipe, we deployed a patch on demand and found we need to run a few tasks to finish the job. We cannot afford to wait in front of the server every time to perform an on-demand patching; hence, what we can do is schedule patch deployment. Because the assessment is run only against data in the VCM database, we must collect patching data from managed machines before and after we run an assessment.

Getting ready

We will need a VCM server that has an Internet connection and has been through the earlier recipes, such as *Prepare VCM for Windows patching* and *Creating a patch assessment template*. For scheduled patches, it is recommended to have machine groups created before we start the process.

How to do it...

As seen in the previous recipe, we need to follow four steps to completely perform the patching job; hence, we will schedule four tasks for completing one single patch maintenance window.

The tasks will be as follows:

- **Initial collection**: Collecting patch status data from machines before patching
- **Initial assessment**: Comparing collected data against the assessment template before patching
- **Deploying patches**: Installing patches according to schedule
- **Final assessment**: Comparing collected data against the assessment template after patching

This is a planned schedule that will look like this:

Sr. no.	Name	Schedule	Reason
1	Initial collection	First Sunday at 08:00 am	12 hours before the actual patch
2	Initial assessment	First Sunday at 02:00 pm	6 hours before the actual patch
3	Deploy patch	First Sunday at 08:00 pm	Scheduled patch maintenance window
4	Final assessment	First Sunday at 11:00 pm	3 hours after patching to give time for automated collection (happens after 30 minutes of patching and reboot)

Initial collection

We can't install a patch unless VCM knows whether it is required; in the initial collection, we will update the VCM database with this information. VCM creates a filter set called **Patching – Windows Security Bulletins** and updates it after each new patch released by Microsoft.

In this example, we will use a machine group called `VCM-CookBook-MW01`, which we have created for this demonstration.

Follow these steps to start automatic Windows patch deployment configuration:

1. To perform initial collection, we need to log in to VCM with admin privileges and go to **Administration** | **Job Manager** | **Scheduled**, click on **Add**, and select **Collection**.
2. Provide a proper name and add description.
3. Make sure you select **Patching – Windows Security Bulletins** as the **Filter Set**.
4. Select the correct machine group for this scheduled maintenance window.
5. Provide a proper schedule, as described in the table at the start of this recipe.

Once the initial collection against the required filter set has been scheduled, we can move to the next step, initial assessment.

Initial assessment

The initial assessment involves checking the status of patches against the machines whose data has been collected in the previous step. We are giving 6 hours to VCM to properly collect the data from all the machines; hence, this job can be scheduled after 6 hours of initial data collection and 6 hours before actual patch time. Follow these steps:

1. Navigate to **Patching** | **Job Management** | **Windows** | **Scheduled** | **Assessment** and click on **Add**.
2. Provide a proper job name related to the maintenance window and a proper description.

3. Select the correct template.

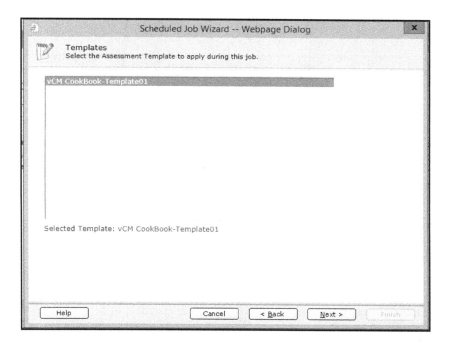

4. Select an associated machine group.
5. Select an appropriate schedule, as discussed at the start of this recipe.

Deploying patches

At this moment, the VCM server has information about which patches are missing on the machines that are a part of the machine group, and now, we can schedule the actual patch deployment task by following these steps:

1. Navigate to **Patching** | **Windows** | **Automatic Deployment**. Click on **Add**.
2. Select the correct machine group responding to the maintenance window.
3. Select the required assessment template.
4. On this page, select **Scheduled Automatic Deployment Run** and, if your company policy approves, select **Reboot immediately after deployment**.

5. For **Threshold Data Age**, we can go ahead with the default of 2, as we have already scheduled jobs to collect data and perform the assessment 12 hours before the actual patch time.

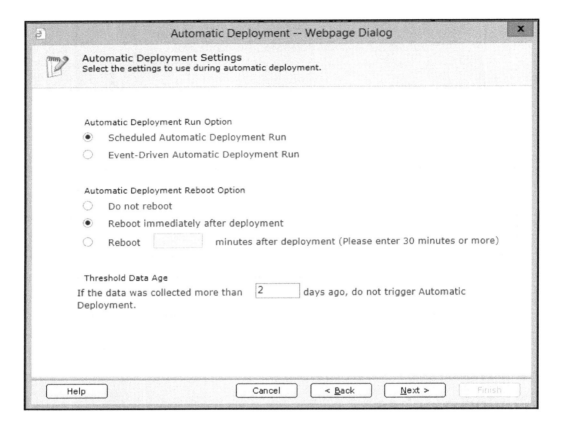

6. Finally, select the schedule we decided on at the start of the recipe and click on **Next**.
7. We will be done with the third step once we click on **OK**.

Final assessment

So far, we have scheduled data collection and assessment and then done the actual patching. Now, we will schedule a task that will update the VCM database with these updates. In the previous recipe, we learned that after performing a patch deployment, when the machine reboots, VCM starts a collection job to collect details of the machine after patch installation. So, we just need to schedule an assessment the same way we did in the initial assessment step; we just need to make sure the name and description indicate that this is the final assessment and it is scheduled some time after the patch installation (3 hours, as decided at the start) to give some time to the VCM server to finish the job. Follow these steps:

1. Navigate to **Patching | Job Management | Windows | Scheduled | Assessment** and click on **Add**.
2. Provide a proper job name related to the maintenance window and a proper description.
3. Select the correct template.
4. Select the associated machine group.
5. Select the appropriate schedule, as discussed at the start.

Once we are done with the final assessment, VCM will update the current details on the user interface and in the reports.

How it works...

This makes life much easier for the admins, who are responsible for patching. All the activities required for patching can be and are scheduled so that admins don't need to sit in front of the VCM console and push patches.

We scheduled an initial collection, which used the **Patching – Windows Security Bulletins** filter set, which made sure we have the latest details of the managed servers in the VCM database. Based on the data collected, we performed an initial assessment. This performed a check against the patching template and provided us with information about the patch requirements.

This is followed by actual patches being downloaded from the Internet if missing on the collector server and then being staged on the managed machine. Once the time is right, the VCM agent installs the patches and performs a reboot as configured. After the patches are installed, VCM initiates the data collection again using the same filter set, **Patching – Windows Security Bulletins**, but this time, we have updated details as the patches have been installed now.

This updated information is added to the VCM database and used in the final assessment to obtain the status of the current patch.

There's more...

Apart from the regular options, there are some additional settings that you should pay attention to if you plan to manage a medium-to-large infrastructure.

Here are the details you need to configure your infrastructure. You need to log in with VCM admin privilege and go to **Administration** I **General Settings** I **Patching** I **Windows** I **Additional Settings**.

Sr. no.	Setting	Explanation
1	Automatic patch deployment – the threshold data age (days)	This sets the automatic patch deployment to trigger based on the threshold data age. When the data age of the patch bulletin is greater than the threshold data age, VCM does not deploy the patches. To update the data age for the patch bulletin, you must run a new collection and assessment. The default is 2 days, which you can modify if required.
2	The timeout in minutes for the entire patch deployment job	The time for which to run the patch deployment job before the process times out. The default is 60; if you have large number of machines getting patched in one go, then this needs to be changed to a higher value, such as 120 or 180, depending upon how many machines you have and the approved maintenance window.
3	The wait time (in minutes) before performing the post collection, for patches that require a reboot	This determines how long VCM will wait before collecting patch status data from rebooted managed machines after the patch deployment is finished. The default is 30 minutes; if you think this is too much or too little, you can change it.

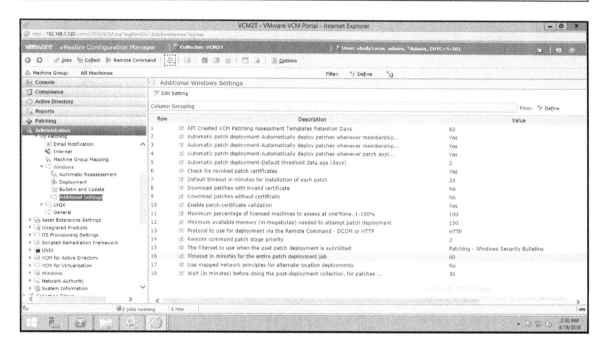

You need to log in with VCM admin privileges and go to **Administration** | **General Settings** | **Patching** | **Windows** | **Deployments**.

Change the value of the maximum concurrent agent installs from 21 to a higher value.

If in the additional settings you have selected 60 minutes as the timeout in minutes for the entire patch deployment job and you have this maximum concurrent set to the default 21, then there are chances that some machines might get a timeout and not get the patches deployed if you have a very large assessment template. This can create some issues, as we might have some machines without patches in a month.

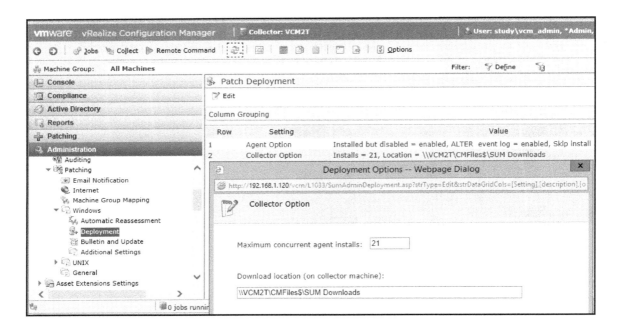

Patching machines in multi-domain environments and workgroups

Typically, in medium-to-large organizations, more than one Active Directory domain exists. We can use VCM to patch servers in multiple domains. Here is what you need to do that.

Apart from multiple domains, there are machines that are part of none, or they are in a workgroup. To manage and patch the machines in a workgroup, you need a network authority account assigned to a machine group populated with machines in a workgroup.

Getting ready

We need to follow the *Adding a network authority account to manage machines in multiple domains* recipe in `Chapter 2`, *Configuring VCM to Manage Your Infrastructure*, with correct domains and their respective NAA accounts for patching multi-domain servers.

For patching machines in a workgroup, we need to create a machine group with static memberships and add all machines that are not in the domain.

Open the necessary ports between the VCM server and the managed servers either in a workgroup or in another domain.

How to do it...

We will approach this recipe in two ways:

First, we will discuss multiple domains.

The first thing we need to do is configure all the required **Network Access Account (NAA)** accounts as per the *Adding a network authority account to manage machines in multiple domains* recipe from `Chapter 2`, *Configuring VCM to Manage Your Infrastructure*.

Then, you can follow the *Windows patching – on demand* recipe from this chapter for on-demand patching or the *Windows patching – scheduled* recipe for scheduled patching.

The second way is for workgroup servers.

We need to add an available account with a . (dot) domain and a username and password common to the workgroup machines. Follow these steps:

1. Go to **Administration** | **Settings** | **Network Authority**, under **Available Accounts** and click on **Add**.

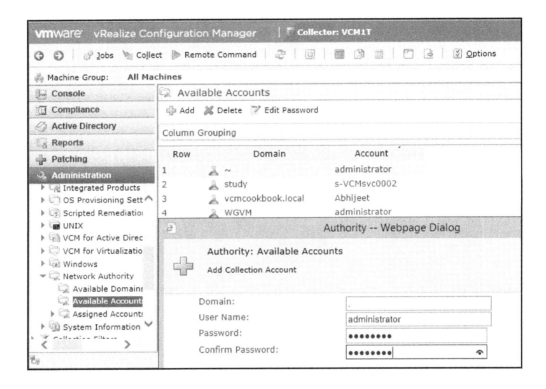

2. Once the accounts have been added, we need to associate them with the machine group created for workgroup machines.

3. If there are no common accounts available, then we can add one account per server in following format. Here, **Domain** is the name of the machine:

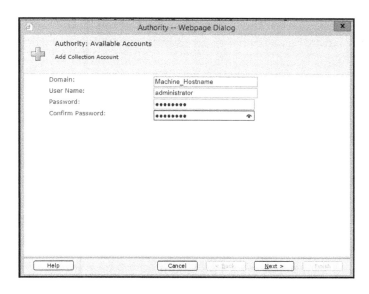

4. So now, go to **Assigned Accounts** by **Machine Group**, select a machine group for the workgroup machines, and assign the accounts added earlier.

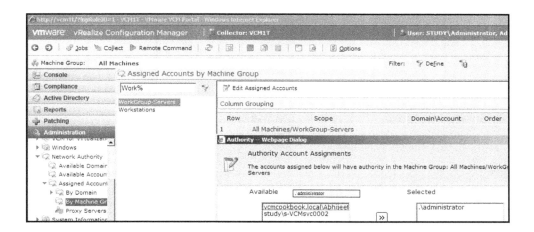

As explained in the previous recipe, VCM tries all the accounts until it finds a working account; there is no problem in assigning all the accounts to the machine group.

 Note that we cannot have multiple accounts with the same account name and domain, so for the . (dot) domain, we can't have more than one administrator as a user registered in the available accounts.

There is another alternative: if, for some reason, you do not wish to assign all the accounts to the machine group, you can create network authority accounts and then assign one account to each machine, making sure that when adding the available account, the domain is defined as the machine name.

1. Once you have added the required accounts, go to**Administration | Licensed Machines | Licensed Windows Machines**.

2. Select the machine whose network authority account needs to be changed; click

   on the   symbol in the menu, and it will launch the wizard.

3. Make sure the machine whose NAA we are changing is available under **Selected**.

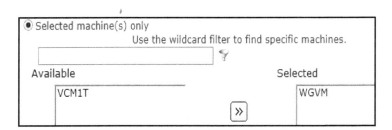

4. Select the associated network authority account for this machine.

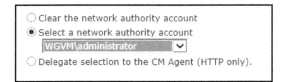

5. Click on **Next** and then complete the wizard.

6. To make sure the account has been changed correctly, scroll to the extreme right and validate under the **Network Authority** column for the machine.

Network Authority
study\s-VCMsvc0002
WGVM\administrator

After this change, we can successfully manage the machine from VCM, which includes collecting data, installing software and patches, and checking and enforcing compliance.

Then, you can follow either the *Windows patching – on demand* or *Windows patching – scheduled* recipes, based on your requirements.

How it works...

The defined network authority account will be used by VCM to manage the patching of the machines in the workgroup.

Patching VM templates

It is essential that when VMs are first provisioned, the virtual machine template to be used is up to date. This will reduce the downtime for the end consumer of the VM when they come to patch, and reduce system-wide vulnerabilities.

How to do it...

Follow these steps to patch a VM template:

1. To patch a VM template, convert it into a VM, provide an IP, and make sure it can reach the VCM server.

   The agent installer should be available on each template.

2. Once the agent has been installed, license the machine in VCM and perform a collection.

3. The machine should be a part of a machine group called **Template Patching**. Perform on-demand patching.

4. After patches have been installed and the VM rebooted and validated by VCM for the patch status, uninstall the agent.

5. Purge the VM in VCM.

6. Convert the VM back into a template.

How it works

This is a completely manual process, where we convert the template in to a virtual machine, install the agent, and then install patches. After patching is over, we purge the machine from the VCM console after uninstalling the agent and finally convert the machine to a vCenter template.

Patching reports

Once the infrastructure has been patched, what we need are fancy reports to show to the management that we are all green in terms of patching. VCM does not disappoint you when it comes to reports–there are multiple preconfigured reports, which can be either scheduled or run on demand and exported to multiple formats such as `.xls`, `.doc`, `.csv`, and `.pdf`.

Getting ready

We must have a compliance template ready before we can begin with the recipe.

How to do it...

Once logged in to VCM, go to the reporting section.

1. Navigate to **Reports** | **Machine Group Reports** | **VCM Patching**.

These are the default reports available in VCM for Windows patching:

Ser	Name	Description
1	VCM Patching Assessment Based	These reports use data generated by VCM patching assessments (on the VCM Patching slider) to generate their patch status results
2	Patch Status Summary	This displays the patching status across the enterprise for Windows and Unix
3	VCVP Windows Patch Status Details	This displays details of virtualization machines' Windows patch statuses
4	Windows Patch Assessment by Bulletin Information	This enables VCM patching by bulletin
5	Windows Patch Assessment by Product Information	This enables VCM patching by product information
6	Windows Patch Assessment Results Details	This displays the details of the VCM patching assessment by machine, bulletin, or template
7	Windows Patch Assessment Results Details By Bulletin	This displays Windows patch assessment results details grouped by bulletin
8	Windows Patch Assessment Results Details By Machine	This displays Windows patch assessment results details grouped by machine
9	Windows Patch Assessment Results Details By Template	This displays Windows patch assessment results details grouped by template
10	Windows Patch Assessment Results Trends	This displays the trends for VCM patching assessment templates by day, week, month, or quarter
11	Windows Patch Assessment Trends	This displays the trends for VCM patching assessments by day, week, month, or quarter
12	Windows Patch Status	This displays the Windows patch status
13	Windows Patch Status by Template Details	This provides the VCM patching patch status by template details

14	Windows Patch Status by Template Summary	This provides the VCM patching patch status by template summary
15	Windows Patch Status Details	This provides Windows patch status details

2. From the VCM console, select the report you want to run, and click on **Run**; the wizard will start. Once the details are filled in, it will show the report. As discussed, the report can be exported into multiple formats to be used by the administrator.

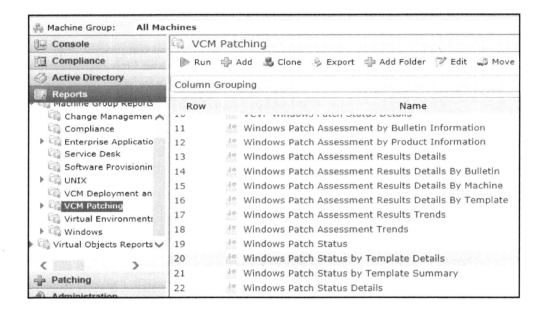

3. The important thing we need to remember here is the machine group selection on the top; this filters the machines that will be included in the report.

4. We can schedule reports as well. We will have more details about that in `Chapter 8`, *Integration with vROps and Scheduling*, in the *Scheduling reports* recipe.

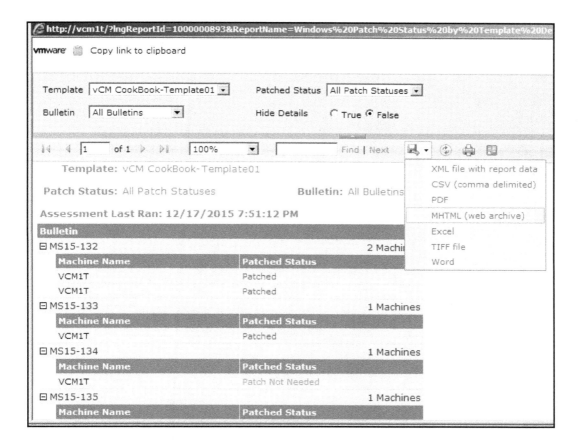

How it works...

There is a big list of existing reports that we can run and export. We can even schedule those reports, and then, they can be either exported to a location or mailed to a specified e-mail id if working SMTP is configured.

There's more...

You can have a look at scheduling reports in the *Scheduling patching reports* recipe of Chapter 8, *Integration with vROps and Scheduling*.

5
Software Provisioning for Windows

In this chapter, we will cover the following recipes:

- Installing a software repository on Windows
- Deploying additional components on agents
- Creating software packages
- Publishing software packages to a repository
- Adding a repository to VCM
- Adding repository sources to package managers
- Deploying a package

Introduction

VCM's software provisioning provides tools, resources, and mechanisms for creating and managing packages for the software you plan to distribute and finally installing the software on managed machines. VCM's software distribution works only with Windows and not other OSes.

In this chapter, we will be looking at a software provisioning overview and the steps required for installing software on managed machines via VCM.

Software provisioning is the process by which we can create software packages, publish those packages to repositories, and then install them on target machines.

To support the provisioning process, the VCM software provisioning components consist of the following:

- Software package repositories
- Package manager
- VMware vCenter Configuration Manager Package Studio

The Windows software repository

The Windows software repository is the shared location to which packages are published by **Package Studio** and the location from which package manager downloads packages for installation.

Package manager for Windows

Package manager is the application installed on each machine to manage the installation and removal of the software contained in packages. Package manager is configured to use one or more repositories as a source for packages.

This figure shows the relationship between the VCM Collector server, software repositories, and package manager instances:

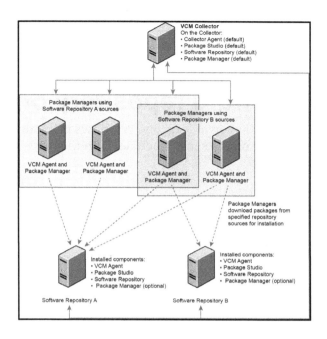

 The definitions and figure are taken from the vCenter Configuration Manager administration guide (http://www.vmware.com/pdf/vcenter -configuration-manager-57-administration-guide.pdf).

VMware vCenter Configuration Manager Package Studio

Package Studio is the application used to build software packages for installation on target Windows servers and workstations.

A software package provides the files and metadata necessary to install and remove programs. One of the most useful features of a package is the metadata regarding dependencies, conflicts, and other relationships, which are not represented by software installation files. This metadata is used to determine whether the necessary dependencies are in place so that an installation is successful, and if not, what is necessary to make it successful.

After a package has been created and is ready for distribution, it is published to a software repository. We then use package manager to download the package from the repository to the local machine and install it on Windows systems.

Installing a software repository on Windows

The software repository is installed on at least one Windows machine in the infrastructure, and Package Studio needs to be on the same machine, with the repository being installed before installing Package Studio.

Getting ready

As the repositories are installed on the Collector server by default, if we need another repository, then we need to install another Windows server with IIS. IIS requirements are the same as that of the Collector server, mentioned in Chapter 1, *Installing VCM*, in the *Preparing our VCM deployment – installing and configuring IIS* recipe.

How to do it...

To deploy a software repository on any other server, follow this process:

1. First, we locate Repository.msi at the following location:

    ```
    X:\Program Files (x86)\VMware\VCM\AgentFiles\Products (on the VCM
    collector Server)
    ```

2. When we double-click on the `Repository.msi` file, it will launch the wizard, and after accepting the EULA and selecting the installation location, it will ask you to provide a virtual directory:

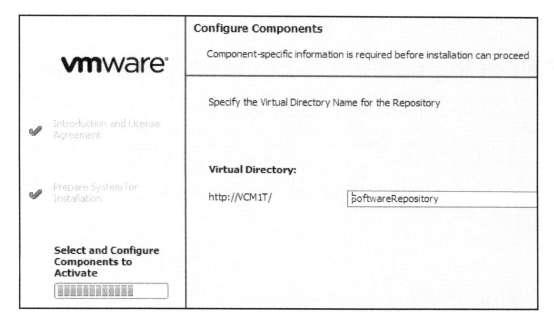

We can either go with the default name or change it.

3. Follow the wizard to finish the installation.

How it works...

A repository is used by Package Studio to store created packages that will be used to provision the managed machines. We can create multiple repositories and keep them close to the managed machines to avoid bandwidth consumption over WAN; also, local provisioning will be much faster.

As repositories will be used to store the installer, you need to provision enough disk space, depending on how many and which applications you are planning to distribute. This acts like a file server, from where all the VCM-managed machines will copy the packages and then install them. A server with two vCPUs and 8 GB of RAM should be enough to cater to the needs of a dedicated software repository.

Deploying additional components on agents

Package manager, which is installed on the target machines, manages the installation of software packages. It does not contain the software packages, only pointers to the packages in the repository sources of which it is aware. When directed to install, the package is copied from the repository to the `cratecache` folder on the target machines. Package manager unzips the files to the `%TMP%` directory and runs the configured installation.

> This is applicable for VCM 5.7.3 or earlier; ignore this if you are already at 5.8.0 or later.

Getting ready

For this recipe, we need a working VCM server and managed machines where VCM agents are installed.

How to do it...

We will follow the process to check whether agent extensions for provisioning are installed or not. If they aren't, we will install them.

This only applies to VCM 5.7.3 or earlier. The steps are as follows:

1. Once logged in to VCM with admin privileges, go to **Administration | Machines Manager | Licensed Machines | Licensed Windows Machines**.
2. In the data grid, locate the machines on which you are verifying the existence of the necessary agent extensions, and verify that the **Agent Ext. For Prov. Version** column contains a value of 5.3 or later.
3. You need to scroll right to see the **Agent Ext. for Prov. Version** column:

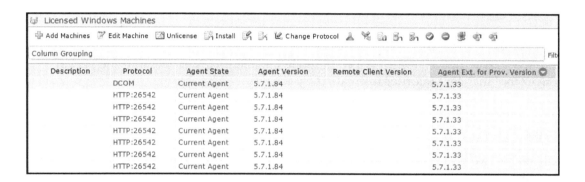

Description	Protocol	Agent State	Agent Version	Remote Client Version	Agent Ext. for Prov. Version
	DCOM	Current Agent	5.7.1.84		5.7.1.33
	HTTP:26542	Current Agent	5.7.1.84		5.7.1.33
	HTTP:26542	Current Agent	5.7.1.84		5.7.1.33
	HTTP:26542	Current Agent	5.7.1.84		5.7.1.33
	HTTP:26542	Current Agent	5.7.1.84		5.7.1.33
	HTTP:26542	Current Agent	5.7.1.84		5.7.1.33
	HTTP:26542	Current Agent	5.7.1.84		5.7.1.33
	HTTP:26542	Current Agent	5.7.1.84		5.7.1.33

4. If it does not, you need to either install or upgrade the VCM agent from the VCM console. Follow the *Upgrading VCM agents* recipe from `Chapter 7`, *Maintenance of VCM*.

How it works...

Agent extensions for provisioning are required to be installed on the managed machine where we need to provision the software. By following this process, we make sure they are there, and if they're missing, we take the necessary action to install them.

Note that package manager is installed on target machines while the VCM agent version 5.3 or later *is installed from the Collector*.

Creating software packages

Package Studio is the application used to build software packages for installation on target Windows machines managed by VCM.

 Note that the software we want to create a package for must be able to install and uninstall without user interaction. This is referred to as **quiet or silent installation**. Typically, command-line options are used.

Getting ready

Before we start with this, we need a completely installed VCM server and the package manager tool installed in order to create the package.

How to do it...

In this recipe, we will create a package for `WinRAR.exe`, downloaded from `http://www.ra rlab.com`.

To do so, follow these steps.

Start VMware vCenter Configuration Manager Package Studio. Go to **Start** | **VMware vCenter Configuration Manager** | **Package Studio**.

 Note that for running Package Studio on a Windows 2008 server, we must run the application as an administrator.

Click on **Manage Packages**, and configure the package contents based on the options in the following tabs:

1. Click on **Properties** and type a **Name**, **Version**, and **Description**, and select the **Architecture**. These fields are required. You have the option of updating the other fields, depending on you requirements:

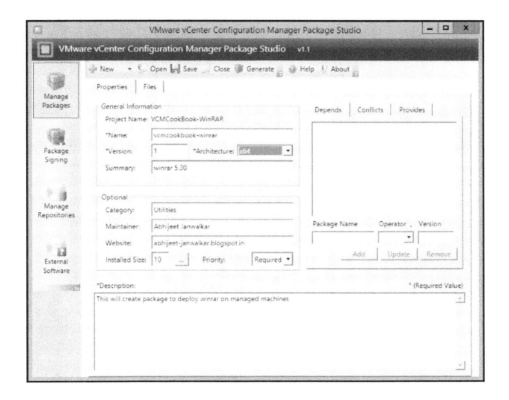

2. Click on **Files**, import the installation files, and configure the command, as follows:
    1. Click on **Select Folder** and go to the location where the installer is kept.
    2. Click on **Import** Files.
    3. Click on **Set Command**, and then, in the **Command** textbox, a command will be created. In our case, it will be `winrar-x64-530.exe`.

Provide any additional arguments; in this case, `/s` is used for a silent installation of winrar.

You can get the required options from the vendor of the software you are trying to install, or you can visit sites such as `www.itninja.com`.

Refer to the blog at
`http://www.itninja.com/question/what-switches-to-use-wit`
`h-exe-files-in-silent-mode`.

4. We have two options: **Installation** or **Removal**. In this case, we will choose **Installation**:

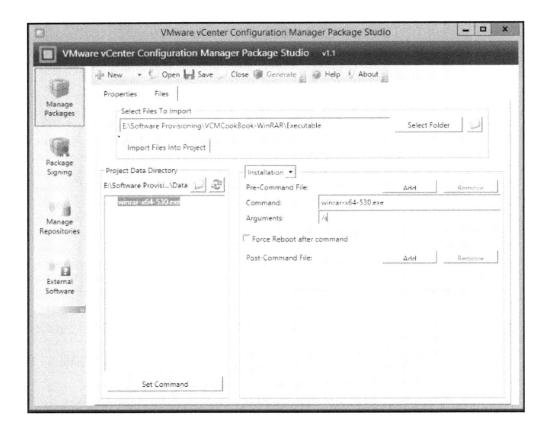

5. Click on **Save** to save the project file so that, if required, we can come back and edit it:

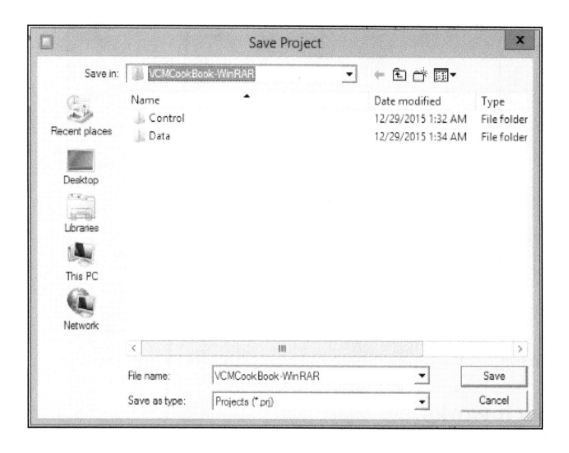

6. Click on **Generate**; this will generate a `.crate` file, which will be used to provision winrar on managed machines:

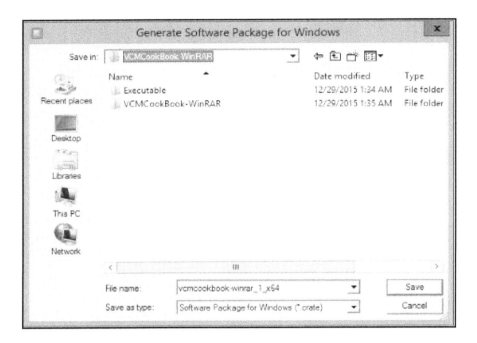

This is how we can create a software package that can be used for provisioning.

How it works...

By following this recipe, we can create a software package in a VCM-recognized format (`.crate`), which will be published on multiple repositories and then downloaded and processed by the VCM agents on the managed machines in order to install the actual software.

Publishing software packages to a repository

In the previous recipe, we created a package in the `.crate` format. The first thing to do after this is distribute the package to the repositories and from there to the managed machines' temporary folders to get it installed.

Now, we will publish the package we created in the previous recipe to the repositories for further processing.

Getting ready

We need a package created in Package Studio, such as the one we created in the previous recipe, and a repository installed by following the *Installing a software repository on Windows* recipe in order to complete this recipe.

How to do it...

We can continue where we left off in the previous recipe or relaunch Package Studio and open the previously created project file.

Follow these steps to publish the package to your repository:

1. Click on the **Manage Repositories** button on the left-hand side. Once on the **Repository** page, click on **Add Platform**. Basically, this is how we can determine which package goes in which folder. These platforms and sections are assigned to managed machines (or package manager in the following recipes).

We can create multiple platforms, such as Windows Server 2008 or Windows Server 2012:

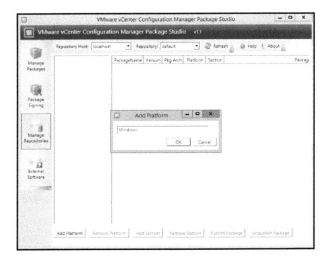

2. Each platform has multiple sections; we can add any number of sections and name them as we want. It is recommended you name them x86 and x64 to categorize your software accordingly:

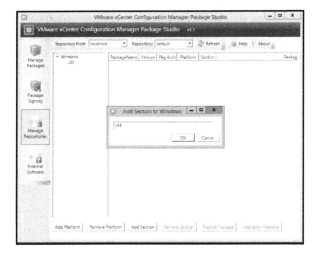

3. Once the sections have been added, select the appropriate section – either x86 or x64 – and hit **Publish Package**. Browse to the location of the .crate file and select it:

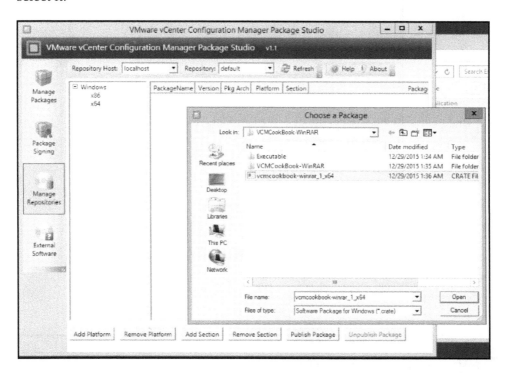

4. Choose the section(s):

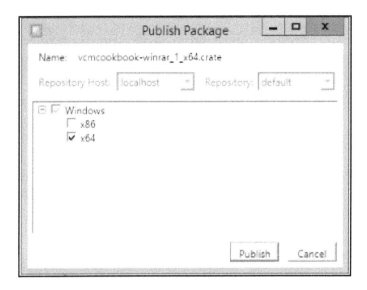

5. We are now good to go:

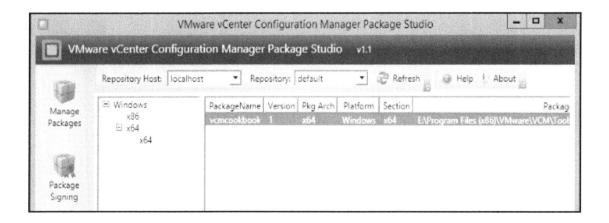

You can check whether the package has been published or not by doing either or both of the following:

1. Go to `X:\Program Files(x86)\VMware\VCM\Tools\Repository\Crates\`.

   You will find a folder with a single-letter name. The letter will be the first letter of our `.crate` file.

   There, you will find a `.crate` file ready for deployment:

2. From Internet Explorer, go to `http://<Repository Server name/ IP>/SoftwareRepository/Crates/X`.

   Again, *X* is a letter, which is the first letter of the `.crate` filename.

How it works...

In this recipe, VCM copies the `.crate` files to the proper locations on the repository server so that they can be accessed by package manager when it tries to deploy the published package.

About platforms: The platform value can be used to define the operating system architecture on which the package can be installed. We can create and use platforms to help manage our software package distribution based on the operating system platforms on which they can be installed. When we use a greater level of specificity, it results in smaller groups of packages and increases the predictability of which packages are installed.

About sections: Sections are used to further refine how your packages are organized on each platform. They are used to specify the repository sources for package manager, allowing us to control which packages are available to which machines. How you use sections can be adapted to your particular business needs. The following are examples of how you can use sections:

- **Line-of-business groups**: Marketing, sales, HRD, and engineering
- **Development state**: Development, acceptance, and production
- **IT software management structure**: Software publishers, departments, and business groups

Adding a repository to VCM

Once a package has been created and published on the repository, we need to assign the repository to managed machines so that they can download and install the package.

To view information about packages and package manager in VCM, we must collect package manager data from managed machines.

Getting ready

We need the agents ready with package manager installed, that is, we need to follow the *Deploying additional components on agents* recipe, and the repository should be published with the software we plan to provision by following the previous recipe.

How to do it...

This is a two-step process. In the first step, we will collect data from all the managed machines that need the software to be provisioned and check their status, and in the second step, we will collect data from the repository servers to check which packages are available for provisioning.

Collecting software provisioning package manager data

We need to run this against all the machines on which we need to provision the software and on which package manager has been installed. Follow these steps to collect data:

1. Once logged in to VCM as an administrator, click on **Collect** in the top-left corner of the VCM console:

2. This will launch the wizard; select **Machine Data**, and in the next step, select all the machines from which you need to collect the details.

3. Under **Data Types**, make sure **Software Provisioning – Package Managers** has been selected:

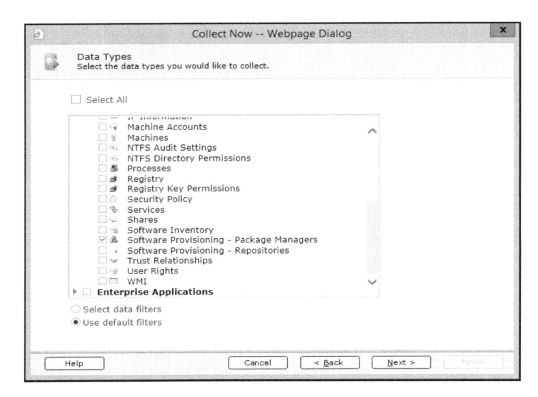

Make sure there are no conflicts, and let the job finish.

4. You can go to
   Administration | **JobManager** | **History** | **InstantCollection** | **Past 24 Hours**
   and check for the job status. It should be successful. You can look at more details
   by clicking on **View Details**:

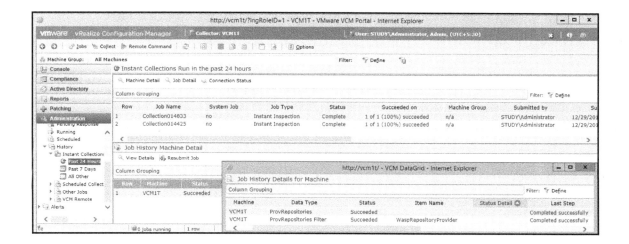

5. Once the data has been collected, the details can be viewed by going to **Console**
   | **Operating System** | **Windows** | **Software Provisioning** | **Package Manager**:

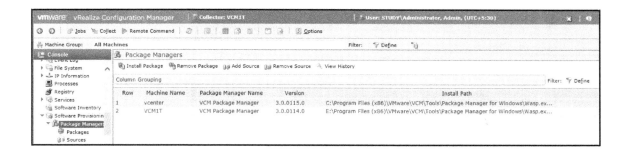

Collecting software repository data

Collect the repository data to identify which software packages are in which repositories. From the collected information, you can determine which repositories to assign to machines based on the available packages.

We need to run this against the machines that have software repositories created.

The process is similar to the previous step, but with two differences:

- We run this against all the repository servers
- The **Data Types** value is changed to **Software Provisioning – Repositories**

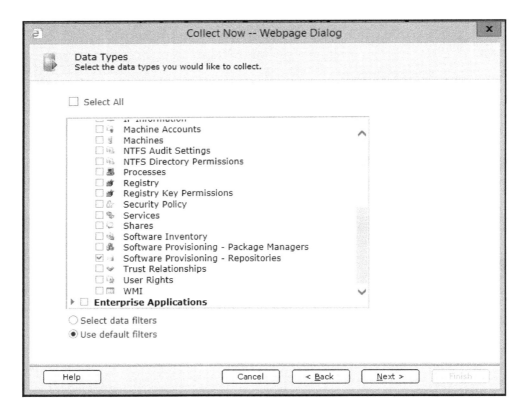

You can go to **Administration** I **Job Manager** I **History** I **Instant Collection** I **Past 24 Hours** and check the status of the job. It should be successful:

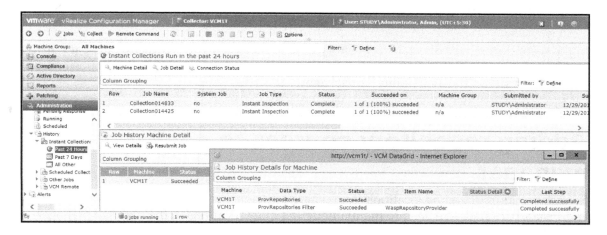

This is how it looks under **Console** I **Operating System** I **Windows** I **Software Provisioning** I **Package Manager** I **Repositories**.

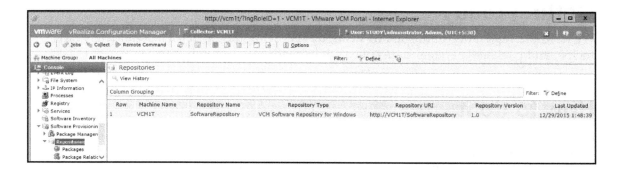

How it works...

In this two-step process, we are collecting data both from the managed machines and software repositories. In the first step, we collect details from all the managed machines to obtain the data about packages and package manager in VCM.

In the second step, we collect the repository data to identify which software packages are in which repositories. This information comes in handy when we need to assign repositories to machines based on the availability of packages.

Adding repository sources to package manager

Repository sources are the locations from where package manager will be able to download and install packages. We need to manually define those locations in the package manager (managed machines), and we can define more than one. Then, VCM package manager will follow its process to download the packages.

Getting ready

We need the repository published to VCM, by following the *Adding a repository to VCM* recipe, and package manager data collected, in order to assign repositories to it.

How to do it...

Adding a source gives the package manager instance on the selected machines access to the packages available in a specified section. The sources are numbered by priority. When you add a new one, you can specify whether to add it to the beginning or to the end of the list. You can also remove sources.

By following these steps, we can add sources to package manager:

1. Log on to VCM Server with administrative privileges and go to **Console | Windows | Operating System | Software Provisioning | Package Managers**.

2. Click on**Add Source**:

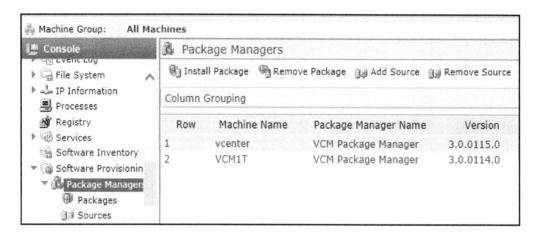

This will launch a wizard.

3. On the **Select Machines** page, verify that the machines displayed in the lower pane are the machines to which you want to add the source, and click on Next.

4. On the **Browse Source** page, select **VCM Managed Repositories**, select the repository, and click onOK:

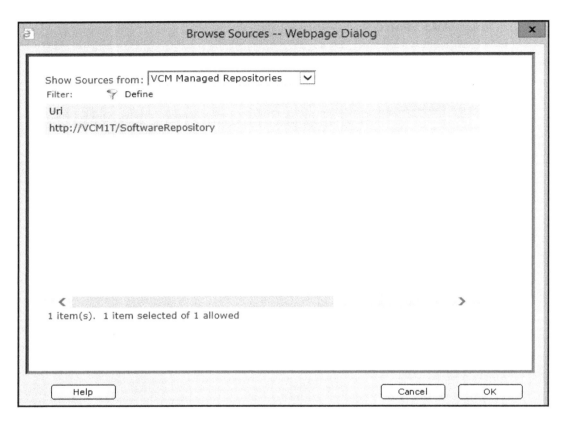

If there are multiple repositories, either select **Add source at the beginning of existing source lists** or **Add source at the end of the existing source lists**, depending on the proximity between package manager and the repository.

5. Verify that the platform name and the section name are exactly the same as those used in the repository when publishing the package:

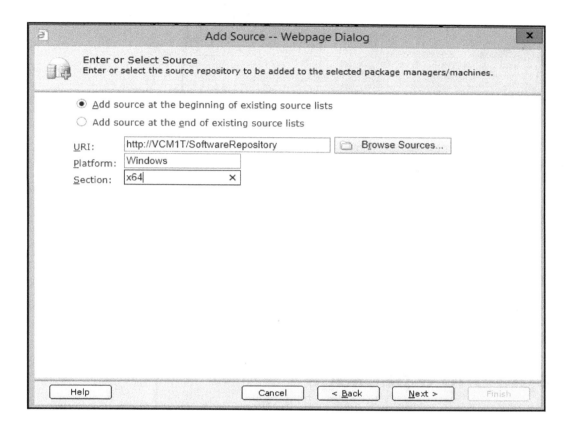

6. On the **Schedule** page, select one of the scheduling options and configure it as needed.

7. On the **Confirmation** page, review the information and click on **Finish**.

8. The added source is displayed in the **Package Managers – Sources** data grid.

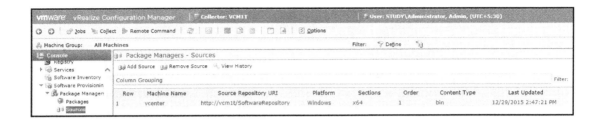

How it works...

Instead of depending on the location from where package manager downloads published packages, we simply assign the repositories and decide the order of the locations from which they can be fetched.

There's more...

Once a repository has been added to package manager, the only thing left is to install the package.

Deploying a package

Finally, we are ready to deploy the package—in other words, we are ready to provision the software.

Getting ready

We need to complete all the previous recipes in this chapter in order to work on this recipe.

How to do it...

To provision the software on managed machines, follow these steps:

1. Log on to VCM Server with administrative privileges and go to **Console** | **Windows** | **Operating System** | **Software Provisioning** | **Package Managers** | **Packages**.

2. Select the package you want to install and click on **Install Package**:

3. Follow the wizard and add more machines on which you want to install the selected package (winrar in our case) if required, or click on **Next**:

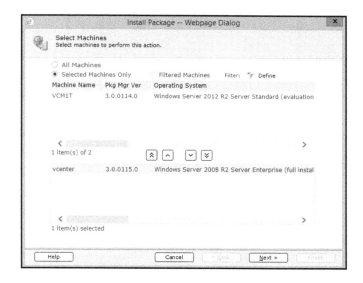

4. As we have not signed the package, accept the warning and allow the unsigned package:

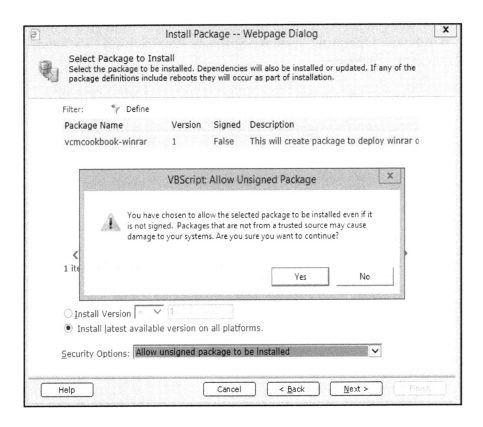

5. Schedule the action or select **Run Action Now**.

6. Accept the confirmation, and you are good to go:

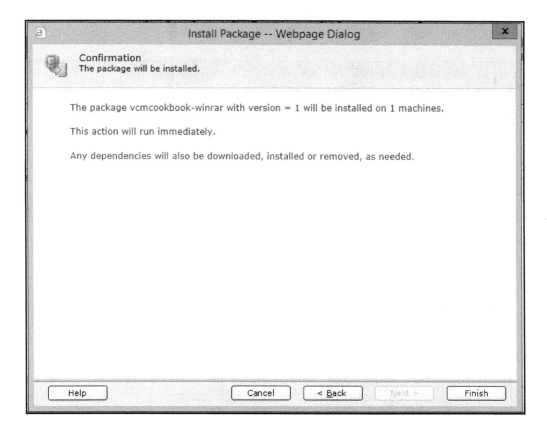

This will start the package installation process immediately if you selected **Run Action Now** or at a later time if you set a schedule.

How it works...

If you have followed everything, then you will have understood the relationship between various VCM components for software provisioning, created and published a software repository, created and published a software package, and added the repository source to package manager.

Let's look at the final step of installing a package.

The `.crate` file is copied to `C:\Program Files (x86)\VMware\VCM\Tools\Cratecache` on the managed machine:

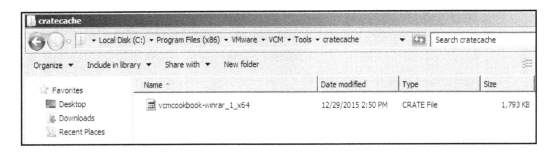

From here, package manager unzips the `.crate` file and uses the installation command and the arguments provided while creating the package to install the application.

The application can be seen installed in **Programs and Features**:

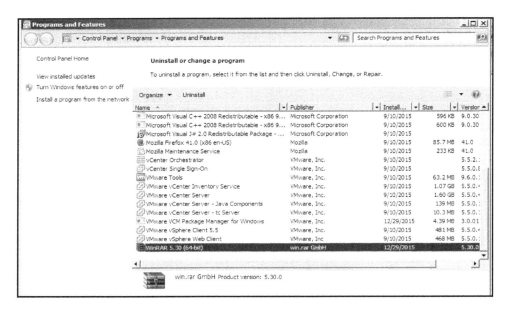

This concludes our exploration of software provisioning using VCM.

6
Compliance Management

In this chapter, we will cover the following recipes:

- Importing compliance packs
- Creating compliance rule groups
- Creating custom compliance rules for Windows
- Creating custom compliance rules for Linux
- Creating custom compliance rules for virtualization
- Modifying the default filter set
- Creating compliance templates
- Checking the compliance of the infrastructure
- Exporting compliance rules
- Compliance reports
- Creating compliance exceptions

Introduction

Compliance means meeting requirements. It is also used to refer to industry-wide or government rules and regulations that mention how data should be managed, and the need for organizations to be compliant with those regulations.

Consider a rule for password complexity, such as the length of the password not being fewer than 12 characters. Now, you need to check whether this is true for all the machines in your infrastructure. Let's assume you have a few thousand machines to check and, if they aren't in compliance, reconfigure.

You can understand how much time it would take to go through each machine, check the setting, and correct it if it's to be found noncompliant. Now, multiply those efforts for a few hundred rules—how do you document all the statuses to show the auditor? This becomes more complex when you want to be compliant for various government and industry standards such as ISO, HIPPA, and Suburban Oxley. They have a few hundred rules per standard and changes per operating system. Also, you may have your own compliance rules, which may be different from the various standards; you need to check them as well. With some rules, there is the possibility that you need a deviation approved by your security team, and hence, being noncompliant with the rule should not affect your compliance score, so you need to add these as exceptions.

Now that the complexity of compliance is clearer, we need something that can do all this for us easily. There are other tools in the market, such as System Center Configuration Manager, BMC BSA, and Puppet, that are capable of doing this, but VCM is much better than these, for the following reasons:

- There are more than 50 ready-to-use industry and government standard compliance packs available
- Creating your own compliance pack is a very easy process
- The rules are processed on the data captured and stored on the VCM server, so that we get the setting configured on the server
- It is much more cost effective, as it is part of the vRealize Operations suite
- We can check the compliance of the VMware virtual infrastructure, as well as supported managed machines, in one console
- We can enforce compliance for noncompliant rules (although not all rules and OSes are supported)

In my opinion, this list is enough to understand why we should use VCM instead of any other tool to manage the compliance of the infrastructure.

The constructs of VCM compliance

To measure compliance, we need to create various elements in VCM. Let's get introduced to them.

Rules

We have learned that compliance means meeting the requirements put forth by a standard, so to check compliance, we need to create a rule. Basically, a rule is the interpretation of the requirement put forth by the standard, which can then be understood by VCM. To continue with our previous example, our requirement was to have a password length of at least 12 characters. When we convert this requirement, what we get in VCM is a rule.

Rules can be basic or complex. A basic rule just checks the contents of data properties while with a complex rule, we can use logic to check for conditions.

Filters

Filters are used to filter machines for conditions. For example, we create some rules and we want those rules to only be checked against a certain OS. So, we create a filter for that OS.

Rule groups

Rules are grouped together under rule groups; for example, we can group all the rules that are applicable to Windows Server 2012 R2 under one rule group.

Templates

Templates are used to group multiple rule groups together. They are used to check the compliance of machine groups.

Here's an example: in our company, we have rules, and they might be different for different versions of Windows. We can create the required rules groups for each OS that will be filtered on the basis of the filters created in each rule group. Then, all the rule groups will be grouped in a single template and that template can be used to check the compliance of the infrastructure.

Importing compliance packs

There are more than 50 compliance packs available for download, and the list keeps on growing as VMware keeps on adding new compliance packs.

Getting ready

We will need an Internet connection for the VCM server in order to download the compliance packs from VMware. The Content Wizard tool will use a proxy configured at the system level; have a look at the *There's More...* section of this recipe for proxy details.

How to do it...

We will now download a compliance pack from the Internet:

1. Log in to the VCM server's OS.
2. Launch the **Content Wizard** tool from the desktop (**Start** | **VMware vRealize Configuration Manager** | **Content Wizard Tool**).
3. On the next page of the wizard, select **Get Updates from Internet**.

   The other option is **Get Updates from Local File System**; for this, all files must be available in the `C:\ProgramData\CM\Content` folder. You must obtain updated files from VMware and manually copy them to the directory. Download the files from `https://vcmupdates.vmware.com/CPC/VCM/5_7/`.

4. The wizard will check for an Internet connection and will start downloading the `Updates.xml` file from VMware.
5. Next, it will present the list of packs that are available for download. Select the packs required for your infrastructure; in this example, we are selecting **ISO 27001-27002 for Windows**:

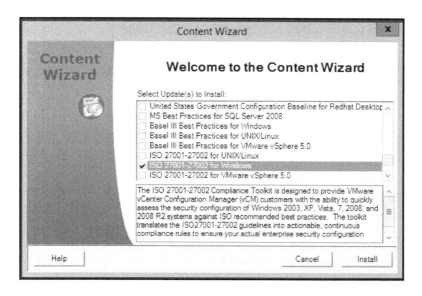

6. The selected pack will be downloaded and ready for import.
7. Once downloaded, it will start the import as a part of the wizard.
8. Once the import is complete, it will present the **Log Result** page and you have an option to save the logs. Click on **Close**.
9. On the next page, click on **Finish** to complete the importing of the compliance pack.

10. You can check the imported compliance packs by logging in to the VCM console and going to **Compliance | Machine Group Compliance | Templates**:

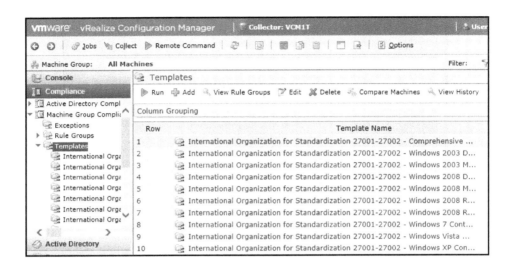

How it works…

As explained in the introduction, we can either create our own compliance rules or import rules by importing compliance packs created by VMware. This gives us all the necessary constructs required to measure compliance against standards such as ISO 27001, SOX, and HIPPA, to name a few.

The tool downloads the rules in XML and they are then imported to the VCM database. The pack includes rules, rule groups, filters, and templates responsible for the selected standard; in our case, it is ISO 27001-27002 for Windows.

Once the compliance pack is imported, we can use the newly created templates to check the compliance of our infrastructure against the ISO 27001-27002 industry standard. Refer to the *Checking the compliance of the infrastructure* recipe from this chapter.

There's more...

If your Internet access requires you to use a proxy, you can do that by changing some registry settings. Go to `HKEY_Current_User\Software\Microsoft\Windows\CurrentVersion\Internet Settings Proxy Server` to check proxy details; if there is a proxy configured and you are in an environment that does not need a proxy or the proxy has been changed, you need to check this before you start troubleshooting why the content wizard is failing to connect to h `ttp://www.vmware.com/`.

Creating compliance rule groups

In the previous recipe, we imported a compliance pack, which created the required rules, rule groups, filters, and templates. When we want to check compliance against our own standards, we need to create each of them. In this recipe, we will create a compliance rule group.

Getting ready

We need a working VCM server and credentials to log in as administrator on it.

How to do it...

This is a two-part recipe; first, we will create a rule group and then will create the required filters.

Creating a rule group

Here are the steps to create a rule group:

1. Log in to VCM using an admin account.
2. Go to **Compliance | Machine Group Compliance | Rule Group**.
3. Click on the green plus sign to create a new rule group.
4. It will launch a wizard; fill in an appropriate name and provide a description. It is best practice to have some naming conventions while creating such things. We will look at naming conventions in detail in `Appendix A` – *Defining Naming Conventions*. In this case, we are creating a rule group for Windows Server 2012 for our company rules, so the following names will be used:

   - **Rule Group Name**: `01_MyCompany_Win2k12`
   - **Description**: Provide an appropriate description
   - **Filter Set**: Use the **Default** filter set

Note that the selected collection filter set is used when calculating the data age for the rules in the compliance templates. The filter set must collect the same data types that are included in the rules in the rule group. If the filter set does not collect the same data types, no data age is calculated.

5. Accept the rule group creation confirmation box by clicking on **OK**.

Once the rule group has been created, we need to create the necessary filters so that only expected machines will be checked for the rules in this rule group.

Creating a filter

This is the second part of this recipe; here, we will create the necessary filters for the rule group. Here are the steps:

1. Click on the newly created rule group, that is, `01_MyCompany_Win2k12`, and then click on **Filters**.
2. Click on the green + button to add a new filter.
3. Provide a proper **Name** and **Description**.
4. Select a data type.

   Our imagination is the limit for selecting the correct data type; all the attributes captured by the VCM agent are available in the VCM database, and all of those can be used to create filters. In our case, we will be using the operating system name as the filter criteria; hence, we have selected **Machines**. You can browse and check the other available options:

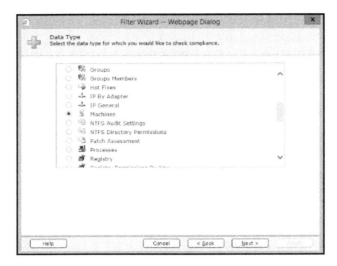

5. Now, the selected **Data Type** will be used to create the rules. As we just need to check the OS name, we are going with **Basic**:

6. Here too we have multiple choices to filter, and we will select OS Name Full, then we have conditional operators, and then the value.

As we are creating a filter for Microsoft Windows Server 2012, we are choosing **OS Name Full = Microsoft Windows Server 2012** % (% is a wildcard):

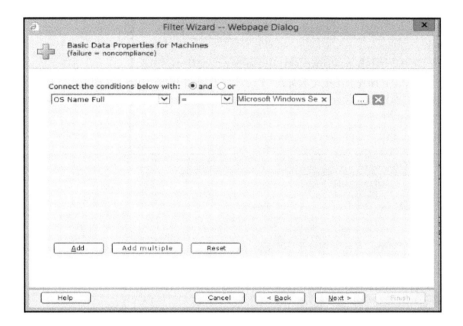

Wildcards in VCM:

Wildcard	Meaning
%	Match all characters
_ (underscore)	Match a single character
*	Equivalent to %
?	Equivalent to _

7. Click on **Finish** to complete the filter creation.
8. To validate our filter, click on **Preview**, and it should display all the machines with Windows Server 2012 in the infrastructure, as our rule is only looking for such machines:

Note that if you have created multiple filters in a single rule group, they work as logical **AND**, that is, if all the conditions are **True**, only then will it display the machines, so be careful when creating multiple filters.

How it works...

In this recipe, we just created a rule group that will include our company security rules to be measured via VCM and selected the default filter set as the information will be collected as a part of the default filter set.

After that, we created a filter that will filter only Windows Server 2012 machines in the VCM.

Creating custom compliance rules for Windows

VCM divides compliance into two broad categories:

- *Machine group compliance*
- *Virtual environment compliance*

Machine group compliance

In this category, compliance is checked at the operating system level, such as for all the supported versions of Windows or Linux.

Virtual environment compliance

In this category, the compliance of the ESXi hosts, vCenter, and virtual machines present in vCenter is checked.

Now, as we are ready with the rule group, let's start populating it with the rules for our organization. There are two ways we can create the rules: either copy what is created in the standard compliance packs we downloaded in the first recipe and modify it as per our requirement or create the rules from scratch.

In this recipe, we will create a custom compliance rule based on machine group compliance.

Getting ready

We will need a fully ready VCM server, and to copy the rule from another rule group, we should finish the *Importing compliance packs* recipe. We will need our own rule group created so that we can create our rules there.

How to do it...

We will continue our example of our requirement of having a complex password and a minimum password length of 12 characters; first, we will try to find the rule in the imported compliance pack and then, we will create our own rule.

Copying a rule from another rule group

We can copy a rule from the compliance packs we have downloaded and added to VCM and then modify them as per our requirement or club rules from various compliance packs or standards as required to support our internal company standards.

Follow the next steps to copy a rule from another rule group:

1. Log in to VCM with admin privileges and go to **Compliance** | **Machine Group Compliance** | **Rule Groups**.

2. As we want to copy a rule, we must know where the original rule is; in our case, the rule is in the **Best Practises – ISO 27001-27002 Windows 2008 R2 Mbr** rule group, so we will go there and select the required rule:

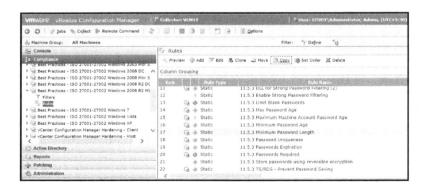

3. Click on **Copy**, and as the wizard starts, select the rule group that you want to copy the rule to:

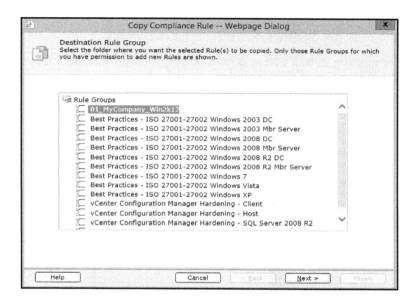

4. In next step, confirm the rule/rules you want to copy and click on **Finish**.
5. The rule will be copied in our rule group now.
6. It should look like the following screenshot:

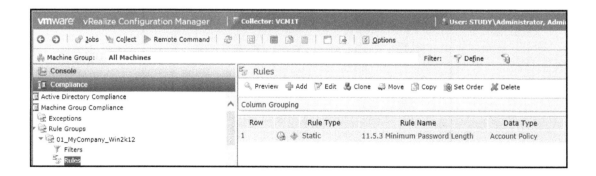

Creating a new rule

Now, as you have seen how to copy a rule, we will continue considering that we are not able to find a rule we want and thus need to create it.

Follow these steps to create the required rule:

1. Once again, log in to VCM and go to **Compliance** | **MachineGroupCompliance** | **RuleGroups**.
2. Select the machine group created for storing our rules and go to **Rules**, click on **Add**, and follow the wizard.

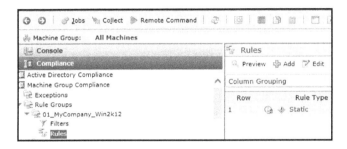

3. Provide a **Name** and **Description** for the rule.

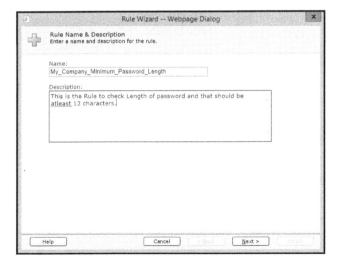

4. Select the correct **Data Type**; in our case, it is **Account Policy**.

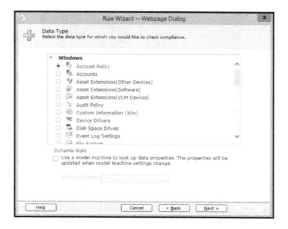

5. Select **Basic Rule**.
6. (For more details about the types of rules, refer to the *Rules* subsection of the *The constructs of VCM compliance* recipe).
7. Select a **Min Length** value greater than (**>**) 12 as a condition so that if the condition fails, it will flag as noncompliant.

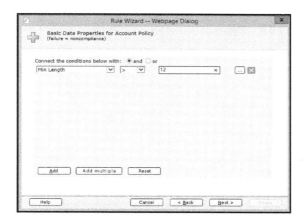

8. Select **Moderate Severity**, confirm the rule creation and click on **Finish**.
9. We just created our first rule for our internal standards for Windows.

How it works...

To measure compliance, we need to create rules for each stated requirement; in this recipe, we first copied a rule from a standard that we imported, and then, to understand the process, we created the same rule. The rule will be stored in the rule group and will check the compliance of the Windows machine for password length.

Creating custom compliance rules for Linux

In the previous recipe, we looked at a rule created for Windows for checking minimum the password length; we will continue with the same requirement here, except for Linux. The process will be similar; only the data types will change.

Getting ready

We need a fully functional VCM and a rule group created to store our Linux rule.

How to do it...

Like in the earlier recipe, here too we have two ways to create such rules, that is, copy them from another imported compliance pack rule group or create our own. The copying process is the same as for Windows; hence, we will not repeat it again.

We will create a new rule for Linux to check the minimum password length by completing these steps:

1. Once again, we need to log in to VCM with admin privileges and go to **Compliance | Machine Group Compliance | RuleGroups**.

   Go to the machine group created for Linux rules, click on the arrow in front of the rule group name, and select **Rules**.

2. Click on **Add**, and it will launch a wizard to create a new rule.

3. On the first page of the wizard, provide a name and description.

4. On the next page for data types, go to **Unix** | **Custom Information**.

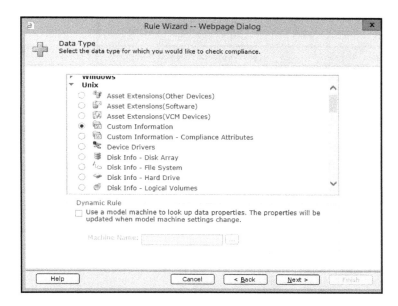

5. If you are a Linux admin, you already know where to find the required details; if not, consult your Linux admin.

   In our case, I filled in the details after consulting my Linux admin.

Here is what we filled in:

- **Information Type:** `builtin:login.defs`
- **File Path :** `/etc/login.defs`
- **Internal Path:** `/builtin:login.defs`

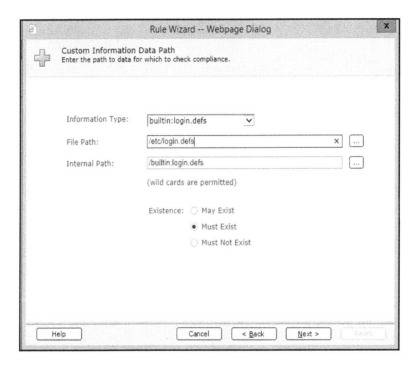

6. Select the PASS_MIN_LEN condition to be greater than (>) 12, so if the value found is less than 12, then we are noncompliant and VCM will let us know.

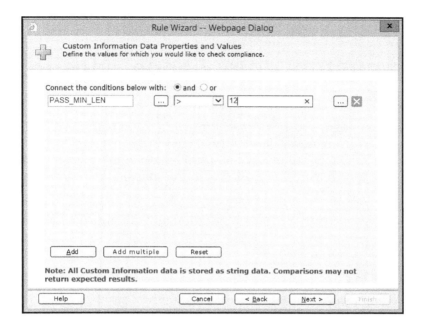

7. Set the **Severity** to **Moderate**, follow the wizard, and accept the creation of the rule and finish it by clicking on **Finish**.

How it works...

Just like Windows compliance rules, this rule will be stored and will process the stored data collected from Linux machines and give us their compliance status.

Creating custom compliance rules for virtualization

So far, we created compliance rules for machine group compliance, that is, for Windows and Linux. Now, we will create a rule for virtual environment compliance. We can't continue with our example of minimum password length in this virtual world, so we will change it to another requirement we have, that is, the snapshot for a VM should not be retained for more than 10 days.

So, let's start and see how many VMs are noncompliant with our rule by first creating one.

Getting ready

We need a rule group created to store the virtualization compliance rules in a fully deployed and functional VCM server.

How to do it...

Like our previous experience with rules, this one can also be copied from another standard pack if you know where to copy from; the process is similar to that for Windows rules, so we will not repeat it here.

We will start creating a new rule using the following steps:

1. Once again, we need to log in to VCM with admin privileges and reach **Compliance | Virtual Environment Compliance | Rule Groups**.

2. Select the rule group created for storing virtual environment compliance rules. Click on the arrow to the side of it and go to **Rules**.

3. Click on **Add** to start the wizard. Fill in the name and description for the rule to be created, and click on **Next**.

4. Check the screenshots in the previous recipes where we created rules for Windows and Linux, and make appropriate changes for virtualization as described in those steps.

5. On the next page of the wizard, **Data Type**, select **vCenter – Guests – Snapshots**, as we want to check the snapshot age.

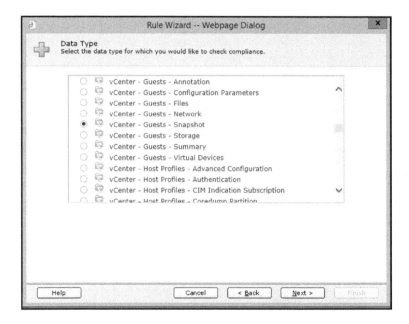

6. Select **Basic** as the rule type and click on **Next**.
7. To form a condition, select **Snapshot Age** less than or equal to (<=) 10, that is, if the snapshot age is less than 10, then we are compliant, but if it is more than 10, then we are noncompliant and that needs to be flagged. Click on **Next**.

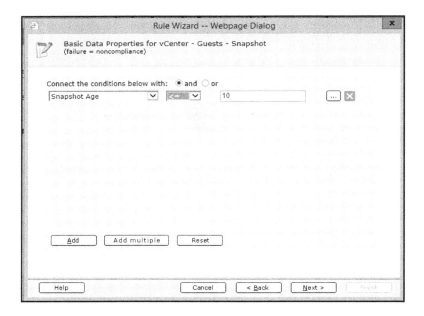

8. Select **Moderate Severity**, confirm the rule creation, and click on **Finish** to close the wizard.

This completes the creation of all types of rules for compliance.

How it works...

The process is the same as machine group compliance and rules for Windows and Linux; in a virtual environment situation, the data to be used will be collected from vCenter servers, and the compliance score of the vCenter server will change instead of individual virtual machines'.

Modifying the default filter set

Now you know that VCM checks compliance on the data collected and available in the database it has and not directly on the live machine. This causes limitation: if a particular data type is not collected, it will not be available, and then, we cannot measure the compliance for the rule and VCM will tell you that the data has not been collected for the rule in the results.

To overcome this situation, we can set lots of collections with different types of filter sets created by VCM or we can modify the default filter set and add required filters.

 Note that modifying a default set is not recommended by VMware. Create your own filter set that includes the required filters and use that to perform the collection.

So, what are filters and filter sets?

VCM filters: Filters define what data a VCM agent should collect while performing the collection; examples are a registry setting, service status, file permission, and so on.

VCM filter sets: These are collections of filters, which can be used to collect data from managed machines. Most of the time, we use the default filter set, but there are a few more created by default when we install VCM, and a few are added when we import compliance packs from the Internet. Compliance packs create the required filters and filter sets so that the data is collected and can be processed when we run the compliance check.

We need to select the correct filter set while performing a collection so that the required details will be added to the VCM database, modify the default filter set, or create a new one and use this single filter set to collect data.

Getting ready

We need a fully functional VCM server, and we should know which data filter is required to add to the default filter set, so we should import the compliance packs as we did in the first recipe.

How to do it…

We will be adding a Linux filter to collect the required data type used in the *Creating custom compliance rules for Linux* recipe, where we used details from the `:/etc/login.defs` file, and those are not part of the default filter set. In this example, we are modifying the default filter set, but you can use the same process to first create a filter set and then add the required filters to it.

Let's jump into the VCM console to modify the default filter set then:

1. To start, log in to VCM and go to **Administration** | **Collection Filters** | **Filter Sets**.

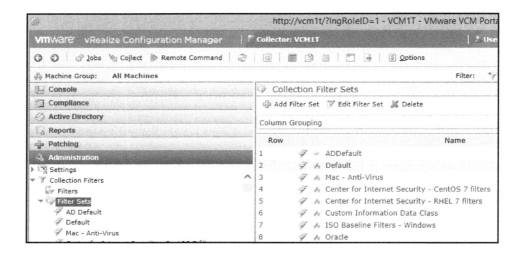

2. Select the default filter set and click on **Edit Filter Set**.

3. The wizard will start; as you can see, there are 9000 filters available; we really can't search through them, so create a **Filter**, click on **Define**, and it will open a pop-up.

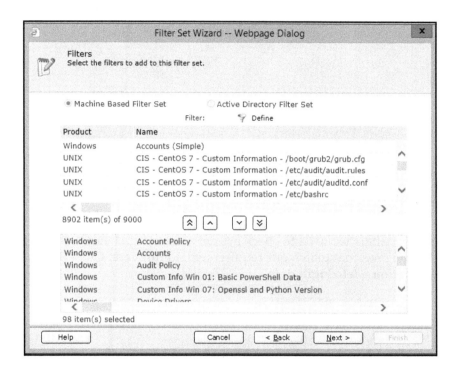

4. As we want to look for login details in the **Filter**, create a filter like **Name** like
%log% (% acts a wildcard).

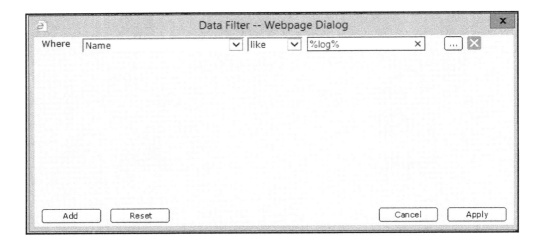

5. Now, the filters we need to check are only 169 in number. Go through them and
select the ones that match our requirement, in this case, **CIS – RHEL 7 – Custom
Information – /etc/login.defs**.

5. Select and click on the downward arrow and then on **Next**.

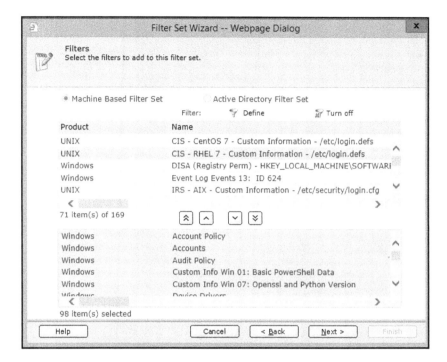

7. Make sure there are no conflicts, and click on **Next**.

8. On the next page, it will show you the list of filters in this filter set; accept them by clicking on **Finish**.

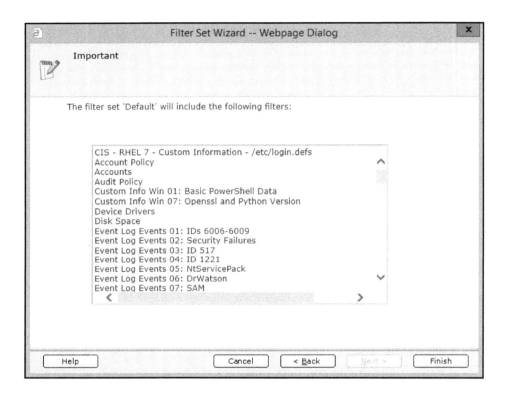

How it works...

As mentioned earlier, we need to instruct VCM what data needs to be collected; else, we will miss the data collection and cannot check compliance for those rules. We can do this in two ways: collecting data multiple times with multiple filter sets or as we did here, adding required filter sets and preparing a master filter set to collect all the details.

We chose the second option. Now onwards, whenever we collect data with the default filter set, it will collect from Linux/Unix managed machines details about `/etc/login.defs` file, which we can use.

Creating compliance templates

Now that we are ready with all the required rule groups with the necessary filters and they have been populated with all the rules to fulfill the requirements given by the security officer, we need to move ahead and start checking compliance. But wait, we can't check compliance against a rule or rule groups; we will need a compliance template, which can have all the required rule groups.

So let's start by creating our compliance template for Windows-related rule groups.

Getting ready

We will need all the required rule groups created and they should be populated with the associated rules in a fully functional VCM server.

How to do it...

By now, you must already know where you should go to create your compliance template; if not, just follow this process and you will be learn that as well:

1. Go to **Compliance** | **Machine Group Compliance** | **Templates** and then click on **Add**.

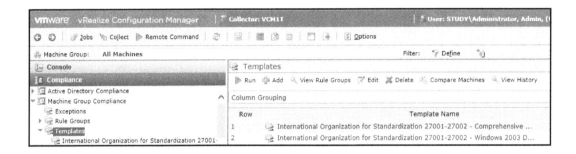

2. Once the wizard for creating a new template is launched, provide a proper **Name** and **Description** value.

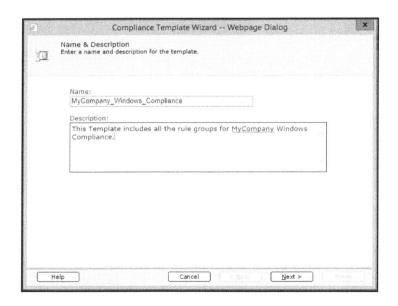

3. Select all the rule groups that should be part of this template.

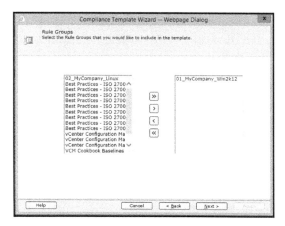

4. Make sure it provides results on both compliant and noncompliant details and processes compliance exceptions (more about this is in the *Creating compliance exceptions* recipe at the end of this chapter).

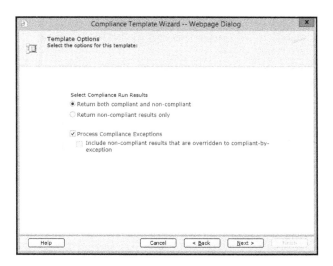

5. Confirm the creation of the template and hit **Finish**.

How it works...

We can create rule groups for each version of Windows, such as Windows Server 2003, Windows Server 2008 and one for 2008 R2, and Server 2012 and 2012 R2. Each will have its own filters so that the rules in those rule groups will be applied to only the specific OSes they are created for. Now we can have a single template to run against a huge machine group that includes all the Windows machines in the infrastructure; VCM will pick the correct rule for them, and we can avoid having multiple templates and associated machine groups to check compliance against (checking infrastructure compliance is our next recipe).

When a rule that is called complaint is passed and it fails, then we are noncompliant for a setting. Now, there are chances that we need to make some exceptions to the rules, like in the last recipe of this chapter, *Creating compliance exceptions*, where we create such exceptions.

Checking the compliance of the infrastructure

We did the hard work of creating all the rules, rules groups, and templates to reach up to this: checking the compliance of the infrastructure. Now, we are ready to check how compliant we are against our internal standards, or we can directly use the standard compliance packs we downloaded and imported in the first recipe.

As we have only created test rules, we will use a standard template we imported in the first recipe.

Getting ready

All the heavy lifting should have been done on the VCM server; for instance, it should be ready with the templates and at least one machine group that will have the machines for which we need to check compliance, or we can use the default machine groups available. The preferred alternative is our own machine group.

How to do it...

As mentioned earlier, we will use an imported standard template called **International Organization for Standardization 27001-27002- Windows 2008 R2 Mbr Server Controls**, and we will run this against the default machine group, **All Machines**.

Follow this process to check the compliance of Windows servers:

1. Once logged in to VCM, go to **Compliance | Templates**.

Note that you should make sure the correct machine group is selected at the top; this is how VCM decides which machines to apply the template to in order to measure compliance. If you want to change the machine group, click on the machine group, and in the pop-up, select the correct machine group.

2. Select the required template on the right-hand side and click on **Run**.

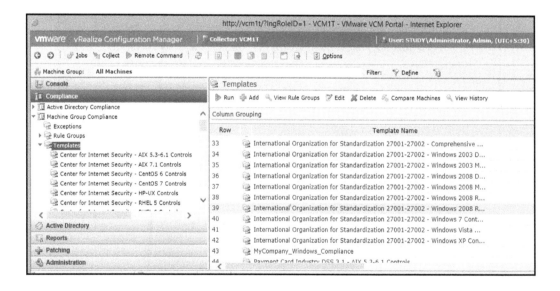

3. Depending upon the organization's policies, decide to enforce or not enforce compliance.

Note that not all rules are enforceable; also, we can create issues, such as breaking a working application. For example, if the print spooler service is required to be disabled, and when we enforce the compliance, we disable the service, this will create an issue in the printer farm as it will stop functioning. So it's better that we first learn what is noncompliant, then make necessary exceptions, and then enforce it from VCM or ask the respective server owners to take necessary action.

4. In a few minutes, depending on how many machines you have in the machine group to check, the compliance run will finish. Click on **Close**.

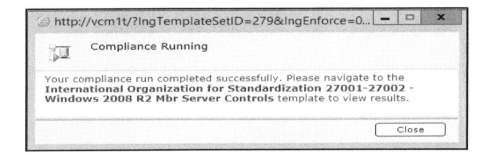

5. The compliance status can be viewed by navigating to the template on the left-hand side and selecting the correct machine group from the top.

   In our case, our support team needs to work a lot as we are noncompliant.

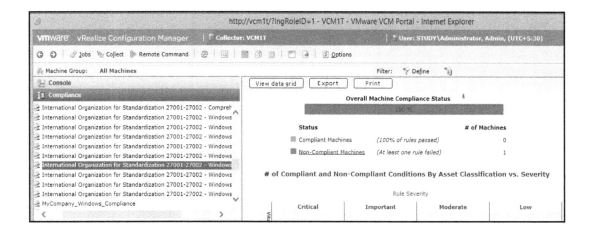

How it works...

When we ask VCM to check compliance, it first applies the filters available in the rule groups and then, only the machines that pass those filters are considered.

The compliance checks are performed on the data collected by VCM and available in the database, unlike some other tools, which performs the checks at the client end and the client submits the data. The process followed by VCM is better as this can be performed on servers that are offline at that point in time, and when we check the result, we get the value because of which a machine is noncompliant for a rule.

Again, this has some issues: firstly, we need to make sure our VCM is clean; by that, I mean that when a machine is decommissioned, it is purged from VCM; else, we will have the details of the machines that are not present in the infrastructure and that could play with our final compliance score.

The second issue is that it does not give us live details as it works on data that is in its database; again, this can give us some false positives.

To encounter this issue, we can schedule a compliance check after a full data collection for that machine group; in this way, we will not have stale data to process.

Once the compliance has been checked and if we have selected to enforce compliance, it will create jobs to enforce them and will start executing on the managed machines; for example, if we have rules to check the status of a service and we expect certain services in the running state, then VCM will start those services.

Exporting compliance rules

I don't know about you, but I am a lazy admin–I like to do things once and use them as many times as I can. Creating a complete compliance configuration is a huge task and can take up to months; now consider you have another VCM deployed and you want to recreate all the rules, rule groups, and templates again. Nobody will approve few months of rework and you won't enjoy the repeated work either.

This is where VMware's Export Import tool bundled with VCM comes in handy. You can export all your settings in a single XML file and then import as many VCM deployments as you want, and once they have been imported, you can modify them if required as well.

In this and the next recipe, we will have a look at those two things. First, we will export the configurations in an XML file and then import them again.

Getting ready

To start with the recipe, we need a completely functional VCM, and all the required rule groups with filters, rules, and templates should be ready before we start.

How to do it...

To work on the recipe, you don't need to log in to the VCM console, but you need to launch the **Import Export** utility from the VCM server's desktop. Follow these steps:

1. Once the **Import Export** tool has been launched, click on **Connect to source**.

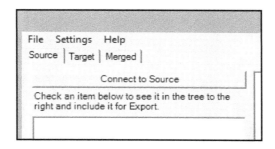

2. Select the database server and click on connect. Select the **VCM** database and click on **OK**.

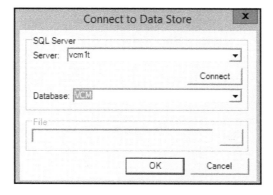

3. As we want to export the compliance template (this will include all the rule groups, filters, and rules), click on **Compliance Template**; the tool will show the available compliance templates on the right-hand side.

4. Accept the dependency alert–we need proper documentation if we modify or create new filter sets in order to recreate them on the new environment where we will import this template again.

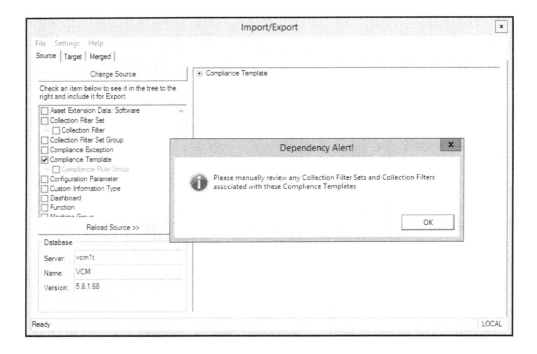

5. Select the compliance template you have created and want to export and then go to **File** | **Save Source Document**.

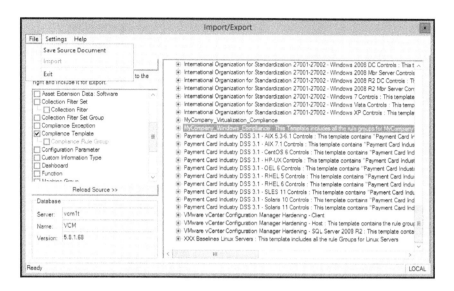

6. In the next step, use the arrow buttons to move the templates you want to export, and then click on **OK**.

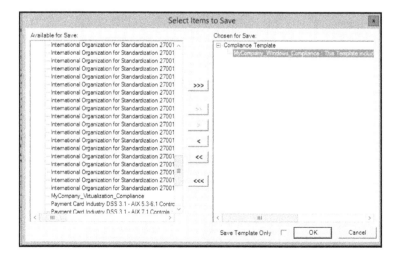

7. Enter a comment under **Save Options**.

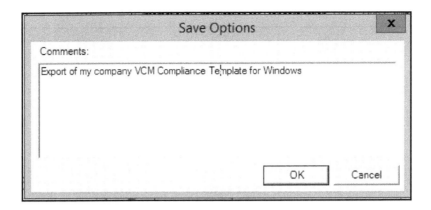

8. Provide a descriptive name and click on OK.

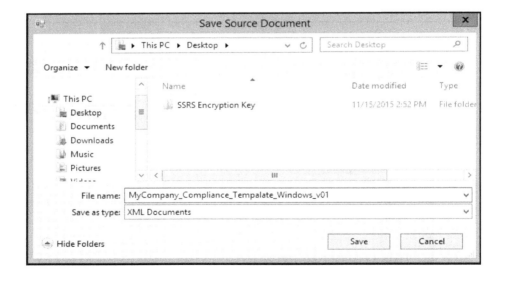

9. Click on **OK** to complete the save.

10. Now, we are done with the export and are ready to share our hard work with the world.

How it works...

The data is exported in XML format, which can be used with the same utility again in any other environment to recreate the compliance details, which could have taken a few months to recreate.

Compliance reports

It does not matter how compliant you are unless you can give a full report showing all the details of the infrastructure. VCM does not let you down here as well: there are 15 default reports available to be exported. We will look how we can do that in this recipe.

Getting ready

We will need a fully deployed VCM server, and we should have finished checking the compliance of the infrastructure so that we can look at the options to get the reports.

 Note that if we have not run the compliance run, we cannot see the reports-quite obvious, but we do miss this.

How to do it...

To get the reports out of VCM, follow these steps:

1. Log in to the VCM console and go to **Reports | Machine Group Reports | Compliance**.

2. Select the required report; use this list to understand what can be seen in the report:

Sr. no.	Name	Description
1	Compliance badge mapping result by object	Displays the compliance badge mapping result by object in detail
2	Compliance badge mapping result by template	Displays the compliance badge mapping result by template in detail
3	Compliance badge rollup detail	Displays the compliance badge rollup in detail
4	Compliance badge rollup summary	Displays the compliance badge rollup summary
5	Compliance change history	Compliance change history for a series of compliance runs
6	Compliance machine group summary	Displays compliance summary broken down by machine group
7	Compliance results detail by machine	Displays results of compliance run grouped by machine and includes rule description
8	Compliance results detail by rule	Displays results of compliance run grouped by rule name and includes rule description
9	Compliance results details	Compliance results details by compliance template
10	Compliance results machine group details	Displays results of compliance run grouped by machine groups
11	Compliance results summary	Compliance results summary by compliance template
12	Compliance results summary for rules	Compliance results summary for rules by compliance template for asset classification and rule severity
13	Compliance results trends	Compliance results trends for selected templates
14	Compliance rule details by rule group	Shows existing compliance rule details and the rule groups that contain them
15	Compliance template listing	Compliance template listing by template with rule group details

3. Once the report is selected, click on **Run** in the top menu. This will launch a wizard for you to follow.

> Note that you have to make sure you have selected the correct machine group from the top; if you have never run a compliance check against that machine group, there won't be any options in the dropdown for the next window.

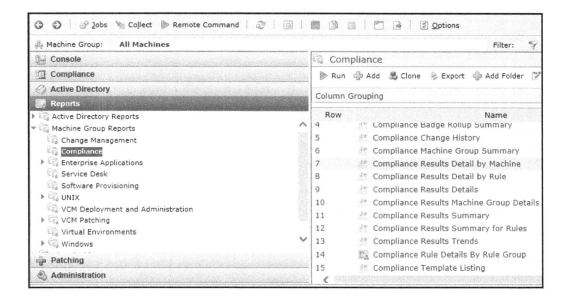

4. Select the options (they will differ for each selected report); the dropdown options will vary depending upon which template you have used to check the compliance.

5. The rest you can choose depending upon your requirement; once all the required options have been selected, click on **View Report**.

6. The report will be displayed, and it can be exported to various formats, such as XML, CSV, PDF, and MHTML.

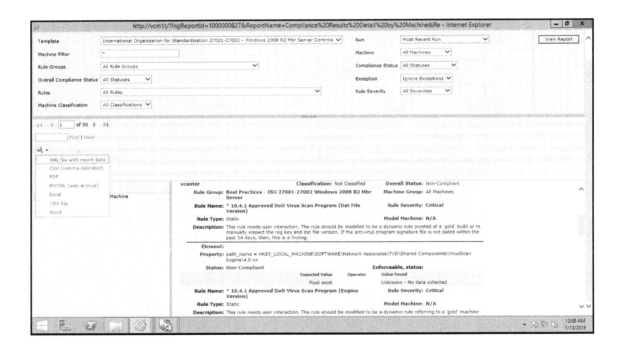

How it works...

VCM uses SSRS for its reporting functionality. When we click on the Run button, in order to display the report, VCM launches another Internet Explorer window, which takes us to SSRS. Then, the report asks us for options, such as the compliance template, the machines, and severity (they vary per report), and then goes to the VCM database and fetches the data. The data is presented in a nice report on the screen or can be exported to the formats shown in the previous screenshot.

Creating compliance exceptions

As you know, every rule has an exception, and this is applicable to compliance as well. You create a rule for disabling the print spooler service on all servers, and then you have print servers that need this service running. Now, we can't disable this service if we know this is a known and accepted deviation, and we don't want our compliance score to get a hit because of this. What we can do is add an exception so that this will not create issues when checking compliance.

Getting ready

Our organization has a policy to disable unwanted services on servers, and the print spooler is considered an unwanted service, so it must be disabled on all the servers. Of course, the exceptions are the print servers. We will create an exception for the print server machine group to be excused from this mandate.

We will need the required rules created in VCM along with a machine group that includes all the print servers.

How to do it…

Let's create an exception for our print servers by following these steps:

1. Log in to VCM and go to **Compliance** | **Machine Group Compliance** | **Exceptions**.

2. Click on **Add**.

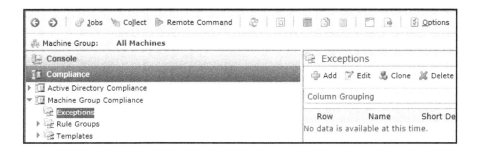

2. Provide a descriptive name and description, and click on **Next**.

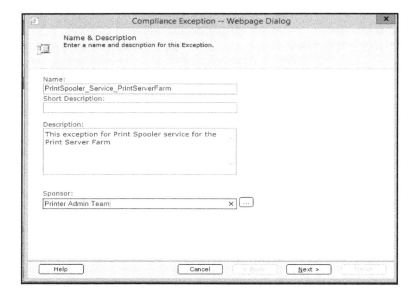

3. Select the template for which you want this machine group to be excluded.

4. In this case, we are selecting the one created by our organization rules; click on **Next**.

5. Select the machine group created for this exception–in our case, it is named **Print Servers** – and click on **Next**.

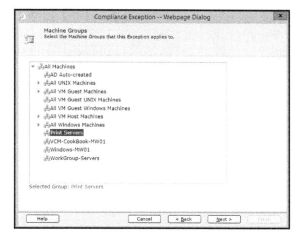

6. Select **Override non-compliant results to compliant**.

7. I really don't know why there is another option, but there must be a use case that I am not aware of.

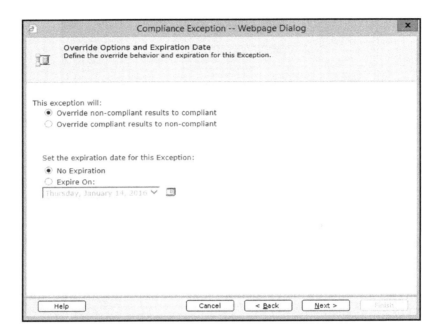

8. We want this exception only for our rule for the print spooler server, called **Service_Print_Spooler**, so selected that rule. Depending upon your requirement, you can have an exception for a complete rule group as well. But an exception to a single rule is sufficient in our case.

9. Click on **Finish**.

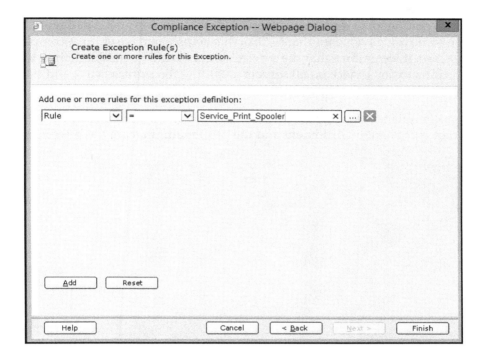

10. You can enable/disable this exception as required.

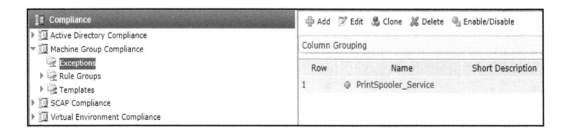

How it works...

Exceptions are considered when we perform a compliance check, and a final score is calculated. By creating an exception, we make sure that we don't get a bad score because we need to have some things noncompliant. Also, this helps when we enforce compliance. Like in the earlier case, if we enforce that the service status should be disabled, then VCM will disable the print spooler service on all servers including the print servers, and that will affect productivity.

So, creating a compliance exception is a win-win situation for both the teams–the security team has a nice compliant environment and the printer admin team has a working print farm.

7
Maintenance of VCM

In this chapter, we will cover the following recipes:

- Upgrading VCM from a previous version – in place
- Upgrading VCM from a previous version – parallel
- Migrating VCM from another domain
- Applying a new license key
- Upgrading VCM agents
- Changing service account passwords
- Managing users
- Decommissioning VMs – manual VM purge
- Decommissioning VMs – scheduled VM record purge

Introduction

After installation and configuration, another extremely important aspect we need to look at is the lifecycle management of VCM. VMware will keep on improving VCM, and to have those improvements implemented, we also need to invest our time to maintain the infrastructure we have built.

This is not just limited to VMware updates and upgrades but also to our own infrastructure changes; for example, relocating a datacenter might need us to change IP or we might have decided to change our Active Directory domain and we need to migrate our management servers to the newly created domain. All this falls under maintenance, and we will have a look what we can do for VCM.

Apart from this, we are managing our infrastructure, and it has its own lifecycle to manage; for example, once the server is decommissioned, we need to remove it from VCM, and after upgrading VCM, we need to upgrade VCM agents on the managed servers.

To manage VCM, we will have a support team; everyone does not need to have admin access on the server. In order to adhere to the security principle of least privilege, we need to create some groups and give them proper access to VCM.

We will have a look at those points in this chapter to make sure we have a maintained VCM infrastructure so that it can manage our infrastructure better.

Upgrading VCM from a previous version – in place

In this recipe, we will upgrade VCM in place, meaning we will do a regular upgrade without changing the OS underneath. If you want to change the OS underneath, have a look at the following recipe.

Getting ready

To start with this activity, you must have all the user accounts in place, and they must have permissions as described in the *Service accounts* subsection under the *Understanding the requirements of VCM* recipe in `Chapter 1`, *Installing VCM*. You must have a user apart from the service account, which may be your own account, with admin privilege on the VCM Collector server.

If you are using a physical server, then take a backup of the server with the tool you are using in your infrastructure; otherwise, if that Collector server is a virtual machine, take a snapshot of the VM.

Take a backup of the databases (`Excel VCM_Raw`) so that if something goes wrong, you can get back to where you were before the upgrade. If you don't know how, you can get help from your SQL admin to take a backup of the databases.

You must have access to `https://my.vmware.com` to download the latest VCM installation ISO files.

How to do it...

In the following example, we will perform an in-place upgrade of a two-tier VCM deployment:

 Note that you should not use a VCM service account to upgrade VCM. Use any domain account that is an admin on the VCM server. You can use your own account to log in to the VCM Collector server if you have those privileges; if not, assign them to your account for the time being.

1. Mount the ISO downloaded from the Internet on your VCM Collector VM.
2. Log in to the Collector OS with a [user right/role].
3. Open an Explorer window and navigate to the CD-ROM drive just mounted.
4. Right-click on `setup.exe` and select **Run as Administrator**.
5. Select **Upgrade** and click on **Next**:

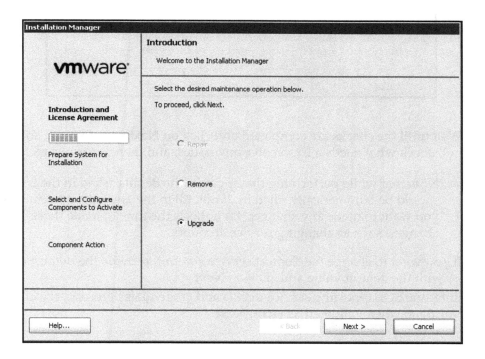

6. Accept the license agreement, and click on **Next**.

7. Confirm the components to be upgraded, and click on **Next:**

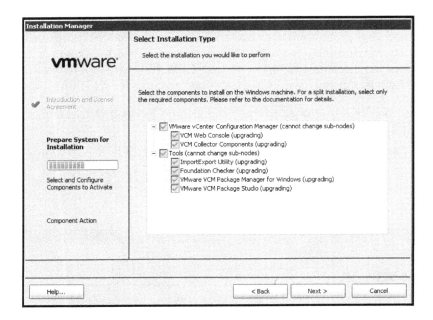

8. Wait until the checks are completed and click on **Next** once they are successful; if not, check what needs a fix, resolve any issues, and then perform a recheck.

 Note that while performing the upgrade, the details asked in the wizard should be automatically filled in. If not, fill in the appropriate details; if you want to make any changes, then this is the time to make those changes, such as changing service accounts.

9. If you want to change the Tomcat service account, provide the details; otherwise, go with the default value and click on **Next**.

10. Enter the SQL reporting service details and credentials here, and click on **Validate**; when validated, click on **Next:**

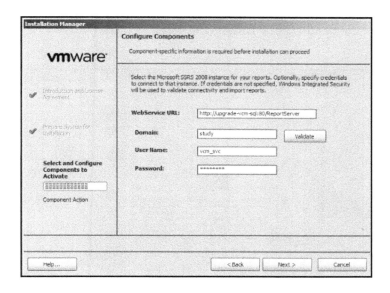

11. Enter the Collector service account (if required) and click on **Next**.
12. If not populated automatically, enter the default network authority account and click on **Next**.
13. The certificates should be selected automatically already. If not, select your certificates by clicking on **Select**, and once done, click on **Next**.
14. If not populated automatically, enter your remote virtual directory details and click on **Next**.
15. If not populated automatically, enter your virtualization client plugin details and click on **Next**.
16. If not populated automatically, enter the installation directory, and click on **Next**.
17. There is no option for you to change this path for the local packages cache location; click on **Next**.
18. The option for the path for the software repository is preselected and can't be changed; click on **Next**.

19. Enter the Package Studio folder location and click on **Next**.

20. Confirm the details and click on **Upgrade**:

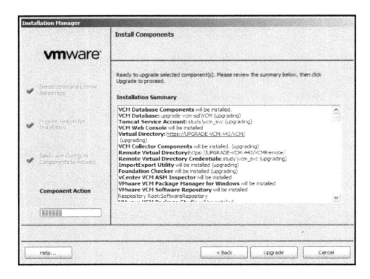

21. The process of upgrading all components can take half an hour or more.

22. Check whether the upgrade was successful by checking the version of VCM.

23. Once the installation is complete, log in to VCM and check the version; it should be **5.8.2.160**, as in the following screenshot, or the version you downloaded from `http://www.vmware.com/`:

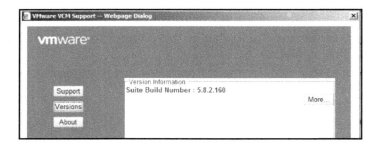

How it works...

We installed the latest version of VCM on the same server, using the old data collected for our infrastructure.

Here are the upgrade options to upgrade the version:

- Upgrade directly from VCM 5.6 or later by running VCM 5.8.x Installation Manager
- Upgrade VCM versions earlier than 5.6 to VCM 5.6 and then upgrade from VCM 5.6 to VCM 5.8.x

Earlier versions include VMware VCM 5.5.x, 5.4, 5.3, 5.2.1, EMC Ionix SCM 5.0 or later, or Configuresoft ECM 4.11.1 or later.

Aftercare

After upgrading VCM, we need to upgrade the agents to the latest versions; have a look at the *Upgrading VCM agents* recipes in this chapter to do that:

- There is a small bug with the agent upgrade to version 5.8.1 (resolved in 5.8.2) from an older version; have a look at the *Troubleshooting agent upgrade* issues recipe and the one after that in `Chapter 9`, *Troubleshooting VCM* for how to solve it
- Once the upgrade is complete, roam through the VCM console to have a look at whether all the servers that were managed earlier, such as vCenter, vCloud, and VCNS, are visible

There's more...

If you have designated a managing agent in your infrastructure, then after an upgrade, there is a chance that the trust between the managing agent and the VCM Collector will be broken. To fix this issue, follow these steps:

Follow the steps of the *Issue 1 – mutual authentication failure* subsection of the *Troubleshooting agent communication issues* recipe in `Chapter 9`, *Troubleshooting VCM*.

To re-enable the server as a managing agent, we need VCM Collector to trust the server again; for this, log in to VCM console and follow these steps:

1. Go to **Administration | Certificate** and select the managing agent server. Click on **Change Trust Status** at the top.
2. In the wizard, select the managing agent machine and tick the **Check to trust and uncheck to untrust the selected machine** option.

   You should see a handshake sign in front of managing agent server.

Now, we need to re-enable the old managing agent to do its job again as was done in the *Configuring a managing agent machine for virtual environment management* recipe in `Chapter 2`, *Configuring VCM to Manage Your Infrastructure*.

Upgrading VCM from a previous version – parallel

If you want to upgrade not only VCM but also the OS underneath it, this is the recipe to look at. VCM 5.8.2 now supports Windows Server 2012 R2, and it's a good chance to perform an upgrade.

Getting ready

To start with this activity, you must have all the user accounts in place and they must have permissions as described in the first chapter. You must have a user apart from the service account, which may be your own account, with admin privileges on the VCM Collector server to perform the installation.

If you are using a physical server, then take a backup of the server with the tool you are using in your infrastructure; if that Collector server is a virtual machine, take a snapshot of the VM.

Take a backup of the databases so that if something goes wrong, you can get back to where you were before the upgrade. If you are not aware, you can get help from your SQL admin to take a backup of the databases.

You must have access to `https://my.vmware.com` to download the latest VCM installation ISO files.

Deploy another server with the latest supported OS available with you, that is, Windows Server 2008 R2, Windows Server 2012, or Windows Server 2012 R2. Check the VCM requirements in the *Software requirements* subsection under the *Understanding the requirements of VCM* recipe in `Chapter 1`, *Installing VCM*.

How to do it...

In the following example, we will perform a parallel upgrade of a two-tier VCM deployment.

This recipe splits into multiple sections.

Migrating the VCM certificate

First, we will export the VCM Enterprise certificate and then we will start installing VCM.

So, let's log in to the old VCM server and follow these steps to export the certificate:

1. Launch `mmc.exe` and add a snap-in for **Certificates (Local Computer)**.

2. Go to **Trusted Root Certification Authority** | **Certificates**; select **VMWare VCM Enterprise Certificate...** and right-click on the certificate under **All Tasks** | **Export...**:

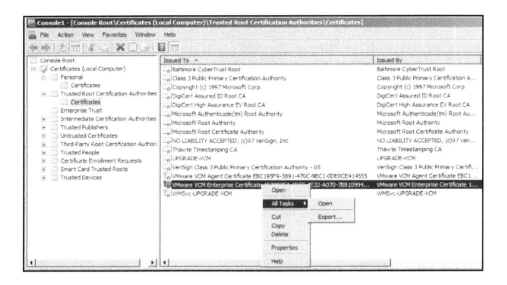

3. This will launch the wizard; export the private key.
4. For the file format, select **Personal Information Exchange** and do the following:
   1. Include all certificates in the certification path if possible.
   2. Export all extended properties.
5. Type and confirm the password; copy it to a safe place–we will need it later.
6. Provide a name and path to save the file to, and you are done with the certificate export.
7. Follow the same process for the Collector certificate, under **Personal** | **Certificate**.
8. Copy the certificates to the new VCM server and then import them to the respective folders from where they were exported. Use the same password given earlier while importing both the certificates.
9. *Shut down* the old VCM server after *disabling and stopping VCM services* on the server.

Migrating VCM to the new server

Once the certificate is available, we can start deploying a new VCM instance by following these steps:

1. Log in to the newly created VCM server and mount the VCM installer ISO downloaded from `https://my.vmware.com/`.

2. Navigate to the mounted ISO, right-click on `setup.exe`, and select **Run as Administrator**.

3. Choose **Advanced Installation**.

4. Click on **Next** for the introduction page.

5. Click on **Next** for the patent information page.

6. Read and accept the license agreement and select **I am an authorized agent and/or representative of the customer/end user** and **I have read the terms and conditions stated above**.

7. Under **Select Installation Type**, select the following:

   - **VMware vRealize Configuration Manager**
     - **VCM Web Console**
     - **VCM Collector Components**
   - **Tools**
     - **Import Export Utility**
     - **Foundation Checker**
     - **VMware VCM package manager for Windows**
   - **VMware VCM package Studio**

8. The installer will perform a prerequisite check and present the results on successful checks. Click on **Next**; if there are failures, click on **View Results**, remedy any errors and warnings, and perform a recheck.

Do not proceed further until there are zero errors.

9. On the next page, enter the serial key.
10. On the **Configure Components** page, provide the hostname of the SQL server that was used with the earlier VCM instance and VCM as the database name (if you have named the VCM database with a different name, then provide that name) and click on **Validate**:

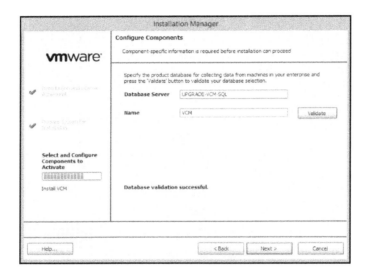

11. On the next page, provide the Tomcat service account and its password.

12. On the next page, provide the details in **WebService URL** (this is the path to the SQL server–the same as the old VCM deployment). Provide the path to install the web console. Check out the following screenshot for more details:

13. Provide a URL to the application; the default is fine.
14. We can provide an SMTP address; the default is the Collector server's. If you don't know it right now, this can be configured in the VCM console later.
15. Provide the path for installing the Collector component and accept the SSL3 warning.
16. Provide the path to store staging data; this is the path where data is temporarily stored before adding it to the database.
17. Provide the details of the Collector service account; this account will be given rights to log in as a service; accept the prompt.
18. Provide details of the network authority account; we can add as many accounts as we want later. We need at least one for the time being. More details about this account can be found under the *Service accounts* section in Chapter 1, *Installing VCM*.
19. The next page is for the certificate; here, we need to reuse the certificate exported from the old VCM server.
20. Click on **Select** and provide the Collector and Enterprise certificates:

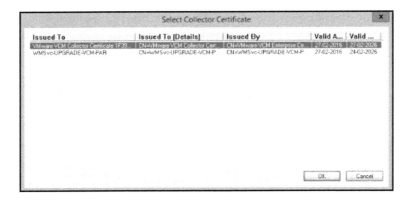

21. Provide details about Virtual Directory and the credentials to access it.
22. Provide the credentials for the Virtualization Client plugin.
23. On the next page, provide the path to install the package manager components to.
24. On the next page, provide the path to the local package cache.
25. On the next page, provide the path for the software repository and local cache.
26. Provide a Virtual Directory name.
27. Provide the path for the Package Studio components.
28. Finally, you will reach the summary page. Check the options and click on **Install**:

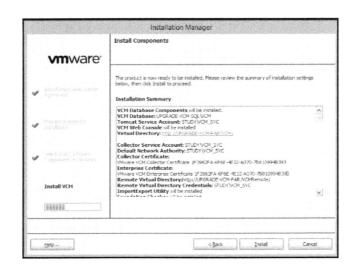

29. Once VCM is installed successfully, log in to the console with the account you used to install VCM. Check whether all the managed machines are available and all the virtual infrastructure elements you configured are present.
30. Also check the version–it should be **5.8.2.160**, as in the following screenshot:

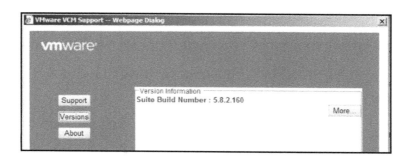

31. Perform a collection of any managed VMs available on the console.

How it works...

We went to the latest Windows OS and then migrated the VCM installation to give us the edge, that is, if you are on an older version of the OS that is not supported by Microsoft or not supported as a *base* OS for VCM, then you can migrate retaining all the old data. You can perform a hardware refresh if your old server was on a physical server.

When we perform a parallel upgrade, we migrate from the old operating system but still using the old database. As we keep the old database, all the data collected is retained after the upgrade. We have all the agents and all the already configured vCenter servers. This helps in keeping our old configuration with the latest build of VCM and the latest supported base OS.

Selecting the right certificate is the key to success here. As you know, the certificate is used by agents when we install them. If we regenerate or use the wrong certificate, the agent-server communication will break and we will be forced to install a new agent with the latest certificate from the server.

Aftercare

Refer to the corresponding section of the previous recipe for aftercare instructions.

There's more...

Refer to the corresponding section of the previous recipe. The same steps need to be followed.

Migrating VCM from another domain

There are scenarios in which we need to migrate from one domain to another and can't afford to lose all the historical data of our managed machines. In this recipe, we will look at how to migrate the VCM server from an old domain to a new domain.

Getting ready

Make sure that the network and DNS (forward and reverse) is correct for the VCM Collector server. Add the VCM Collector to the new domain and create or identify the domain account that you want to use, as described in *Service accounts* subsection under the *Understanding the requirements of VCM* recipe in `Chapter 1`, *Installing VCM*.

How to do it...

To change VCM service accounts to run under a different domain account, follow these steps:

1. On the VCM database server, run the following SQL update queries against the core VCM database. Make the appropriate name substitutions:

```
DECLARE     @collector_service_account NVARCHAR(128)
SET @collector_service_account = N'domain-name\account-name'

DECLARE     @collector_config_id INT
SELECT @collector_config_id = c.configuration_id
    FROM dbo.ecm_sysdat_configuration_values c
    WHERE c.configuration_name = 'collector_service_account'

EXEC dbo.ecm_sp_configuration_values_update
    @configuration_id = @collector_config_id,
    @configuration_value = @collector_service_account
EXEC dbo.ecm_sp_security_collector_service_account_setup
    @collector_service_account = @collector_service_account
```

2. Select and stop the following services:

    - **VCM Collector**
    - **VCM Database Service**
    - **VCM Patch Management**

3. Right-click on each service, select **Properties**, and select the **Log On** tab.
4. Change the account credentials to the new account, and click on **OK**.
5. Go to **Start | Administrative Tools | Component Services**.
6. On the left, go to **Console Root | Component Services | Computers | My Computer | DCOM Config | LicenseDcom**.
7. Right-click, select **Properties**, and select the **Identity** tab.
8. Select **This** user, enter the new domain account credentials, and click on **OK**.
9. From **Start | Administrative Tools | Services**, restart the services you stopped.
10. Go to **Start | Administrative Tools | Server Manager**.
11. On the left, navigate to **Server Manager** (hostname) **| Configuration | Local Users and Groups**.

12. Double-click on **Groups**.

13. Select VCM_LDP_GROUP, right-click, and select **Properties**.

14. Remove the old account and add the new one.

15. Navigate to **Server Manager** (hostname) | **Configuration** | **Services**, double-click on **Groups**, select CSI_COMM_PROXY_SVC, and repeat the process for replacing the account.

> Note that if you run the **Repair** option of the VCM installer, account changes revert to what you specified during installation.
>
> Note that if you run the VCM installer to upgrade to a newer version of VCM, account changes default to what you specified during the older installation. Enter the account changes that you want during the upgrade process.

16. Add the new domain to the network authority in VCM.

17. Add any new users required for the new domain.

How it works...

VCM runs its services under accounts that you specify during installation. After installing VCM, the conditions at your site might require that you change from running under the initial domain account to a different domain account.

This procedure also applies when you need to change from running under a built-in Windows account to a domain account. To change from domain accounts to built-in accounts, refer to the next recipe, where we provide new credentials to run services in the new domain and retain historical data in VCM.

Applying a new license key

You might have had a temporary license key when you installed VCM or the infrastructure might have grown more than you expected and you now need to provide new licenses to manage the infrastructure. This is where you need to provide new keys, and entering a new serial key is not a straightforward console option; there is a command-line utility called **jlicense.cmd** available to do this.

Getting ready

Get the new key to be used. You must have VCM admin access on the VCM console.

How to do it...

Log in to the VCM server with VCM admin privileges, and follow these steps:

1. Launch CMD with administrative privileges and go to X:\Program Files (x86)\VMware\VCM\Tools (*X* is the drive where VCM is installed).

2. Run jlicense.cmd -k xxxxx-xxxxx-xxxxx-xxxxx-xxxxx (this is the new key you want to add to VCM), as shown in the following screenshot:

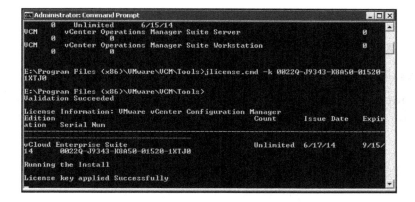

How it works...

It will append to the already available capacity of VCM, that is, the number of machines we can manage and the expiration date of the key.

Using the **jlicense.cmd** utility, you can:

- Update a single license key for servers
- Update a single license key for workstations
- Enter two keys for servers and workstations
- Enter a single license key for servers or workstations or enter two license keys for both servers and workstations

Here's how to use the JLicense tool:

- To display the JLicense help information, run this command: `jlicense -h`
- To evaluate the license key but not to install it, run this command:

    jlicense -n -k xxxxx-xxxxx-xxxxx-xxxxx-xxxxx

    Here, xxxxx-xxxxx-xxxxx-xxxxx-xxxxx is the license key

- To change a license, run this command:

    jlicense -k xxxxx-xxxxx-xxxxx-xxxxx-xxxxx

    Here, xxxxx-xxxxx-xxxxx-xxxxx-xxxxx is the license key

Upgrading VCM agents

After an upgrade of the VCM server, you need to upgrade the VCM agent. This recipe deals with the Windows and Linux VCM agent upgrades from their previous versions.

Getting ready

You must have some old agents to be upgraded to the latest version and they should be communicating with VCM server.

How to do it...

There are two ways to upgrade the agent in the case of Windows. From the console, you can choose **Upgrade** as an option, or you can choose Install and in the wizard choose **Remove Current Agent** from the machine. Both the processes do the same thing–upgrading the agent to the latest build–but **Install with Remove Current** version takes more time. Both the options retain all the old collected data.

We will use the **Upgrade** method in this recipe.

Windows

This is the way to do it in Windows:

1. Log in to VCM with administrative privileges.
2. Navigate to **Administration** | **Machines Manager** | **Licensed Machines** | **Licensed Windows Machines**.
3. Right-click on the machine and select **Upgrade Agent**:

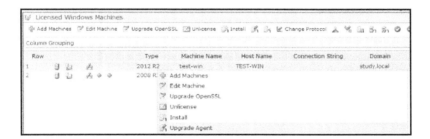

4. On the **Machines** page, select the Windows machines to upgrade and click on the arrow to move the machines to the selected pane. Click on **Next**.

5. On the installation options page, select or verify the option for the agent installation, and click on **Next**.

6. On the **Schedule** page, schedule the operation and click on **Next**.

7. On the **Important** page, verify the summary and click on **Finish**.

8. Click on the **Jobs** button and see whether the job is completed successfully.

9. Once the job is finished, check the console for the agent version. It should be the latest one, as in the following screenshot:

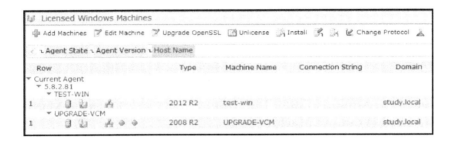

Linux

Here's how to do it in Linux:

1. Log in to VCM with administrative privileges.

2. Click on **Console** and go to **UNIX Remote Commands** | **UNIX Agent Upgrade**.

3. In the **UNIX Agent Upgrade** data grid, click on the appropriate remote upgrade package for the operating system and the version of the machines to upgrade:

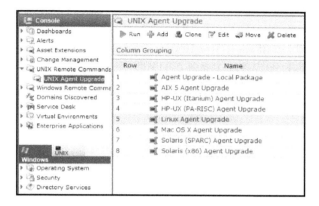

4. Click on **Run** and follow the wizard to send the remote command and upgrade packages on the agents on the selected machines.

   The agents will execute the package upgrade.

5. Select the managed machine whose agent you want to upgrade.
6. On the **Schedule** page, select **Run Remote Command Now** or schedule the operation for later and click on **Next**.
7. On the **Important** page, verify the summary and click on **Finish**.
8. Verify that the job completes successfully.
9. Perform a collection on the managed machine.
10. Check the status of the agent on the console of VCM; it should look something like the following screenshot:

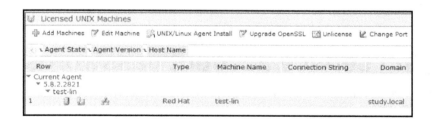

How it works...

We push the latest installer from the VCM console, it gets copied to the managed machine, starts upgrading the old agent files, and finally creates a VCM service on the managed machines and comes back with a status of success.

You can perform a collection after the agent is installed to be sure nothing was broken during the upgrade.

In case of a Linux upgrade, the process copies the latest agent installer from the VCM console along with the remote command to run on the Linux/Unix machine. Then, it executes the script to install the agent.

There's more...

It is observed that after most of the agent or server upgrades, we need to perform the steps as described in the *Issue 1 – mutual authentication failure* subsection of the *Troubleshooting agent communication issues* recipe in Chapter 9, *Troubleshooting VCM*, as the trust between the upgraded agent and VCM Collector is broken.

You will see the error message described in the previous recipe, so simply follow the steps to resolve it.

See also

- There is a small bug with the agent upgrade to version 5.8.1 (resolved in 5.8.2) from an older version; have a look at the *Troubleshooting agent upgrade* issues recipe in Chapter 9, *Troubleshooting VCM*

Changing service account passwords

There are occasions when we need to change passwords for service accounts; in this recipe, we will learn how to.

Getting ready

You must have new passwords available to be replaced.

How to do it...

We'll look at the various service accounts used by VCM that we can change if we want to.

To update a password for VCM service accounts, follow these steps.

Collector service accounts

1. On the Collector, go to **Start** | **Administrative Tools** | **Services**.
2. Select and stop the following services:

   - **VCM Collector**
   - **VCM Database Service**
   - **VCM Patch Management**

3. Right-click on each service, select **Properties**, and select the **Log On** tab.
4. Update the account password and click on **OK**.
5. Go to **Start** | **Administrative Tools** | **Component Services**.
6. On the left, go to **Console Root** | **Component Services** | **Computers** | **My Computer** | **DCOM Config** | **LicenseDcom**.
7. Right-click, select **Properties**, and select the **Identity** tab.
8. Under **This** user, update the password and click on **OK**.

VCM remote service accounts

We provided details about the VCM remote user when we performed the installation.

The VCM remote service account is used by the VCM remote client for anonymous access to the VCM remote virtual directory on the web server. Follow these steps:

1. On the web server, go to **Start** | **Administrative Tools** | **IIS Manager**.
2. On the left, navigate to **{web-server-hostname}** | **Sites** | **Default Web Site** | **ECMRemoteHTTP**.
3. Double-click on **Authentication**.
4. Select **Anonymous Authentication**.
5. In the **Actions** pane on the right, select **Edit**.
6. Click on **Set**.
7. Enter the existing domain/username, then the new password, and click on **OK**.
8. Navigate to **{web-server-hostname}** | **Sites** | **Default Web Site** | **VCMRemote**, and repeat the steps to change the password.

Network authority accounts

Follow these steps for a network authority account:

1. In VCM, click on **Administration** and go to **Settings** | **Network Authority** | **Available Accounts**.
2. Click on **Edit Password**.

SSRS

For an SSRS account, run the RSConfig command to change the embedded account information.

How it works...

VCM runs its services under accounts that you specify during installation. After installing VCM, conditions at your site might require that passwords on the accounts be changed, making it necessary to update the passwords in VCM as well.

We can make those changes using the steps we just went through.

Managing users

You need to manage VCM logins and assign roles to users who have access to VCM. Roles determine the level of access for each user and can be adjusted for access to specific machine groups and VCM functionality.

Getting ready

If you are planning to create custom roles, they must be ready before starting this recipe.

How to do it...

Follow these steps to add new users and groups and give them appropriate permissions:

1. Navigate to **Administration** | **User Manager** | **VCM Logins**.
2. Click on **Add Users**.

> Note that you cannot add the Collector service account as a VCM login.

3. Select **Enter Domain Account** and click on **Next**.

> Note that individual Active Directory accounts can also be added. Adding a group ensures that role-based access is governed by Active Directory.

4. Enter the security group in the `DOMAIN\Group` format and click on **Next**.
5. Double-click on **Admin** (or a lesser role for general access) and click on **Next**.
6. Click on **Finish**.

How it works...

When VCM is installed, the user who installs it gets administrative access on the console. We need to add users or groups to give them access. By following this recipe, we can add users who need access.

 Note that when a user starts VCM, if more than one role is assigned to their login, a drop-down list appears and allows the user to select the desired role. To automatically log in to VCM using a particular role, users can check the **Automatically log in using this role** option. To switch roles or not log in automatically, users can select a different role or uncheck this option.

Default roles

This is the list of default roles available with VCM and a short description of each of them:

Sr. no.	Name	Description
1	Admin	Top-level role. Admin has rights to everything in the database.
2	Domain Controller Manager	Role with full access to the Domain Controllers dynamic machine group.
3	Read-Only	Role with read access to all machines and data.
4	Help Desk	Only allows password changes on domain controllers.
5	IIS Admins	Role with full access to the Microsoft Internet Information Servers dynamic machine group.
6	Server Managers	Role with full access to the Servers dynamic machine group.
7	SQL Server Admins	Role with full access to the Microsoft SQL Servers dynamic machine group.
8	Workstation Managers	Role with full access to the Workstation dynamic machine group.
9	VCM Auditor	Role with read access to License Manager.
10	AD_Admin	Built in role with access to AD data and Administration for AD.
11	AD_User	Built in role with access to AD data only.

12	Change Restricted	VCM **Change Restricted** role. With this role, users can discover machines, collect data from them, assess them, display bulletin and template details, check for updates, and view history. Users can add, edit, and delete reports, compliance rules and rule groups, and compliance and patch assessment templates. Users with the **Change Restricted** role can also install the VCM agent, upgrade VCM, and uninstall it.

There's more...

When creating a role, we need to understand access rules as they define the areas of VCM that users can access and the actions that they can perform.

VCM roles and access rules go hand in hand; roles define which areas can be accessed by whom while rules define what kind of access is provided to the user, such as **None, Read Only, Full Access**, or **Custom**. When you select **Custom**, it goes to a very granular level and you can select a single privilege, such as only **Add Automatic Deployment** or **Run a Report**.

You can either use the 14 default access rules or you can create new ones as per your requirement:

1. To create a new access rule, log in to the VCM console, go to **Administration | User Manager | VCM Access | Access Rules**, and click on **Add Rule**.
2. Provide a nice name and description.
3. Under **Rule Type**, select **Basic Rule** (this defines data types and areas of VCM to access) or **Admin Access Rule** (to access administrative areas of VCM).
4. For **Basic Rule**, under **Data Type**, include what type of data, that is, machine data or Active Directory data, and then define access to the VCM console, except the **Administration** tab.
5. **Admin Access Rule** defines what type of access is defined in the **Administration** tab, such as **None, Read Only, Full Control**, or going granular with **Custom**.
6. Lastly, click on **Finish** on the **Important** page of the wizard to close and create this new access rule.

As seen previously, there are 12 default roles created, but if you still have a use case that requires a different role, then you can create your own role. Follow these steps:

1. Log in to the VCM console and go to **Administration** I **User Manager** I **VCM Access** I **Roles**.
2. Click on the **Add Role** button and follow the wizard.
3. When creating a role, you will need some information. To start with, provide a name and description for the newly created role.
4. For **Role Access**, we can select either **Machine Data** (access to data based on the selected machine groups), **Active Directory** (access to Active Directory objects based on the AD structure), or **Admin** (access to administrative functions) access.
5. On the next page, under **Machine Data Access**, you can filter which machine group this new role user can access.
6. On the **Active Directory** page, under **Enterprise**, select the **Access Rule** that will be applied at the root of AD, if you have configured any.
7. For **Admin Access**, select a proper rule to provide access.
8. Under **Logins**, select any logins to assign this role to and, after reviewing it under **Important**, close the wizard to finish it.

Decommissioning VMs – manual VM purge

As a part of the lifecycle management of a managed machine, we need to remove the details of the managed machine from the VCM console.

Getting ready

You must have the name of the machine that you want to remove from VCM.

How to do it...

It's a two-step process: First, free up a license and keep the data. Next, purge everything and remove the managed machine from the VCM database.

Unlicense a managed machine

1. Log in to VCM with administrative privileges.
2. Go to **Administration** | **Machines Manager** | **Licensed Machines** | **Licensed Windows Machines** or **Licensed UNIX Machines**.
3. Right-click on the name of the machine you want to remove from the display.
4. Select the **Unlicense** option and follow the prompts.

 Note that this returns the machine to the **Available Machines** list and frees up the machine's license for reuse.

Purge the machine

1. Log in to VCM with administrative privileges.
2. Go to **Administration** | **Machines Manager** | **Available Machine**.
3. From here, if required, we can license the machine and move it to **Licensed Windows Machines** or **Licensed UNIX Machines** or remove it from the VCM database.
4. Select the machine and click on **Purge** in the top menu.
5. Follow the wizard; it will remove the machine completely from the VCM database.

How it works...

The process will obtain records as well as collected data from the VCM database and help us clean the clutter in the VCM, as the machines we want to delete have already been decommissioned. If those machines are not deleted from VCM, we could have an incorrect compliance score. We will always have machines that will fail patch installation and we will never reach the score we want.

There's more…

If you are good with vRealize Orchestrator, VMware had released a package for VCM (which is available for download at `https://my.vmware.com`). With the help of this package, you can create a workflow to remove/purge managed machines.

Decommissioning VMs – scheduled VM record purge

In the era of the cloud, we would like VM decommissioning to be done automatically so that our operations team can do more creative stuff than cleaning up the VCM database.

Getting ready

You must have access to the SQL server where the VCM database is hosted. You must know the basics of SQL Management Studio.

How to do it…

The following stored procedure can be implemented on the VCM database (VCM) as a scheduled task. This will purge the records of the VMs that haven't been contacted in the last 3 weeks.

Change the value of `@expire int = xx` (the number of days for which the machine has not been contacted) in the script:

```
USE [VCM]
GO
/****** Object:  StoredProcedure
[dbo].[ecmSVC_sp_remove_noncollected_machines]    Script Date: 11/20/2012
11:40:58 ******/
SET ANSI_NULLS ON
GO
SET QUOTED_IDENTIFIER ON
GO
ALTER PROCEDURE [dbo].[ecmSVC_sp_remove_noncollected_machines]
@expire int = 21,
@value NVARCHAR(5) = 'True'
 AS
/***********************************************************************
```

```
/
Procedure:  dbo.ecmSVC_sp_remove_noncollected_machine
------------------------------------------------------------------------
REVISION HISTORY
Modified:   <YYYY.MM.DD> by <Author>
    Description -
    Issue/ATS# -
Created:    2006-05-11 by Chris Lennon
------------------------------------------------------------------------
DESCRIPTION
    Check for machines not pingable and haven't been collected over x amount
    of days
    Removed from the Licensed Machines into the Available Machines and as an
    option purge from ECM.
    -------------------------- Copyright Notice ----------------------------
This code may not be copied, altered, reused, or redistributed in any way
without the express written consent of Configuresoft, Inc.
    Copyright 1998-2006 Configuresoft, Inc.  All rights reserved.
    -------------------------- Configuresoft, Inc. -------------------------
    *********************************************************************/
BEGIN
    DECLARE
        @uids VARCHAR(8000),
        @creator_id int,
        @owner_id int
    SELECT @uids = ''
    --Locate machines with no ping and not collected over x amount of days
    SELECT @uids = @uids + ISNULL(LTRIM(CAST(machine_id AS NVARCHAR(32))),
    '') + N'|'
    FROM ecm_view_rpt_machine_info_all
    WHERE (connection_state = 'ICOStatusConnectionNoPing16'
    or connection_state = 'ICOStatusConnectionNoName16')
    and [date last contacted] < DATEADD(dd, -@expire, GETUTCDATE())
    and managed = '1'
    -- remove trailing pipe if it exists
    IF RIGHT(@uids, 1) = '|'
    BEGIN
        SELECT @uids = SUBSTRING(@uids, 1, LEN(@uids) - 1)
    END
    IF @uids <> ''
    BEGIN
            --Remove from Licensed Machines
            exec dbo.ecm_sp_machines_set_state @uids, N'|', 5
            --Purge from ECM if @value is TRUE
            IF @value = 'TRUE'
            BEGIN
                SELECT @creator_id = dbo.userid()
                SELECT @owner_id = dbo.role_current()
```

```
                    exec dbo.ecm_sp_machine_delete_all_data @uids, 1, N'|',
                    @owner_id, @creator_id
            END
     END
END
```

Schedule a job in SQL

1. Expand the **SQL Server Agent** node, right-click on the **Jobs** node in **SQL Server Agent**, and select **New Job**:

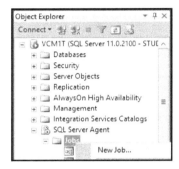

2. In the **New Job** window, enter the name of the job and a description in the **General** tab:

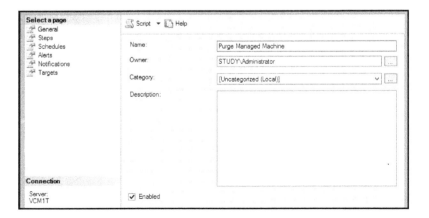

3. Select **Steps** on the left-hand side of the window and click on **New** at the bottom.

4. In the **Steps** window, enter a step name and select the database you want the query to run against:

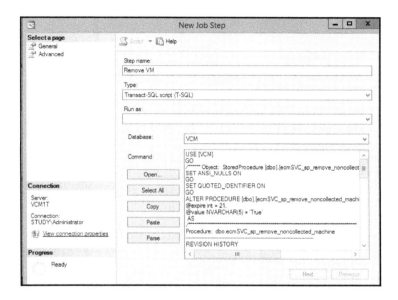

5. Paste in the T-SQL command you want to run in the command window, and click on **OK**.

6. Click on the **Schedule** menu to the left of the **New Job** window and enter the schedule information (for example, daily and a time).

7. Click on **OK**, and that should be it.

How it works...

The job will run on the schedule provided by you and clean the managed machines that have not been communicating for the last 21 days; if this seems too much, then the number can be changed in the script to a suitable number as per your requirements.

8
Integration with vROps and Scheduling

In this chapter, we will cover the following recipes:

- Installing and configuration of vROps Management Pack for VCM
- Configuring vROps – VCM compliance mapping and scheduling
- Scheduling OS and compliance data collection
- Scheduling compliance
- Scheduling reports
- Scheduling vCenter collections
- Scheduling vCenter discovery

Introduction

We will be discussing two different topics in the chapter. First, we will install the VCM adapter in vROps and integrate them so that we can send compliance data from VCM to vROps.

Nobody likes to be in front of any console to do the work, and automation is the key to everything. In this chapter, we will take a look at the scheduler feature of VCM, such as scheduling jobs to collect the data from managed machines, pushing the compliance details to vROps, or exporting a report and saving it on a share or sending to someone on e-mail.

So, let's begin with vROps and VCM integration.

Installing and configuration of vROps Management Pack for VCM

Integrating VCM with vROps provides compliance and event details from VCM to the vROps console. This means that you can have an idea about what's going on with a particular server when you are troubleshooting. An event can give information, such as when the server was rebooted, when the pathing was done, or when the software was installed from VCM. Apart from this, VCM can push compliance details about the managed machine with the mappings that have been created.

Getting ready

We will need a configured VCM that has compliance configuration completed, and a working vROps server where we have admin access. We will also need user credentials that can log in to VCM and have admin access in the VCM application. We need to download the latest VCM solution from https://solutionexchange.vmware.com/.

vROps must be monitoring the same vCenter server that is managed by VCM.

How to do it...

In this recipe, we are going to install the VCM adapter for vROps. We will be logging into vROps and following the given steps:

1. Log in to vROps with an admin account, or another account that has admin privileges, and go to **Solutions**. Click on the green plus symbol under **Solutions**, as shown in the following screenshot:

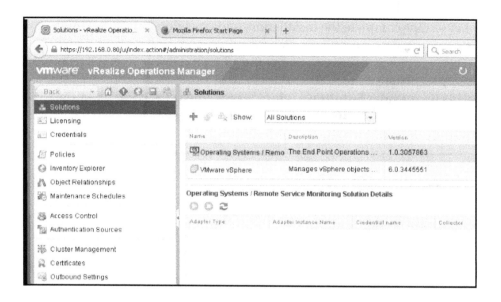

2. Click on **Browse** and go to the location where you have downloaded the VCM solution from the Internet and click on **Upload**. You will then get a screen similar to the following screenshot:

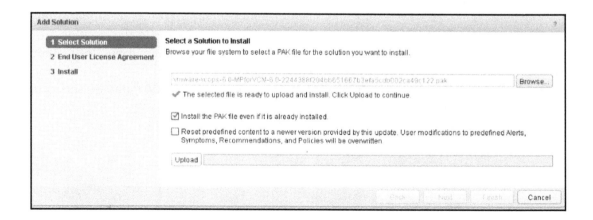

3. Accept the unsigned solution warning if displayed by vROps.

4. Accept the EULA.

5. Let vROps complete the installation, and once done, click on **Finish** to complete it.

6. This completes the installation of the adapter. Now we need to configure the adapter instance.

7. This time, under **Solutions**, select **Management Pack for VCM for vSphere** and click on the **Configure** button at the top with two gears:

8. Provide the following details:

   - **Display Name**: This will be the name displayed for the adapter
   - **Description**: Provide a good description so someone can understand what it is, when you are not around
   - **Database Host:** This is the IP or name of the VCM database server (for single-tier, it's the VCM Collector server)

- **Database Port:** This is the SQL port on the VCM server
- **Database Name:** This is the VCM database name; the default is VCM
- **Database Instance:** If you have installed SQL as **Instance**, provide the name that can be kept blank for default

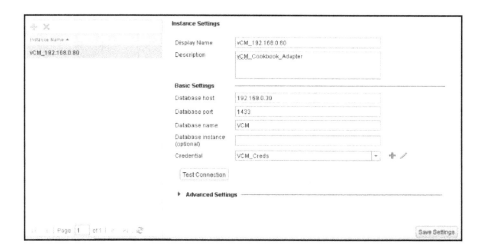

9. Provide the following details for the **Manage Credential** window:

- **Credential Name**: This is a descriptive name for the credential
- **Database Username**: This is the database user account for the VCM database

Note that you have to create a dedicated service account in the Active Directory for this, and give this account an admin role in VCM.

- **Database Password**: This is the password for the user account
- **Database Authentication**: This will be either SQL or Windows authentication (recommended)

- **Windows Domain**: In case of Windows authentication, provide the domain name, as shown in the following screenshot:

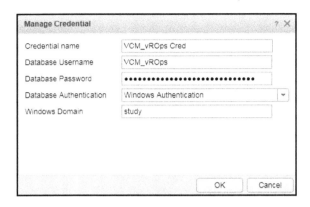

10. After the information is provided, click on **Test Connection**.
11. Once the test is successful, click on **Save Settings**. Don't worry about the advanced settings, you can keep the default settings for time being.
12. Wait 2 minutes and check **Admin** | **Cluster Management** whether objects and metrics are collected:

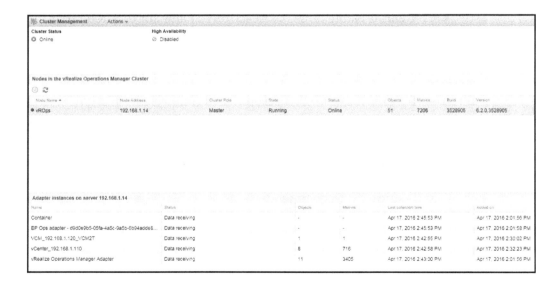

How it works

Now we are ready to connect to the VCM database and fetch the required information to be displayed on the VCM console. vROps goes to the VCM database and starts collecting the required details, such as compliance score or events; these are posted on the vROps console:

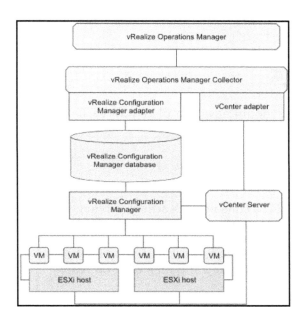

Image Source: www.vmware.com

There's more...

The account used for adapter configuration must not be the account that is used for an interactive user login. The adapter account frequently logs in and out of VCM. If you use it as an interactive account, you must regularly refresh the connection, which affects your VCM experience.

Configuring vROps – VCM compliance mapping and scheduling

Once VCM is integrated with vROps, we need to move ahead so that it can run the compliance and send the compliance score to be displayed on the vROps console. We will create a mapping in the VCM that will run the compliance check and update it with the details in vROps.

Getting ready

To perform this task, you should have completed the earlier recipe to install the management pack and configure it.

How to do it…

We need to log in to the VCM console with admin privileges in order to perform this recipe. Once logged in, follow the steps to complete the mapping:

1. Navigate to **Compliance** | **Machine Group Compliance** | **vCenter Operations Manager Badge** | **Mapping** and then click on **Add**:

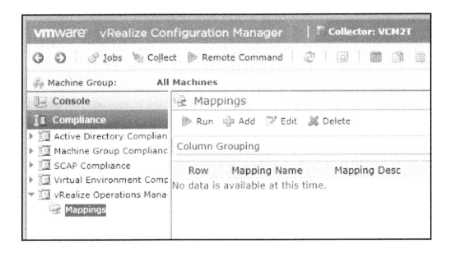

2. Give the proper name and description when the wizard starts:

   - **Select Badge**: **Risk Compliance**
   - **Roll up Type**: **Simple Percentage**
   - **Select Group Context**: As per the requirement

3. Select **Correct Machine Group**.

   When the mapping runs, it will run against all the machines that are part of this machine group.

4. Select **Corresponding Compliance Template**.

   Select the template that is required to check compliance against the earlier selected machine group. You can select either a compliance template created for your organization or any standard template downloaded from the Internet.

5. Click on **Finish**. This will save the mapping.

   Once the mapping is created, we need to run this so that the compliance score is calculated for the machines that are part of the machine group and then informed to vROps in order to be displayed on the vROps console.

6. Select the mapping and then click on the **Run** button at the top.

7. It will first run the compliance check on the **Machine Group**, and then when vROps updates the details via the management pack imported and configured as described in the *Installing and configuration of vROps Management Pack for VCM* recipe, the status will be updated.

   Depending upon how many machines you have in the machine group and the number of rules in the compliance template, it will take some time.

8. To check the compliance tab on vROps, log in to the vROps console and navigate to **Environment** | **vCenter Adapter** | **Virtual Machines** and then select **Machine Go to Analysis** | **Compliance**.

   You will see the compliance status of the machine.

It will show the number of rules passed and failed and the compliance template used for checking the compliance along with the overall compliance status reported by VCM:

Once the mapping is done, we can schedule this mapping so that it will update vROps on schedule. Continue from where we left off:

1. Navigate to **Administration** | **Job Manager** | **Scheduled** and click on **Add**.
2. Select **vCenter Operations Manager Compliance Badge Mapping Run** on the **Job Type** page of the wizard.
3. Provide **Name** and **description**. You can be creative as there is a limit of characters for **Name**, you can use any naming convention as all the scheduled job are going to land at the same place in VCM.
4. Select the mapping that you want to schedule:

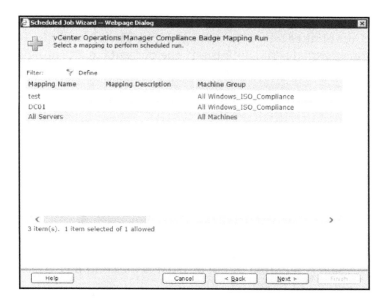

5. Select the schedule and click on **Finish**. As this is related to compliance, make sure that this is scheduled after the OS and compliance data collection, as then we will have the latest data to run the compliance checks.

How it works...

To get the details, the vCenter server must be monitored by vROps and managed by VCM.

When we add and configure the VCM Management Pack, it fetches compliance details from the VCM and then displays it on the vROps console.

The VCM compliance data is based on compliance templates that are run against the data collected from the same vCenter Server objects that are monitored in vRealize Operations Manager. The templates are the configuration settings that must be present on a target object for it to be considered compliant with the template standards. The standards might be the VMware vSphere Hardening Guide, Payment Card Industry standards, Health Insurance Portability and Accountability Act, or other VMware or industry standards.

When we select the mapping, it will first run the compliance check with the selected template(s) and then update the compliance score on the vROps console. The score is visible on the **Analysis | Compliance** tab of the managed VM. The tab will display the compliance status against various templates (if configured), the percentage, the number of rules, and so on. Once we schedule it, the job will make sure that the compliance score is updated on the vROps console.

Scheduling OS and compliance data collection

Collections are fetching the data as requested in the **Filter Set** from the managed machines. As you know, VCM does not go to the managed machine each time it needs to process something against the managed machine such as **Patch** or **Compliance** status, it uses the data that is available in the database, and after processing the data, it gives a result, for example, whether a patch is required or not or what is the compliance level we are at.

If the data about the managed machine is not frequently updated, VCM processes stale data and we can have false positives or a very bad compliance score even though we are compliant.

To overcome this situation, we can go to the VCM console and start collecting the details on our own or schedule the job in the VCM and ask it to do it.

Continuous server management is based on the latest data that you collected from the target servers. Windows and Linux data appears in VCM and is available for several management actions, including **Console** dashboards and reports, **Compliance Views**, and **VCM Patching**.

Getting ready

We need a configured VCM where we have created all the required machine groups as described in the *Creating a machine group* recipe in Chapter 2, *Configuring VCM to Manage Your Infrastructure*.

How to do it...

To perform this recipe, login to VCM with the admin account and follow the steps:

1. Navigate to **Administration** | **Job Manager** | **Scheduled** and click on **Add**:

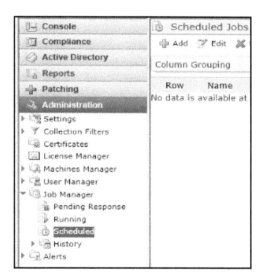

2. Select **Collection** on the **Job Type** page of the wizard.

3. Provide **Name** and **Description**. You can be creative as there is a limit of characters for the **Name**, it will be better if you use a naming convention. Some examples are given in `Chapter 2`, *Configuring VCM to Manage Your Infrastructure* as all the scheduled job are going to land at the same place in VCM:

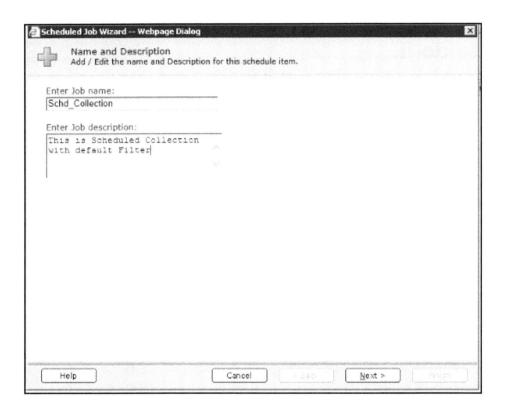

4. Select the filter set as per the requirement. Also select if you want every scheduled collection to collect all the data or just the delta from the last collection. You can decide this based on how frequent you are collecting the data. If the frequency is too high and you have huge infrastructure to manage, you can opt for **Delta** as that will be faster:

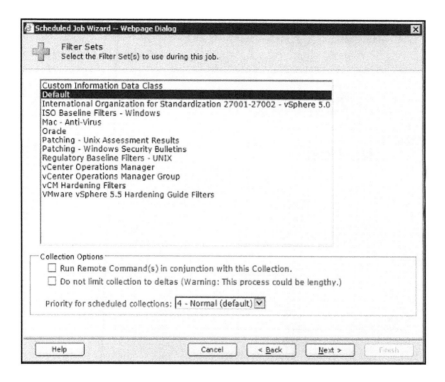

5. Select the machine group that you planned in the *Getting ready* section:

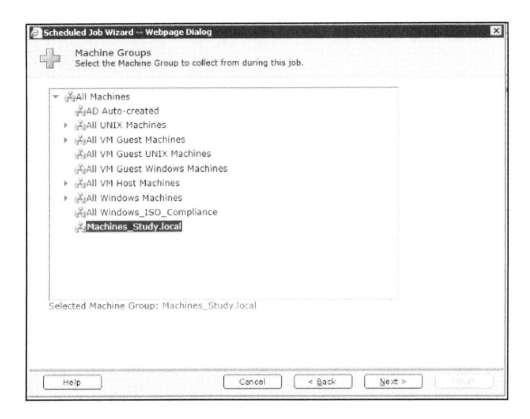

6. Provide the schedule, this will vary as per your requirement and what exactly you are collecting, use your imagination to schedule this job **Daily**, **Weekly**, **Monthly**, or **Once**:

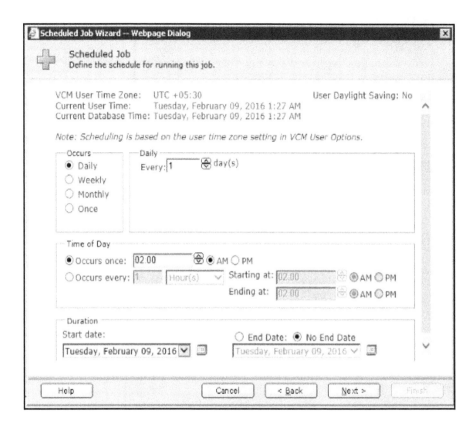

7. Confirm that there are no conflicts and click on **Finish**.

How it works...

Basically, we are creating a scheduled task in SQL that will be triggered as per the schedule we have created. Then this will ask all the managed machines to provide the details as defined in the selected filter set. The data is stored in the VCM database and will be further used for various purposes, such as checking **Compliance**, **Patch Status**, or **Get Reports**.

 Note that the displayed data is only as recent as the last time you collected it.

There's more...

Collection filters control the data that is collected from managed entity by VCM. Typically, collection filters are twinned with a compliance template and collect only the data that the compliance template requires. For example, the ISO baseline filters-Windows collection set defines the extra information that is required to be imported to measure ISO 27001 compliance.

 Note that collections should be scheduled with additional collection filters for the compliance templates used. This process is the same as for Windows and Linux OS collections.

See also

- Before you start creating this scheduled task, make sure that you have created the required machine groups by following the recipe in the *Creating a machine group* recipe in `Chapter 2`, *Configuring VCM to Manage Your Infrastructure*.

Scheduling compliance

Compliance is an ongoing process and we need to check it at regular intervals to know exactly where we are and whether we need any remediation to be in good state. In the earlier recipe, we scheduled the data collection. Now is the time to consume the data.

Getting ready

We need to have the latest data available in our VCM database to be processed, so schedule the compliance check after few hours of data collection to give it some time to update the database.

How to do it...

To perform the following recipe, log in to VCM with the admin account and follow the steps:

1. Navigate to **Administration** I **Job Manager** I **Scheduled** and click on **Add**:

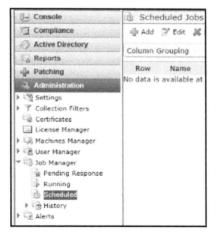

2. Select **Compliance** on the **Job Type** page of the wizard.

3. Provide **Name** and **Description**. You can be creative as there is a limit of characters for the **Name**, you can use any naming convention as all the scheduled job are going to land at the same place in VCM:

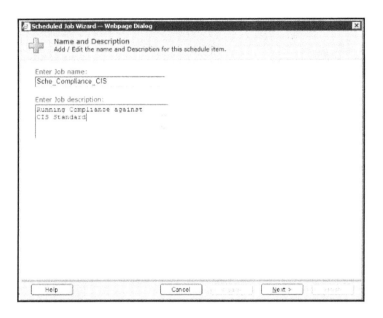

4. Select the template that you want to check compliance for.

5. There are some rules that can enforce the compliance, such as starting or stopping a service, that you can select here if you want to auto enforce the compliance.

Note that only complex rules can be used to enforce compliance. When you enforce compliance, there are chances that it can break working configuration, for example, your security policy wants the Print Spooler service disabled, if you enforce the compliance, VCM will disable the service. However, if you have **Print Servers** managed by VCM and not created exceptions in VCM, this may create issues.

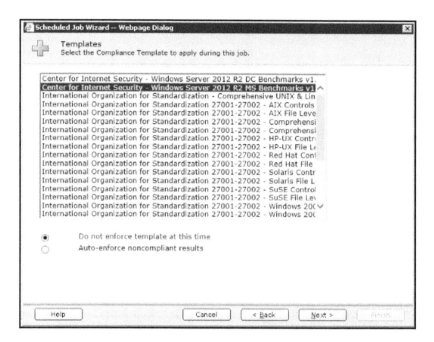

6. Select the appropriate **Machine Group**.
7. Provide the schedule, schedule this after the collection job and make sure that you give some time for VCM to collect the data and insert it in the database.

8. Click on **Finish** to close the wizard:

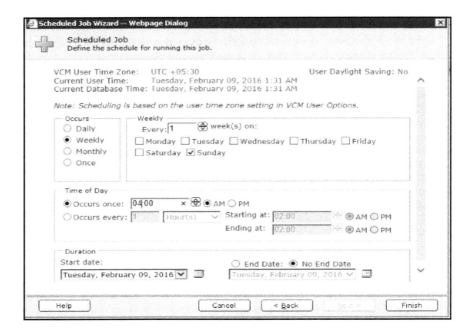

How it works...

Every scheduled job is a scheduled job in VCM database, compliance job uses data from the VCM database for processing. Once the job is finished, it will update the compliance stats on the VCM console and then these can be exported in the form of a report, which can also be scheduled.

Scheduling reports

We don't want to sit in front of the VCM console to get the reports exported. We can schedule them and they can be in our inbox when we login. The patching and compliance reports can also be scheduled to be sent to the security officer to take a look at the infra. As they will be sent automatically, our admins can use this time to fix the actual issues than exporting and sending the reports.

Getting ready

Get a proper name ready for the scheduled report and create machine group against the report that should run. For compliance reports, make sure that a compliance check is already performed so that it can have some data in the report.

How to do it...

To perform this recipe, log in to VCM with admin account and follow the steps:

1. Navigate to **Administration** | **Job Manager** | **Scheduled** and click on **Add**.
2. Check the screenshot from the earlier recipes
3. Select **Run Report(s)** on the **Job Type** page of the wizard.

4. Provide **Name** and **description** You can be creative, as there is a limit of characters for the **Name**, you can use any naming convention as all the scheduled job are going to land at the same place in VCM:

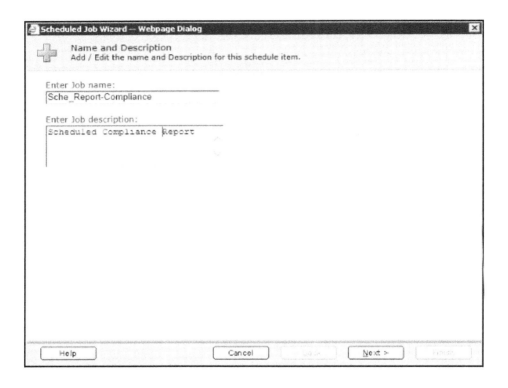

5. On the **Report Folder** page of the wizard, select the report you want to schedule. In this case, we are going to choose patching-related reports.

6. Provide a location to save the exported reports that can be a shared location where all the reports are saved.

7. Select **Select only certain s to run**:

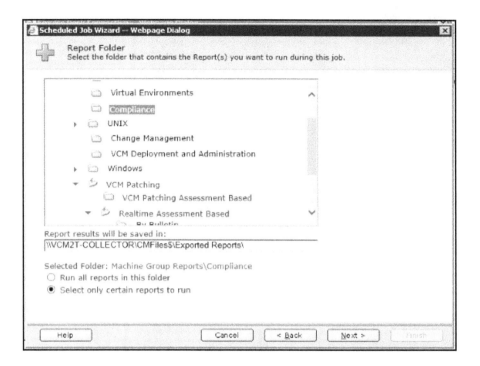

8. Select the reportreports to run: Select the reports you want to schedule, hover over the name of the eporreport to see full name on the top:

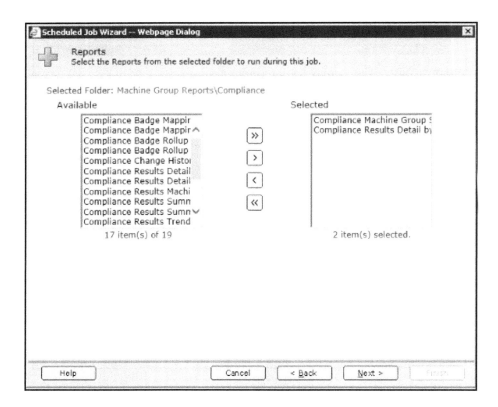

9. Click on the arrows in front of the report names to provide the input details, the details will change depending on the report you have selected in the earlier step:

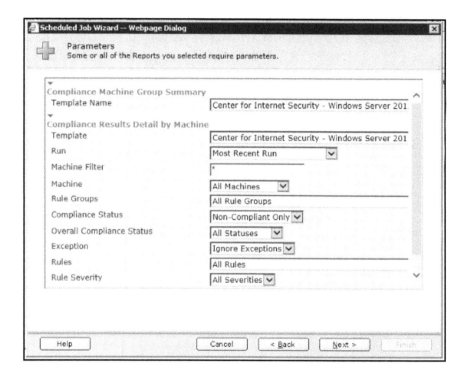

10. Provide the format of the file you want, you can e-mail the report as well if you have SMTP configured and keep few copies of the report on SSRS:

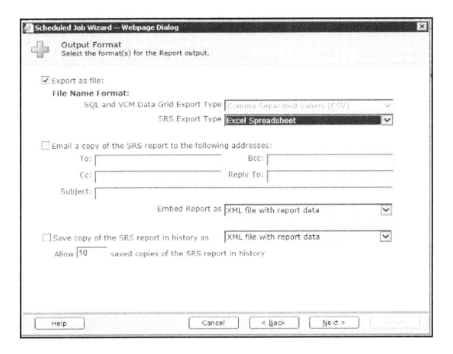

11. Select the machine group against which you want to run the report.
12. Select the schedule and click on **Finish** to close the wizard.

How it works...

VCM goes to the database and prepares the requested report, then depending upon the option selected, it will either dump the report at a shared location in the requested format and/or mail to the configured e-mail IDs.

Make sure that you have scheduled the dependency task earlier and finished before starting this report, like in this case, you should configure the compliance check first, and once it is complete, you should schedule this report or configure patching report once the scheduled patching is finished.

Scheduling vCenter collections

To manage virtual machines, VCM must collect the virtual infrastructure data from the registered vCenters. We can directly add, license, and install agents on the machines added by vCenter collections.

Getting ready

Make sure that vCenter is added in VCM by following the *Adding a vCenter server instance* recipe in Chapter 2, *Configuring VCM to Manage Your Infrastructure*. You have imported the compliance pack for vSphere 5.5 Hardening by following the *Importing Compliance Packs* recipe from Chapter 6, *Compliance Management*. Create a machine group that will include only vCenter Servers by following the *Creating a machine group* recipe from Chapter 2, *Configuring VCM to Manage Your Infrastructure*.

How to do it...

1. Navigate to **Administration | Job Manager| Scheduled** and click on **Add**. Check the screenshot from the earlier recipes.
2. Select **Collection** on the **Job Type** page of the wizard.
3. Provide **Name** and **Description.** You can be creative as there is a limit of characters for the **Name**, you can use any naming convention as all the scheduled job are going to land at the same place in VCM.

4. Select **VMware vSphere 5.5 Hardening Guide Filters**. This collection filter set was downloaded when you prepared yourself in the getting ready section:

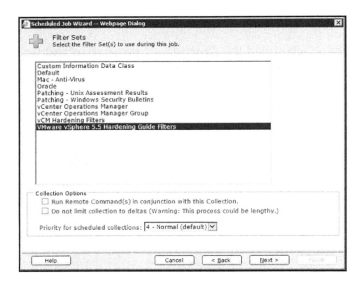

5. Select **vCenter Servers Machine Group**. This machine group was configured when you prepared yourself in the getting ready section.
6. Schedule the vCenter collection for a daily collection.

 Note that this means that any newly provisioned servers will be discovered daily. If you know the machines will be deployed frequently, and you want them to be discovered early, you can change the schedule according to your needs.

How it works...

In this recipe, VCM collects data from the VCM servers that are added in VCM for management and then it makes new VMs available for agent installation by performing a discovery and management such as checking compliance and patching.

See also

- The *Adding a vCenter server instance* recipe in `Chapter 2`, *Configuring VCM to Manage Your Infrastructure*: To make sure that vCenter is added in VCM
- The *Importing Compliance Packs* recipe from `Chapter 6`, *Compliance Management*: To import compliance pack for vSphere 5.5 Hardening
- The *Creating a machine group* recipe in `Chapter 2`, *Configuring VCM to Manage Your Infrastructure*: To create a machine group this will include only vCenter Servers

Scheduling vCenter discovery

Discovery is used to identify if there are any new machines available that can be added to VCM for management. If we don't do it, then we need to manually add and license the machines to be managed.

VCM must discover machines in your environment before you can collect data from them. You can create a discovery rule to discover all machines or you can apply a filter to limit the machines that VCM discovers.

Note that the vCenter discovery must occur after the vCenter Collection. This is counter-intuitive, but simply put, the vCenter discovery is finding new VMs that have come under the vCenter management through the vCenter collection.

Note that for servers and workstations, exceeding the limit on your license key produces warnings but does not restrict the VCM operation.

In this recipe, we are scheduling a vCenter discovery so that all the newly created VMs can be added, and agent can be installed and licensed in VCM.

Getting ready

Check whether you have enough licenses available to accommodate the newly added VMs, make sure that vCenter is added in VCM by following the recipe in the *Adding a vCenter server instance* recipe in `Chapter 2`, *Configuring VCM to Manage Your Infrastructure*. You must have created a discovery rule by following the recipe in *Adding a discovery rule* recipe in `Chapter 2`, *Configuring VCM to Manage Your Infrastructure*. You must have scheduled a vCenter collection before running this discovery. If you are exceeding the limit of your license key, add one by following the *Applying a new license key* recipe in `Chapter 7`, *Maintenance of VCM*.

How to do it...

1. Navigate to **Administration** | **Job Manager** | **Scheduled** and click on **Add**.
2. Check the screenshot from the earlier recipes
3. Select **Discovery** on the **Job Type** page of the wizard.
4. Provide **Name** and **description.** You can be creative as there is a limit of characters for the **Name**, you can use any naming convention as all the scheduled job are going to land at the same place in VCM.

5. Select the vCenter discovery rule created in the *Adding a discovery rule* recipe in `Chapter 2`, *Configuring VCM to Manage Your Infrastructure*:

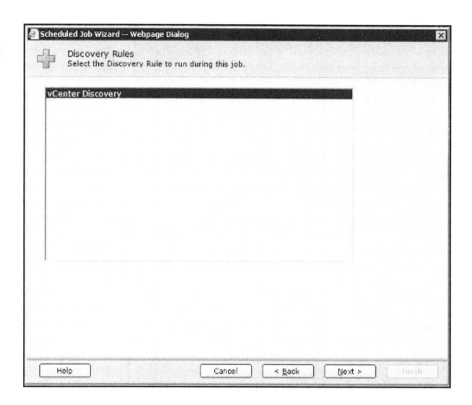

6. Click on **Next** and select a daily schedule.

Note that it is best to schedule the Discovery after the Collection. A two to three hour gap should be sufficient for most environments, but double-check the vCenter Collection job status for large environments.

How it works...

A discovery rule is created; we are just asking VCM to run it on a schedule. If there are too many VM installations on daily basis, we can increase the frequency by selecting **Occurs Every XX hours** and schedule accordingly. This will go in the database and check the details fetched by vCenter collections and add the newly created VMs in the licensed machines. If in the discovery rule we have selected to install the agent, then it will just follow the discovery and install the agent.

See also

- The *Adding a vCenter server instance* recipe in Chapter 2, *Configuring VCM to Manage Your Infrastructure*: To add a vCenter in VCM
- The *Adding a discovery rule* recipe in Chapter 2, *Configuring VCM to Manage Your Infrastructure:* To create a vCenter discovery rule to be used for this schedule
- The *Applying a new license key* recipe in Chapter 7, *Maintenance of VCM:* To add license key if you are exceeding the limit of your license key.

9
Troubleshooting VCM

In this chapter, we will cover the following recipes:

- Troubleshooting tools – EcmDebugEventViewer
- Troubleshooting tools – Job Manager | History
- Troubleshooting tools – Machine Collection Status
- Troubleshooting agent communication issues
- Troubleshooting agent upgrade issues
- Troubleshooting SCR download issues
- Troubleshooting VCM console login failure
- Troubleshooting vCenter and vCloud data collection issues
- Troubleshooting the Recommended Action: Investigate Issue Linux server patch error
- Troubleshooting not being able to see any jobs on the console
- Troubleshooting not being able to see the Monthly option on the Schedule Job page

Introduction

Troubleshooting is the process of identifying the source of a problem and eliminating it. To start troubleshooting, you start with the most obvious possible problem and then pinpoint the exact issue. Doing this requires two things: experience of the entity you are troubleshooting and good tools to look at details such as logs and error codes.

In this chapter, we will talk about both. In the first three recipes, you will be introduced to the tools, as they are necessary to gain some expertise in VCM troubleshooting, and then, we will look at some general issues and their solutions.

The troubleshooting tools we will cover include **EcmDebugEventViewer.exe**, **VCM logs**, **Job Manager | History**, and the **SQL log viewer**. If you are good with SQL, you can try SQL trace as well.

The general issues include issues with data collection, issues faced during patching, and issues with agent communication.

Agent communication messages are too cryptic; they say **Pingfailed** for every issue, You need to check what exactly went wrong.

So, let's get started with troubleshooting VCM.

Troubleshooting tools – EcmDebugEventViewer

You can use the EcmDebugEventViewer tool to have a closer look at all the events that are stored in the VCM database. This will help you find event errors for your environment.

Getting ready

We need access to the VCM OS with admin rights.

The tool is called EcmDebugEventViewer.exe. It is a standalone executable available in `C:\Program Files (x86)\VMware\VCM\Tools` (if you installed VCM with defaults).

How to do it...

This recipe splits is in two parts: starting and filtering.

Accessing events

The tool can be launched from its own location, or you can copy the `.exe` file anywhere and start. Follow these steps:

1. Connect to your VCM OS with administrator rights.
2. Open an Explorer window and browse to `X:\Program Files (x86)\VMware\VCM\Tools` (*X* is the drive where you installed VCM).
3. Right-click on **EcmDebugEventViewer.exe** and select **Run as Administrator**.
4. You are now presented with a blank screen. You can choose from three possibilities: **Database**, **Collector DB**, or **Open File** to open a saved `.dbe` file. For this example, select **Database**.
5. Press *F5*; it will fetch the content of the logs from the database.

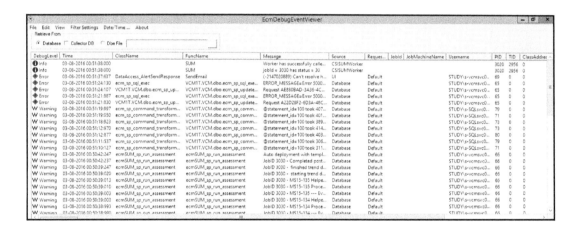

6. Double-click on a line to open more details. The following screenshot shows an error message that the VCM server is unable to resolve the mail server.

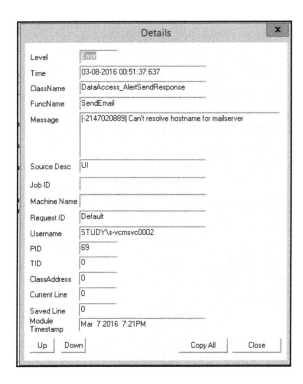

7. You can use the **Up** and **Down** buttons on the details windows to see other log entries.
8. Click on **Close** to close the event details.

Filtering events

As there are lots of entries, you might want to reduce the amount by deploying a filer. Continue with these steps:

1. Click on **Filter settings** and then define a filtering criteria, such as the source or type of the message, as shown in the following screenshot:

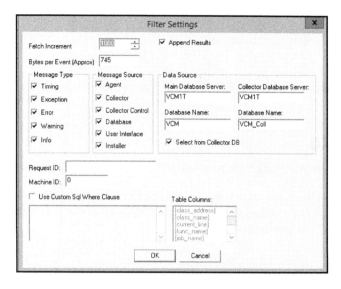

2. You can also select the specific timeframes that should be shown. Click on **Date/Time** in the top menu and modify the duration, as shown in the following screenshot.

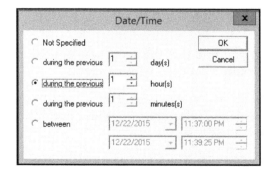

3. You can export the selected logs by going to **File | Save As dbe**. This will save all the lines.

4. To save only selected lines, select the lines and then go to **File | Save Selected As dbe.**

This concludes our overview of the EcmDebugEventViewer tool.

How it works

You can open the main VCM database as well as the VCM_Coll database or any saved files.

When you are troubleshooting VCM issues, this is the first place to start. Always select the main VCM database as it contains the collected system data from the VCM agents along with all the processes it is performing.

Let's take an example:

You are trying to patch a Linux machine and it is failing, and it is giving you the PingFailed error code. You check and find that you are able to ping the managed Linux machine and you can Telnet to the port-everything with regards to communication with the Linux machine is working fine. The small catch here is that VCM first tries to communicate with the SCR server on port 26542, and if that is not accessible for any reason, it just gives you a cryptic PingFailed error. Now, if you start the ECMDebug tool, and you have already enabled the debug log level to info, you can see that it is trying to communicate with the SCR server and failing there.

On further troubleshooting, you find that the agent was not communicating for some reason. After restarting it, you can proceed with patching.

The next option is the VCM collection database. The VCM_Coll database contains information about the UI, such as Collector settings and options. To be frank, I have hardly used it, so I don't really have a use case.

The last option is opening a DBE file. The VCM agent also saves its own logs in the .dbe file format, so to troubleshoot agent issues, you can copy the file from an agent to the server and read it, or someone can send you a saved .dbe file from their VCM installation, and after going through the file, you can provide suggestions. When you work with VMware, they will ask you to generate this .dbe file and send it to them so that they can review it and get back with some solution.

Troubleshooting tools – Job Manager | History

The History tool is built in to VCM. With this tool, you can look at the status of the jobs completed earlier, and it gives you the logs to further troubleshoot.

Getting ready

You will need access to the VCM console and basic understanding of VCM to roam around the console.

How to do it...

To look at details about the jobs completed earlier, launch the VCM console and go to **Administration** | **Job Manager** | **History**.

You have four options here: **Instant Collections**, **Scheduled Collections**, **Other Jobs**, and **VCM remote**. If you are not troubleshooting collection issues, then you most probably need to go to **Other jobs** and select the job in the top-left pane, and the details will be visible in the bottom pane.

Select **Job History** and click on **View Details**. If the job had multiple machines, you will get an option to choose either of them, and then you can see what went wrong.

In the following screenshot, when we hover over **Status**, we can see that there is something wrong with **Mutual authentication**.

We can use the M**enu** option at the top to copy the data, and it can then can be used to search on the Internet or provide an exact log to VMware for further troubleshooting.

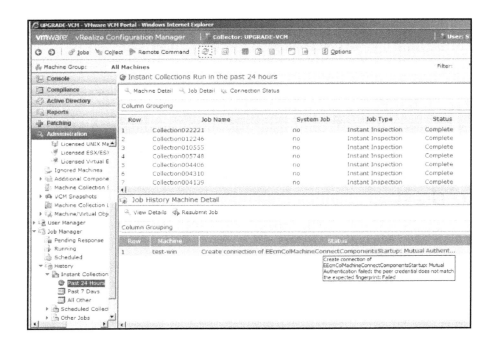

VCM Job Manager | History

How it works

Every time VCM performs a scheduled or on-demand job, it is captured at this location; you can have a look at them and see whether they failed or were successful. If they fail, it will give you errors, which you can use for further troubleshooting.

When you click on a job and select **View Details**, it will give you a popup to either have a look at the selected machine or all machines. You have an option to resubmit the job from here.

Let's have a look at a real-life experience. We were not able to patch a Linux server. We had configured the SCR server and VCM as expected, but it was still failing. After checking the logs here, we found that VCM is looking for a file called `REDHAT-rt.ptoperties`, while as per the documentation, we had configured file called `redhat-rt.properties`. After correcting the name of the file (to capital letters), we were able to patch the server.

Troubleshooting tools – Machine Collection Status

Machine Collection Status in the VCM console is where you can see what data is collected from which server and whether it is a full collection or a delta. This can come in handy when you are troubleshooting data collection issues.

Getting ready

You will need access to the VCM console and basic understanding of VCM to roam around the console.

How to do it...

Go to **Administration** | **Machines Manager** | **Machine Collection Status**.

As mentioned, we can have a look at what data was collected, which filter set was used, and which filters were successful in obtaining the data.

Let's assume you are creating a machine group with a specific dynamic rule and the machines are not getting populated, perhaps because the datatype you are using for filtering was not collected.

You are running a report for compliance and see **Data not Available** for performing the compliance test; as stated, perhaps the data was not collected.

You can see the details by applying lots of filters in the console, as this will be a large table to look at if you have a big infrastructure.

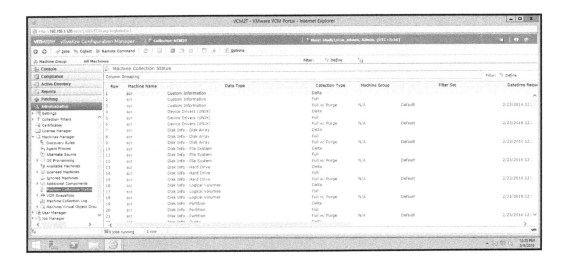

Machine collection logs in VCM under Administration

How it works

When we collect data from managed machines, what we collect and when we made the collection is logged there.

We were working with an RHEL 7 machine to collect the data. The job was successful, but when we tried patching the server, it did not show the status, that is, whether the patch is required or not. When we checked in the Machine Collection Status tool, we did not find our machine, which means that details were not getting captured. After checking the logs, we concluded that the VCM collector was not able to capture details. After resolving the issue with the machine, we performed another collect operation and found that the details are available and the machine is listed in Machine Collection Status.

Troubleshooting agent communication issues

Now, we will have a look at multiple issues faced with agent communication and how they can be resolved.

Getting ready

In this recipe, we will have a look at the following issues:

- *Issue 01: Mutual Authentication failed*
- *Issue 02: Rethrown certificate issue*
- *Issue 03: PingFailed*
- *Issue 04: CredentialsFailed*

Issue 01: Mutual Authentication failed

Mutual authentication failure may happen after an upgrade. When you try to collect data, it fails with the error, as shown in the following screenshot:

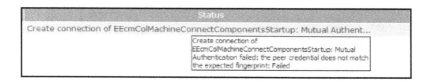

VCM agent communication issue : Mutual Authentication Failed

You can see the error under **Administration** | **Job Manager** | **Instant Collection**.

Then, select the appropriate subsection. After that, select the **Job** in the top-left pane, and you'll be able to see the details in the bottom-left pane.

How to do it...

To resolve the issue, follow these steps:

1. Select the machine for which you are not able to collect data.
2. Click on **Re-establish Mutual Authentication** (the handshake symbol on the menu bar).
3. Select the machine or machines that are facing the issue.
4. Click on **Finish** to close the wizard.
5. Confirm that the issue was resolved by performing the collection again.

Issue 02: Rethrown certificate issue

Agent-server communication is based on the certificate we use while installing the agent; if the certificate on the agent does not match the certificate on the server, then you will get the following error message:

Status	Start Time
Create connection of EEcmColMachineConnectComponentsStartup: [RETHROWN] Cer...	28-02-2016 00:44:13

Create connection of EEcmColMachineConnectComponentsStartup: [RETHROWN] Certificate chain does not contain an authorized certificate.: Failed

VCM agent communication: the rethrown certificate issue

How to do it...

To resolve the issue, do the following:

1. Reinstall the agent with the correct certificate and perform the collection again.
2. In the case of a Linux server, use the installer from the correct VCM server, as the certificate is embedded in the installer.

Issue 03: PingFailed

This issue could be because of many things:

- DNS resolution for the managed machine is not working
- The firewall is blocking port 26542 (either on the agent or between the server and agent)
- The service is not running
- The agent is not installed
- The machine is powered off
- There are issues in routing; hence, the machine IP is not reachable

VCM agent communication issue: PingFailed

How to do it...

To resolve the issue, follow these steps:

1. Make sure the managed machine is powered on.
2. Ping the managed machine with the hostname or FQDN and see whether the IP is resolved.

   Use the following commands:

   ```
   ping -a 10.20.30.40

   ping server01.study.local
   ```

   Make sure the latter two hostnames resolve the same IP, and the first command gives the correct hostname. It has been observed that sometimes the name resolution does not work as intended and needs corrections.

3. Trace the IP from the VCM server to check whether the machine can be reached from the VCM server and there are no routing issues; if there are any, add the required routes.

   Use the following command to do this:

   ```
   tracert server01.study.local
   ```

   From the managed server, run this command:

   ```
   tracert vcm.study.local
   ```

   You must be able to reach from both the sides.

4. Check the Telnet port 26542 from the VCM server; if it isn't working, check the local firewall on the managed machine. If that is disabled as well, check with the networking and security teams whether there is a firewall between the managed machine and VCM server and whether it has port 26542 open.

   From the VCM server, try following command:

   ```
   telnet server01.study.local 26542
   ```

   For more on the required ports, have a look at the *Understanding the requirements of VCM* section of `Chapter 1`, *Installing VCM*.

5. Check the firewall on the local server.

   This should either be disabled or should have the required ports open.

   The procedure is different for Windows and Linux. Have a look at the following articles:

   For Windows:
   https://technet.microsoft.com/en-us/library/cc753558.aspx

   For RedHat: https://access.redhat.com/documentation/en-US/Red_Hat_Enterprise_Linux/6/html/Security_Guide/sect-Security_Guide-Firewalls-Common_IPTables_Filtering.html

6. Check whether CMAgent is installed. This can be done in multiple ways:

For Windows:

1. Check whether the CMagnet service is available.
2. Check whether the `C:\Windows\CMAgent` folder is present and is not empty.
3. Check whether CMAgent is listed in **Add/Remove Programs**.

For Linux:

Run `netstat -an | grep 26542`.

Make sure the service is listening on port `26542`.

Check whether the service is running by executing this command:

```
netstat -l | grep csi-agent
```

The command should return `tcp 0 0 :csi-agent *: LISTEN`.

Monitor processes with the top utility. If the top utility is installed and available, you can use it to monitor processes. Here's how:

1. Start the top utility.
2. Type `u`.
3. At the **Which User (Blank for All):** prompt, type the user account that the agent is installed as (`csi_acct`).
4. Type `s`.
5. At the **Delay between updates:** prompt, type `1`.

7. Check whether the CMAgent service is running.

Follow the OS-specific actions to check the status.

For Windows:

Run `services.msc` and make sure the **CM Socket Listener** service has been started.

For Linux:

Log in to the managed server with root privileges.

Go to `/etc/init.d`.

Execute `./csi-service status` and make sure it is running.

Issue 04: CredentialsFailed

As shown in the following screenshot, you might get an error called **CredentialsFailed**. This happens when the network authority account configured for the managed machine does not have rights on the managed machine.

Chances are, the machine you are managing is either from another domain or in a workgroup, and you did not add the required credentials as the network authority account.

VCM agent communication issue: **CredentialsFailed**

How to do it...

Have a look at the *Patching machines in multi-domain environments and workgroups* recipe in `Chapter 4`, *Windows Patching*, and the *Adding a network authority account to manage machines in multiple domains* recipe in `Chapter 2`, *Configuring VCM to Manage Your Infrastructure*, then add the appropriate network authority account for the managed machine and try collection again.

How it works

We discussed multiple issues here: VCM must communicate with the agents if we want to manage them. VCM agent communication is based on the certificate on the server; if that is not as expected, then the server won't communicate, and we need to replace that by reinstalling the agent with the correct certificate.

We need to make sure that we can resolve the hostname of the managed machine and connect on port 26542, so open firewall ports in between.

Troubleshooting agent upgrade issues

After upgrading VCM to version 5.8.1, you might face some issues while upgrading the agent to the latest version. The upgrade fails, but if you choose **Install with Remove Current version** from the VCM console, then the agent gets installed/upgraded to the latest version.

 Note that this issue has been resolved in the latest version of VCM at the time of writing this book, that is, VCM 5.8.2. This is applicable only if you are upgrading to VCM 5.8.1.

Getting ready

When you select a machine on the VCM console, choose the Upgrade option, and run the job, it should fail while creating the service on the managed machines and throw an error as per the following code, which is present in `C:\Windows\CMAgent`.

```
***   Installation Started 03/03/2016 3:57   ***
```

```
Title: EcmComSocketListenerService
Source: C:\windows\TEMP\GLB90C6.tmp | 03-03-2016 | 03:57:04 | 71680
Rem Wise Error Number: 141
Rem Function Name: EcmCreateService
Rem Error Message: Caught an exception from wise : Call to
EcmCreateService for service CSI Socket Listener failed with error code
of 1072 : error code 141
141
```

How to do it...

In the 5.8.1 release, VMware promoted the HTTP listener module, which stops the listener service before upgrading while the Collector is waiting for it. The Collector contacts the agent for the upgrade status when the listener is being upgraded. As a result, the collector receives a ping failed response, and it signals the collector to FAIL the upgrade job.

The following setting allows the collector to fall back to DCOM when the HTTP connection fails:

1. Run the following query in the SQL management server while selecting VCM as the database:

   ```
   UPDATE dbo.ecm_sysdat_configuration_values SET configuration_value =
   '1' WHERE configuration_name = 'config_allow_http_failover_to_dcom'
   ```

2. Also, correct the module filename of `ECMSocketListenerService` using this query:

   ```
   UPDATE dbo.ecm_sysdat_install_modules SET module_file_name =
   'EcmComSocketListenerService6_6.exe' WHERE module_name =
   'EcmComSocketListenerService'   AND module_version = '6.6'
   ```

3. Restart the SSRS and VCM collector service.

After that, you can upgrade the agent from the console.

Troubleshooting SCR download issues

As you know, SCR is a tool that is used to synchronize patches for Linux/Unix operating systems from vendor sites to local repositories. Sometimes, the synchronization fails and can't download content from vendor sites.

Getting ready

We are able to log in to the RedHat portal with the same account, but the patch download fails with an error. When we try to synchronize patches with vendors (in this case, RedHat) from SCR, it throws an error, as shown in the following code:

```
Nov 19, 2015 9:11:32 AM com.lumension.scr.log.CommonsLogging error
SEVERE: Error processing architecture X86_64
com.lumension.scr.exception.AuthenticationFailedException: Failed to
establish login session with RHN
        at
com.lumension.scr.pojo.SCPackage.getAllPackageFiles(SCPackage.java:508)
        at
com.lumension.scr.pojo.SCPackage.download(SCPackage.java:363)
        at
com.lumension.scr.client.StandaloneSCRepositoryClient.download
(StandaloneSCRepositoryClient.java:596)
        at
com.lumension.scr.client.StandaloneSCRepositoryClient.process
(StandaloneSCRepositoryClient.java:492)
        at
com.lumension.scr.client.StandaloneSCRepositoryClient.main
(StandaloneSCRepositoryClient.java:644)
```

As it indicates an issue with login, the first suspect is, as always, the account used to synchronize the repository with RHN. We can log in with the same account on RHN, and if we try changing to another account, the problem still persists.

How to do it...

The resolution for this is as follows:

1. Resynchronize the SCR Tool with the RedHat repository.
2. Select the SCR Tool output folder and delete all of the `SystemId*.xml` files:

```
cd "PatchRepo/Repos"/unix
rm SystemId*.xml

[root@scr unix]# pwd/opt/vcmpatches/unix[root@scr unix]#
lsSystemId_5Server_i386.xml
SystemId_6Server_i386.xmlSystemId_5Server_x86_64.xml
SystemId_6Server_x86_64.xml
```

Take a backup of the files by running the following command for each file:

```
[root@scr unix]# cp SystemId_5Server_i386.xml
SystemId_5Server_i386.xml.bak
[root@scr unix]# rm -f *.xml
[root@scr unix]# ls
[root@scr unix]#
```

The path to the `unix` folder is located in the `properties` file and is defined using the `folder=value` parameter.

For example, `folder=/PatchRepo/Repos`.

3. Run the replication process manually or allow it to run on schedule:

```
[root@scr unix]# cd /etc/cron.daily/
[root@scr cron.daily]# ./SCR
```

4. The XML files will be created at the earlier location (`/PatchRepo/Repos`) and the synchronization will also start:

```
[root@scr unix]# pwd
/opt/vcmpatches/unix
[root@scr unix]# ls
SystemId_5Server_i386.xml      SystemId_6Server_i386.xml
SystemId_5Server_x86_64.xml   SystemId_6Server_x86_64.xml
```

How it works

The real problem was that the source machine information was changed or deleted on the **Red Hat Network (RHN)**.

When we delete the XML files and restart the synchronization, the machine information is updated again and we are allowed to download patches from RHN.

Troubleshooting VCM console login failure

You are trying to log in to VCM and it throws an error: **Your ID is disabled**.

Getting ready

You will need access to SQL server to resolve the issue.

Consider this: you do not have anyone who can help you enable the ID or, even worse, you were setting up the VCM and still haven't added anyone, so yours is the only account that can log in and make the necessary settings.

No worries; we have a solution.

You will need SQL Managemnt Studio and access to your SQL server that holds the VCM DB.

How to do it...

Follow these steps to unlock the user:

1. Log in to the VCM SQL server and launch SQL Management Studio.

   Select VCM as the database and run the first query:

   ```
   select * from ecm_sysdat_logins
   ```

   This will show all the users with their login IDs.

2. Note the login ID for the user you were trying and run the following query:

   ```
   update ecm_sysdat_logins set login_active = 1 where login_id = X
   ```

   X is the login ID of the user you noted earlier.

The login is now enabled. Try logging in to the VCM console, and if you were the only administrator, start adding others.

How it works

VCM stores all the information about everything it does in the SQL database. In this case, we found that the account we were trying to log in to was locked and needed a reset.

After running the first SQL query, we checked the status of the account in the database, and as it was locked (that is, `login_active = 0`), we ran another query and enabled the account, that is, `login_active = 1`.

After that, we can log in to the VCM console.

It is recommended to have an AD group added to the VCM for administration purposes as described in the *Managing users* recipe in `Chapter 7`, *Maintenance of VCM*.

Troubleshooting vCenter and vCloud data collection issues

The issue: when trying to collect data from vCenter and vCloud Director, the operation fails.

Getting ready

You should have the following problem: when you try to collect data from either vCenter or vCloud Director, it either fails or you are not able to see any details in the VCM console, under **Console | Virtual Environments**.

How to do it...

There could be few reasons for this.

The details of the error or failure can be seen with the **EcmDebugEventViewer** tool or in **Job manager | History**; based on the error codes, you can try any or all of the following solutions:

- The credentials set while configuring vCenter and/or vCloud may not be right; try changing them.
- The certificate thumbprint set while configuring vCenter and/or vCloud may not be correct.

  If this is the case, then under **Job manager | History**, VCM will show the configured thumbprint and expected thumbprint; you can copy the expected thumbprint. Make sure it's correct, and then, change the wrong certificate thumbprint.

- As you know, we have filter sets, and most of the time, we choose the default filter set for performing collection. Validate the default filter set and see whether it has all the vCenter and/or vCloud-related filters present; if not, add them and perform a collection.

  The setting is available under **Administration | Collection Filters | Filter Sets**. Select **Default Filter**, click on **Edit**, and add any missing vCenter and/or vCloud filters, as shown in the following screenshot.

You can define a filter to limit the filters with criteria like in the screenshot:

This will limit the filters to only vCenter, vCloud, and vShield. Make sure these are part of the default filter set; if not, then use the down arrow to add all of them to the default filter, and click on **Next**. Complete the wizard and then perform a collection for vCenter, vCloud, and/or vShield. It will work.

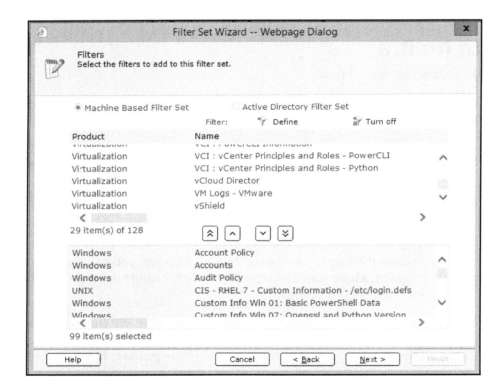

Modifying the default filter set

How it works

VCM uses filter sets, and those include filters to collect data from various managed objects. Filters define what data needs to be collected, such as operating system name, some registry value, or file permissions. There are thousands of filters available, and not all filters are used in one filter set. We have a default filter set, which includes filters for all the managed machine types, such as vCenter, vCloud Director, Windows, and Linux. Sometimes, certain required filters go missing from the filter set. We then need to add them back so that the next time we use them to collect details, VCM will know what data needs to be collected.

In this troubleshooting recipe, we did the same thing and added missing filters to the default filter set.

Troubleshooting the Recommended Action: Investigate Issue Linux server patch error

When trying to patch a Linux server, you might get a message saying **Recommended Action: Investigate Issue** and hence are not able to patch the server.

Getting ready

The error will look like the following screenshot. The recommended action is **Investigate Issue**:

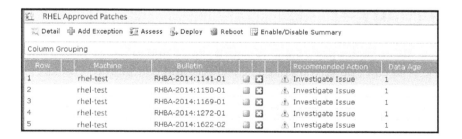

How to do it...

1. To resolve the issue, follow these steps on the VCM database:
2. Run this SQL query to know the `machine_id` for which it shows **Investigate Issue**:

```
select machine_id, machine_name from ecm_dat_machines where
machine_name = '<Machine Name>'
```

3. The machine name is the name of the service creating issues.
4. Update the timestamp for that `machine_id` value using the following query:

```
update ecm_sysdat_imd_machine_timestamp_xref set timestamp = 0 where
machine_id = <>
```

5. Carry out another assessment on that machine, and it will tell you that patches are required.

Troubleshooting not being able to see any jobs on the console

The issue: VCM is not running or showing any jobs. When jobs are started manually, they are not being executed, rendering VCM close to useless.

Getting ready

When we run any job such as data collection, patching, or compliance checks, they might not start and be absent from the **Jobs** window. Because of this, there is no update in the VCM database, you can't patch a managed machine, and compliance checks can't be executed.

We need access to the SQL server hosting the VCM database.

How to do it...

Here is the resolution. To determine whether the SQL Server Service Broker is enabled, run the following script in SQL Server using SQL Server Management Studio:

1. Launch SQL Server Management Studio and create a new query, as follows.

```
USE master;
GO
SELECT name, is_broker_enabled FROM sys.databases;
GO
```

2. Check whether the value of is_broker_enabled is (zero) for the VCM database, and re-enable the SQL Server Service Broker by running the following script in SQL Server:

```
USE master;
GO
ALTER DATABASE {db-name} SET ENABLE_BROKER WITH ROLLBACK IMMEDIATE;
GO
```

Here, db-name is the name of your VCM database. The database name is VCM by default.

How it works

With Service Broker, a feature in Microsoft SQL Server, internal or external processes can send and receive guaranteed, asynchronous messages. Messages can be sent to a queue in the same database as the sender, to another database in the same SQL Server instance, or to another SQL Server instance either on the same server or on a remote server. We fixed the broken broker service on the VCM database so that it can function again.

Troubleshooting not being able to see the Monthly option on the Schedule Job page

Sometimes, it may happen that when we are trying to schedule something in VCM, when we are about to complete the wizard, on the schedule page, the **Monthly** option is disabled (grayed out), and we can't set a monthly schedule.

Getting ready

The **Monthly** scheduling option is disabled, as shown here:

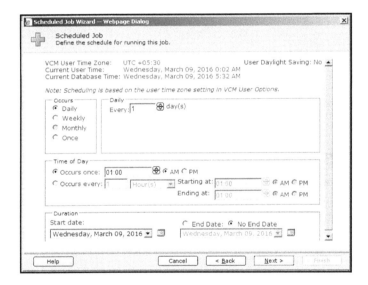

How to do it...

The monthly scheduling option is **disabled** if the time zone setting of the VCM user launching the console is different from the VCM database's time zone setting.

Make sure the time zone of the machine that is used to connect to the VCM server is the same as the VCM database server's.

Defining Naming Conventions

We need to create lots of entities such as machine groups, patching templates, compliance templates, and so on, and to keep all these things tidy, we need to have certain naming conventions. Here is the list of entities we will be creating naming conventions for:

- Machine groups
- Machine group filters
- Patching templates
- Patching jobs
- Patching assessments
- Compliance templates
- Compliance rule groups
- Compliance filters

Machine groups

You can use the operating system and maintenance window a machine belongs to, to create its **machine groups**, such as this example:

```
MW01-Win-xxxxYYYY
```

This is what the sections mean:

- `MW01`: First maintenance window
- `Win/Lin`: Windows or Linux
- First/second/third/fourth (`xxxx`): The number of the week of the month
- Day: The day of the week for which patching has been planned

Machine group filters

A machine group filter inherits its name from the machine group it belongs to, so this will be the same as the machine group name.

Patching templates

Patching templates are a group of patches that we can use by following the naming conventions for them.

For monthly patching templates, use the following naming convention:

```
Win-XXX-YY-Template
```

This is what the components mean:

- The first three characters are for the OS (`Win/Lin`)
- The next three characters (`XXX`) are for the month
- The next two numbers (`YY`) are for the year
- The final word (`Template`) is for specifying that this a template

Scheduled patching jobs

The following naming convention can be used for **scheduled patch jobs**:

```
XXXYY-OS- MWZZ Monthly Patching
```

This is what the sections of the name stand for:

- xxx: Month
- YY: Year
- os: Win/Lin
- zz: Maintenance window number 01/02/03/04
- Monthly Patching: Descriptive label

Scheduled patch status collection

The following naming convention can be used for **scheduled patch status collection**:

OS-MWZZ-XXXPatchStatus

This is what the sections of the name stand for:

- os: Win/Lin
- zz: Maintenance window 01/02/03/04
- xxx: When the assessment will run-pre/post patching
- Last word: Status

Scheduled patching assessment

The following can be used as a naming convention for **scheduled patching assessment**:

WinMWZZ-InitialAssessment

This is what the sections of the name stand for:

- os: Win/Lin
- zz: Maintenance window 01/02/03/04
- Next word: When the assessment will run-Initial/Final assessment
- Last word: Assessment

Compliance templates

The following can be used as a naming convention for **compliance templates**:

```
01-MyCompany-MyCompany ISO 27001-27002 Windows 2003
```

This is what the sections of the name stand for:

- First two numbers: Sequence
- Next three characters: `MyCompany`
- After that: Name/title from where the rule groups are to create this template

Compliance rule groups

The following can be used as a naming convention for a **compliance rule group**:

```
01-MyCompany- MyCompany ISO 27001-27002 Windows 2003
```

This is what the sections of the name stand for:

- First two numbers: Sequence
- Next three characters: `MyCompany`
- After that: Name/title of the rule group

B
Understanding VCM Console

Before you start using VCM, let's have a small primer to the console, as we've used it throughout the entire book and it's better to get familiarized with it.

Here's how to connect to the VCM console:

Sr. no.	VCM deployment	Default console link
1	Single-tier	`https://<VCM Server IP/FQDN>/VCM`
2	Two-tier	`https://<Collector Server IP/FQDN>/VCM`
3	Three-tier	`https://<Web Server IP/FQDN>/VCM`

The only supported browser is IE in various versions, so enter the URL and hit *Enter* in the browser and provide the credentials. Select the role if you have multiple roles, and then you will enter the amazing world of VCM.

The console looks like the following screenshot:

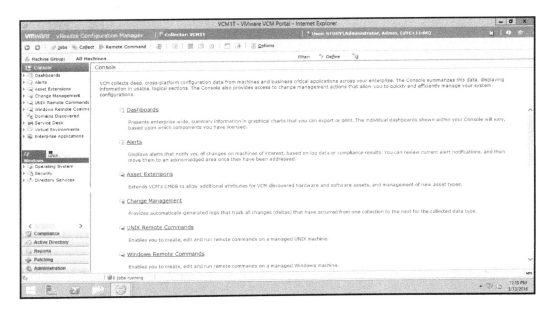

The very first blue row gives you the name of your collector server and the user connected to it.

On the next row, you have menu options. The most important of them are **Jobs** and **Collect**, while the rest allow you to select, copy, and export the data shown in the console.

On the third row, you have **Machine Group:** – this is very important, as all the actions you will be performing from the left-hand slider will be done on the machines that are a part of the machine group you have selected here. For example, if you want to patch a machine that is not visible in the console view, but you are sure the machine is a part of the VCM, have a look at the machine group you have selected–the machine is not a part of the machine group you have selected from the top.

Next up is the slider on the left-hand side; the main options you get here are as follows:

1. **Console**

    As shown on the previous screenshot, this is the default slider whenever you launch. Here, you can perform the following functions–note this is not a comprehensive list, and once you get familiar with VCM, you can explore more:

    - You can have complete summary information about the managed machines
    - You can see all the vCenters, vCloud, and vShield instances and the data collected from them, such as virtual machines, ESX and ESXi servers, and vApps networks
    - You can have a look at various dashboards, which you can use in various presentations
    - You can run Linux remote commands

2. **Compliance**

    This is where you can check the compliance of your infrastructure and create or modify new rules and templates.

3. **Active Directory**

    Here, you can have a look at your Active Directory infrastructure, such as AD domains, AD objects, schema, and Active Directory site lists, including site links, site link bridges, subnets, intersite transports, and servers.

    So, all the stuff related to Active Directory is here.

4. Reports

This is the place where you can export the details fetched from managed objects in various formats, such as XLS, CSV, DOC, and so on.

There is a big list of default reports available; apart from those, you can create your own custom reports as required.

5. Patching

A lot of your time will be spent here and the remaining in administration. This is where you will create your patch assessment templates for the various operating systems you are supporting and want to patch, schedule jobs related to patching, and perform on-demand patching.

6. Administration

This is where you will be spending a majority of your time when working on VCM. This is the core of VCM. You can perform the following functions here:

- Adding/removing any new managed machines, if that isn't happening automatically
- Checking the status of jobs, either running or already finished, to help in troubleshooting
- Changing various settings to fine-tune VCM as per your needs
- Checking your license status so that you don't run out of compliance on the license front
- Checking and approving certificates
- Creating various discovery rules, machine groups, and so on

This is a very limited list; you will explore it further as you start working on it.

Index

www.ingramcontent.com/pod-product-compliance
Lightning Source LLC
Chambersburg PA
CBHW081505050326
40690CB00015B/2934